Praise for *Into the*

"Cassandra's story is heartbreaking and p
brings you on a journey with a young vulnerable child searching for stability and love to a grown woman who has taken back her power and learned to survive and thrive. The journey has not been easy and Cassandra writes in a way that draws you in and keeps you turning the pages wanting to learn more and wanting to wrap her in a huge healing hug. Her light and empathy for others shines through as she brings her message to everyone who meets her. You too can become your own hero!"—Michele Correa

"Every page I turned made me crave the next. My experience with Cassandra's book *Into the Light: Becoming My Own Hero* was a testimony to the resilience of the human spirit and to the strength that we can develop through anything, if we so choose. The pain and heartbreak that she shares with us are as beautiful as they are devastating. Her story resonated with my own and taught me that, while I still have a lot of work to do, it's absolutely possible to create a life worth living."—Jessica Beeching

"Cassandra Love Lambert is a remarkable woman whose resilience and compassion inspire everyone she touches. Having survived the profound trauma of childhood sexual abuse, she has transformed her pain into purpose. Through her somatic work and connecting in a genuine way, Cassandra empowers others to navigate their own healing journeys. Her upcoming book *Into the Light: Becoming My Own Hero*, and her heartfelt podcast, Into the Light, where I had the privilege of being a guest, showcase her courage and dedication to sharing her story. Cassandra's inner strength and commitment to helping others are a testament to the power of hope and healing."—Danette Burzlaff-Haag, RN, BSN, Inspirational Speaker and Author

"Casandra Love Lambert's *Into the Light* is a raw, powerful, and deeply inspiring book that sheds light on the harrowing realities of childhood sexual abuse and the profound strength it takes to heal and move forward. Casandra bravely shares her story of growing up with the trauma of abuse by her mother's boyfriend, offering readers not only an unflinching account of her experiences but also a roadmap to resilience and hope.

I had the privilege of speaking with Casandra on my Don't Shrink to Fit podcast, where she opened up about her journey to reclaiming her life, her sense of self, and her joy. Her courage to face her past and share it with others is nothing short of remarkable. Casandra is a living testimony to the possibility of creating a full and meaningful life after enduring unimaginable pain.

This book is more than a memoir; it's a lifeline for those who have endured similar trauma, reminding them that they are not alone and that healing is possible. Into the Light is a must-read for anyone seeking understanding, compassion, and the inspiration to overcome. Casandra's story will touch your heart and ignite a belief in the power of strength, courage, and transformation.

I encourage anyone who has experienced the tragedy of abuse, or knows someone who has, to read this book. It is a profound reminder that even in the darkest moments, there is always the possibility of stepping into the light."—Claudia Noriega-Bernstein, Abundance, Coach, Author, and host of the Don't Shrink to Fit Podcast

"I have had the pleasure of collaborating with Cassandra in various professional capacities, and I am continually impressed by her passion and dedication to her work. Cassandra is not only brilliant and knowledgeable but also deeply committed to helping others. She approaches her work with conviction, integrity, and expertise. I hold the utmost respect for her skills and the impact she creates, and I would recommend her and refer clients to her without hesitation."—Karen Sarmento, Nurse Practitioner & Success Strategist

"Casandra Love Lambert's *Into the Light* is a deeply moving and courageous account that shines a spotlight on the devastating impact of childhood sexual abuse and the incredible strength required to rebuild and heal.

Through her heartfelt storytelling, Casandra shares her personal journey with vulnerability and determination, offering readers a message of hope and empowerment.

We had the privilege of interviewing Casandra for The Corporate Escapists Magazine and Podcast, where she opened up about the inspiration behind her book and her mission to help others find their own light after trauma.

Her story is not only a testament to human resilience but also a powerful call to action for creating awareness and fostering healing. Into the Light is a must-read for anyone seeking inspiration, courage, and the reminder that no matter how dark life may seem, there is always a path to healing."—Christine Innes, CEO of The Corporate Escapists

"Had it not been for Cassandra and her healing gifts, I wouldn't be here today. She guided me back home to my body after years of disassociation and helped me develop a conscious, compassionate and loving relationship with myself. She connected me to source and opened the floodgates to my spiritual awakening! She taught me how to co-create a magical reality and bust through limiting beliefs. Holy moly! So much fruit has been bared and flowers bloomed from the seeds we planted. Eternally grateful for C-love and your sparkle!"—Chelsea Gay

"I've had such a hard time dealing with a lot of emotional issues around the way I look and some sexual abuse that all happened when I was young. Cassandra was able to get me to pin point specific events that I often think about as if they happened yesterday. It's been hard to let go of those feelings and events since they were such a huge part of my life. Talking through it with Cassandra while tapping I was able to release the pain attached to those events. I cried and cried and I was able to have some clarity talking through it. I recommend this to everyone! Cassandra creates a safe space to share things like that and I appreciate her willingness to help others through their pain and past traumas."—S.A

"Cassandra was a fantastic practitioner to work with. It sometimes takes me a while to sort through and identify what I am feeling and she established an atmosphere of patience that allowed me to get to a place of security and openness quickly. I left the session with a shift in perspective and clarity on my goals!" —Jess Johnson

"Cassandra has such a friendly, personable nature it was easy to let go and immerse in the session. She had a great way of getting into the core of my issue and enabling some unexpected memories and associations to surface, which resulted in some major energetic and perceptual shifts, which I'm now integrating. Definitely a great person to put you at your ease and help guide you through some challenging places in your mind."—Heather Jones

"Working with Cassandra in just one session, helped me to release a deep grief I had been carrying around for almost two months. I had been trying two other talk therapies, and they just weren't doing it. In just one session I felt so so much lighter, felt overall more positive, and got so much reassurance that it was ok to feel the way I was feeling. Its unusual for me to get so far in just one session. Cassandra clearly knows her stuff with EFT and I felt supported and not judged at all during the process. Highly recommended!"—JMCD

"As many of us learn from our most difficult life experiences, Cassandra has had a history of being treated poorly, especially by men early in her life, and it has carried over into her adult life. Through her struggles with learning how to trust people, she has overcome so much, as she has endured more than most. She could have developed into a person with deep anger and resentment, but she has chosen to channel her energies into great healing. When she teaches, it's calming to those that learn from her. As much of the world is now on video, I have witnessed great videos from her on teaching others how to overcome their suffering. She has a unique way of explaining how to think about, and feel into, new ways of being to heal the heart."—Derek Hart

"My first session with Cassadra completely changed my view about myself. When I reached out, I wasn't even sure why I felt so distanced and angry all the time. I didn't know how much I was struggling to express myself after the man I loved left me for my "best friend".

Since we were in the same friends group, I was forced to just swallow the trauma it caused me and never had the chance to speak up for myself. I lost my magic, I didn't feel good enough, I built a wall around myself.

Cassandra amazingly guided me through these painful feelings gently—I felt a burning ball in my throat but she helped me release this bad energy I was holding and completely opened my throat chakra. I was finally able to work through this trauma and realize that there's absolutely nothing wrong with me. I slowly regained my confidence, I started to comfortably speak up for myself in every situation. I found my voice again.

Months later I had an encounter with my ex—we talked for hours, & I was able to honestly talk about my feelings which encouraged him to do the same, he apologized for many things and gave me complete closure. I feel aligned and I am confident in being able to manifest my dreams. I'm not afraid of expressing my ideas anymore. I'm so so so happy that I reached out to Cassandra.

She is beautiful inside and out. I highly recommend connecting with her and guarantee that she will go deep and find the root of your trauma without any judgement.

She will help you heal with the amazing light and generous love she has in her. I am forever thankful for her support & hows she's helped me heal and feel more liberated & empowered!"—Bernadett Cseh

"I met Cassandra a few years back at an art show and we just clicked! She is the embodiment of sisterhood and positivity.

I was really struggling with crippling depression and anxiety after my mom died. It seemed to open the flood gates for all the trauma I had been suppressing since childhood. I was even considering antidepressants.

Therapy helped a little but I felt like they were always trying to slap me with a diagnosis.

Cassandra helped me talk everything out at my own pace in a non-clinical way that re-established my self worth. Her work is validating and relatable. Her energy just flows right through the screen, you almost forget you're on a Zoom call.

I feel like an enormous weight has been lifted from my shoulders. I am inspired to be my authentic self again and Cassandra has given me all of the tools to do so. If you want a holistic approach on how to overcome your trauma and manifest your personal and professional goals through deep self exploration then you must join her longer program. You won't regret letting this light into your life."—Michelle H.

"Cassandra Love Lambert was perfectly named When Love is at the center. That is who she is. She leads with her heart and shares it openly and vulnerably. Cassandra shows us that the pain of abuse, neglect and abandonment do not define who we become. She shows us that our past can hone our hearts into vessels of powerful transformation if we allow it. Cassandra is a powerful healer, taking her clients through the process of releasing their own traumas and stepping into their authentic self and power with Grace, integrity and true authentic Beauty."—Kathy Baldwin, Unlearn The Crap, Life Purpose Strategist & Concierge

INTO THE LIGHT

Becoming My Own Hero

CASSANDRA LOVE LAMBERT

C-LOVE
Spring, Texas

Paperback ISBN: 978-1-917724-02-9
eBook ISBN: 978-1-917724-03-6

Edited by: Raimonda Jankunaite, Women Thrive Media
Cover photo © 2025, Cassandra Love Lambert
Cover Design: Cassandra Love Lambert
Cover Layout, Interior Design, and Formatting: Woven Red Author Services

This book is dedicated to my daughter.
You are my why;
I love you eternally

Table of Contents

Disclaimers and Advisory

The contents of this book are based on the author's personal experiences and recollections, which may include factual events, as well as subjective interpretations and emotional reflections. All names, places, and events depicted in this memoir are either the author's own memories or have been altered for the sake of privacy, narrative flow, and storytelling. Any resemblance to actual persons, living or dead, or actual events is purely coincidental, except where otherwise stated.

This book does not seek to reflect the views or experiences of any individuals or organizations other than the author, and any opinions or statements made within are solely those of the author. The author does not intend to defame, libel, or cause harm to any individual or group through the publication of this book.

This memoir is a work of non-fiction, but creative liberties have been taken for narrative purposes. All quotes, dialogues, and personal events are based on the author's recollections, but may not be exact and should not be construed as a factual historical account.

Readers are encouraged to verify any external facts, claims, or references mentioned within this book independently.

Health and Wellness Disclaimer

The stories and experiences shared in this book are not intended to serve as medical advice or trauma recovery guidance. If you are currently experiencing trauma or any mental health challenges, it is important to seek professional medical advice and support. This book should not be relied upon as the sole resource for healing or treatment. Always consult with a licensed healthcare provider or mental health professional for personalized advice and care.

Sensitive Content Advisory

Dearest Reader & Into the Light Angel,

Thank you for choosing to join me on this deeply personal journey through the pages of my book. As we delve into the intimate details of my life, I want to offer a gentle heads-up: this book explores profound experiences that may resonate deeply, particularly if you've faced similar challenges. It's possible that the content could stir emotions or reawaken past traumas. If you find it overwhelming at any point, please feel free to put the book down and take a break. It's important to process these stories at your own pace and prioritize your well-being.

Additionally, please note that this book is not suitable for young children due to the mature themes discussed. Ensure it is kept out of reach of little ones who are not yet ready to understand such complex topics.

To aid you on this journey, I've created a complimentary workbook/journal designed to accompany the book. I hope it serves as a helpful tool for reflection and healing as you navigate through these pages.

Take care of yourself, and thank you for your courage and trust in sharing this experience with me.

Warm Regards,
Cassandra Love Lambert
Aka C-Love

Claim your Gift HERE:
https://intothelightwithc-love.com/gift

C-LOVE

Foreword

The first time I met Cassandra, I was immediately drawn to her warmth and her unique ability to connect with others in a truly meaningful way. When she joined the Women Thrive community as a speaker, she instantly filled the space with positivity, authenticity, and an undeniable sense of kindness. We shared a deep sense of purpose and a shared quest to support and empower others in life. Having witnessed her presence in our community, Cassandra is the kind of person you simply want to be around—someone who makes you feel seen and heard.

Her extraordinary gift for establishing deep, genuine connections flows seamlessly onto the pages of her book. *Into the Light: Becoming My Own Hero* is a beautiful offering of Cassandra's heart—a testament to her journey and the powerful message that we all have the right to claim our spotlight.

I am deeply proud of Cassandra for doing the hardest thing—sharing her story and speaking her truth on the pages of this book. It is no easy task to be so vulnerable and open, but in doing so, she will no doubt support other trauma survivors and be the guiding light that they too can become their own heroes and find the light at the end of their painful journeys, inspiring hope, healing, and transformation.

I deeply resonated with Cassandra's courage in her introduction, where she openly shares how, despite having some fragmented memories, she felt a deep calling to share her story and help others who are facing similar struggles. This will no doubt be personal and resonate with any trauma survivor who may doubted their experiences and the power of their voice. In this book, she takes us through the painful and transformative moments of her life—childhood abuse, neglect, and the complex relationships and personal challenges she faced as both a teen and an adult.

What makes this book truly captivating are the many personal stories and seemingly small moments that pull you in. Cassandra's writing allows readers to experience her journey in a way that feels raw and real. The language is not only impeccably crafted but also beautifully explains the trauma she endured and its long-lasting effects. This insight is not only enlightening but will also provide much-needed support to other trauma survivors as they search for meaning and healing from their own pain.

Into the Light invites readers into a world where vulnerability meets strength, and where pain is alchemized into power. Cassandra's bravery in sharing her truth is a gift to anyone who has ever felt broken, lost, or unheard. This book is a powerful reminder that healing is possible and that we each have the capacity to become our own hero.

Thank you for entrusting me to support you in bringing this book into the world. It is an honor to know you and to be part of this book being birthed into the world, where it will continue to impact many lives around the globe.

Raimonda Jankunaite
Founder & CEO, Women Thrive Media

C-LOVE

Introduction

Memories, particularly from our younger years, often arrive in small pockets of remembrance. Significant moments tend to stand out, while trauma can lead to memories being sporadic, fragmented, or even entirely absent. This disjointedness can make it challenging to piece together our past, highlighting the profound impact trauma has on our recollections and sense of self.

They are glimpses into an individual's reality. As we grow older, we come to understand that we can coexist—sometimes even side by side—while experiencing the same events at the same time. Yet, the way one person perceives or remembers those events can be vastly different from another's recollection. Even when we share the same space, each of us is navigating our own unique reality, and every perspective is relevant and valid. This complexity of memory highlights the rich tapestry of human experience and the importance of honoring each individual's story.

This is my story, shared through my perspective at each stage of my life, capturing the experiences, trials, and tribulations I faced along the way. It's an invitation into my reality—an opportunity to see through my lens and experience the world as I did, gaining insight into my journey from my point of view.

Writing this book has been a journey into facing myself more deeply than ever before, re-examining the memories and moments of my life, and confronting the vulnerability of sharing openly the things I have carried shame around for decades.

Pursuing this lifelong dream of writing a book has taken a lot of courage. I have known I wanted to write my story for longer than I have been a mom—well over a decade. It has taken until now, at 41 years old, to feel ready to share my story this way and have it come from a place of transformation rather than still being entrenched in the trauma.

Putting my experiences into words has forced me to relive many painful moments, but it has also been incredibly healing. Through this process, I've gained a deeper understanding of myself and the strength that resides within me. The act of writing has allowed me to process and release the weight of the past, turning it into a source of empowerment.

Fears of sharing my truth emerged, particularly around how others in my life who are also part of the story will react or treat me as a result of my openness. I've had conversations with a couple of them, explaining my intentions and expressing my hope for understanding. Standing in my power and owning my right to share my story as I remember experiencing it has been a significant area of growth for me. In the past, these fears have controlled me, keeping me silent and preventing healing and growth.

I've come to understand that anyone or anything that hinders my ability to share my story and speak up vulnerably and authentically is obstructing my healing process and, in essence, contributing to the problem. Speaking out and sharing our experiences can offer medicine and healing to those in similar situations. Those who shame or belittle you for expressing your truth are not individuals to keep close or heed. They inadvertently perpetuate cycles of abuse, whether they realize it or not. By sharing your truth, you break those cycles and create space for healing and transformation—not just for yourself, but also for others who may be struggling in similar ways.

Confronting my fears and choosing to move forward despite them has been a profoundly empowering experience. It serves as a reminder that my voice matters and my experiences are valid. By committing to write my truth, I honor my journey and the person I have become. This decision transcends mere storytelling; it's about breaking the chains of silence that have held me captive for so long.

This book is an act of liberation—a powerful declaration that I am breaking the silence and reclaiming the power that was taken from the little girl I once was. It's a resolute statement that the fear of judgment or rejection will no longer dictate my path. Through this journey, I am reclaiming my voice and embracing my truth.

For so many years, I felt trapped, as if I was moving from one confinement to the next, never experiencing true freedom. It felt like I was living in hell. No matter what I did, it seemed futile; darkness followed me relentlessly, and I felt imprisoned within it. I didn't know how to escape or break free; I felt cursed. That's the insidious nature of abuse. You endure it as a child, and then it seems to shadow you throughout life, making you a magnet for more perpetrators. It's as if you're wearing a blinking sign on your forehead that says, "Me, me, me."

While writing, I've repeatedly bumped heads with my mom. She disagrees with my decision to share certain experiences and perceives some events differently than I do. There are memories I hold that she doesn't recall, and conversely, she remembers things that I have no recollection of. This disparity highlights how trauma affects families and shapes memories. It can obscure specific details or entirely block events, manifesting uniquely for each person involved.

I refuse to stay silent simply because my memories, perceptions, and experiences differ from someone else's perspective. I am committed to sharing my truth and my story, and in doing so, I am reclaiming the power it has held over me for so long. My hope is that by reading these pages, you too will feel empowered to free yourself from the burden of keeping your own story hidden away. May you find the strength to release its hold on you and embrace your truth. Nothing heals in the shadows of silence; it must be brought to the light to truly transform.

We become freer people by sharing openly the hard things; being raw and vulnerable in our humanity and humility. Through this openness, we can truly connect with others and find healing. When we hide our stories, we give them power over us, allowing shame and fear to dictate our lives. But when we share our stories, we reclaim our power and invite others to do the same.

Not every single thing I have ever gone through or experienced is in this book. I had to narrow it down to some of the most impactful moments; otherwise, this would be a trilogy (LOL). The timelines are also a bit squished and muddled. Memories can get so compressed or mangled together, it's complicated to flush them out. So this is my narrative to the best of my ability—the most impactful pieces, the good, the bad, and the ugly—raw and vulnerable.

I've selected the moments that shaped me the most, the experiences that left a lasting imprint on my soul. To capture the essence of my journey, even if it means some details and events had to be left out or condensed. This complexity means that some events might blur together or seem out of order. While this book reflects my real-life experiences, I have also changed some details to protect other people's identities.

May this book serve as a beacon of hope, guiding you toward the light of your own life. If you find yourself feeling trapped as you read this, please remember that there is a way out. Even when it feels impossible, there is always hope and the potential for transformation.

I hope this book serves as a testament to the resilience of the human spirit and the power of embracing one's truth, no matter how painful or challenging it may be.

You are worthy of being in the light; it's your God-given birthright. Through these pages, I hope you feel the goosebumps and the healing energy put into them.

Thank you for allowing my story to be part of your healing path and journey. I pray it brings you strength, courage, and the belief that you, too, can find your way out of the darkness and into the light to become your own hero.

Finding this book is no accident—you were divinely guided to it.

See you on the other side ;-)

Statistics

According to the CDC, 1 in 4 girls experience sexual abuse before age 18.[1]

- 1 in 5 girls and 1 in 20 boys is a victim of child sexual abuse.[2]
- Children are most vulnerable to CSA between the ages of 7 and 13.[2]
- According to a 2003 National Institute of Justice report, 3 out of 4 adolescents who have been sexually assaulted were victimized by someone they knew well.[2]
- 16% of youth ages 14 to 17 experience sexual victimization in a year, and 28% experience it in their lifetime.[2]
- Females ages 16-19 are four times more likely than the general population to be victims of rape, attempted rape, or sexual assault.[2]
- Almost 1 in 5 women in the United States report any contact sexual violence by an intimate partner in their lifetime.[3]

---

[1] "About Child Sexual Abuse | Child Abuse and Neglect Prevention." CDC, 16 May 2024, https://www.cdc.gov/child-abuse-neglect/about/about-child-sexual-abuse.html. Accessed 31 October 2024.

[2] Finkelhor, David. "Child Sexual Abuse Statistics - The National Center for Victims of Crime." The National Center for Victims of Crime, https://victimsofcrime.org/child-sexual-abuse-statistics/. Accessed 31 October 2024.

[3] "New Research: The National Intimate Partner and Sexual Violence Survey 2016/2017 Report on Intimate Partner Violence." National Sexual Violence Resource Center (NSVRC), 11 October 2022, https://www.nsvrc.org/blogs/new-research-national-intimate-partner-and-sexual-violence-survey-20162017-report-intimate. Accessed 31 October 2024.

C-LOVE

Chapter 1

Fragments: Pieces of My Past

Being a spirit, having a human experience and human behavior, has always fascinated me. It's remarkable how our fundamental beliefs, behaviors, and habits are etched into our psyche by the tender age of seven. What fascinates me most is how, despite this early imprinting, I didn't truly feel connected to my own body until my mid-twenties to thirties. Life seemed like a surreal nightmare, with only fleeting moments of brightness shimmering through the darkness. Oh, how I craved those glimmers of light when the world around me seemed like a nightmare. In those times of turmoil, I sought refuge within the sanctuary of my imagination, crafting a safe haven where I could retreat from the chaos and find solace.

Life before I turned five is like trying to recall a dream upon waking, fragments of memories floating in a sea of uncertainty. They're not neatly arranged in a linear timeline. Rather, they emerge sporadically, like pieces of a puzzle waiting to be assembled. There's a lingering question of their authenticity, a whisper of doubt that accompanies each recollection. Yet, when I hear echoes of those early years from others or glimpse snapshots captured in old photographs, it's like finding pieces that fit snugly into the puzzle, reinforcing the reality of the memories I recall.

Anecdotes shared with me reveal that I took two weeks to make my entrance into the world. I was supposed to be a New

Year's baby, but I didn't make my showcase until the 13th of January. I'd say my soul knew this life was about to be very challenging and was trying to prolong the inevitable. I skipped crawling altogether; I went straight from being on the ground to walking, eager to get a head start. By the time I was one, I had a full mouth of teeth and was already a very observant child. Instead of grabbing the breakables in the front room of my Godfather's mom's house, I would just stare at them, taking in all their details with wide, curious eyes.

Flashes of my early memories reveal certain snapshots that stand out vividly. I can still taste the chewed gum from the backyard of a babysitter's house, its vibrant colors contrasting against the wooden fence. At three years old, I experienced a moment of innocent discovery while changing a boy's diaper at daycare, becoming aware of the differences between boys and girls. Yet, amid these glimpses of childhood innocence, a shadow of uncertainty looms. I have a vague recollection of having a baby sister when I was two, but she vanished from my life, never to be seen again.

We were constantly on the move, never settling in one place for long. This meant being cared for by a revolving door of babysitters in various homes. While I can't clearly remember the faces of all those caregivers before I turned seven, flashes of their backyards and glimpses of specific toys remain etched in my memory, easily recalled whenever I reflect on that time.

The upheaval in my life came swiftly and painfully. During a heated argument between my mom and her boyfriend, his mother called Child Protective Services (CPS). In the midst of their dispute, my mother had moved me out of the way, and in doing so, I accidentally fell and hit the corner of a table, resulting in a black eye. When CPS arrived and saw my bruise, they immediately took me into foster care, away from my mother.

The sense of abandonment and confusion that followed was overwhelming. I was suddenly thrust into the home of a stranger, far from the warmth and familiarity of my mother's embrace. This profound disruption left me haunted by nightmares for years, as I yearned for the security of my mom and the comfort of home. The impact of this traumatic event is captured in photos from that time, where the sadness etched on my young face is palpable and heart-wrenching. Even now, my body seems to remember more than my conscious mind can fully grasp, holding onto the echoes of that tumultuous period in my life.

During those turbulent early years, consistency was a foreign concept. It felt as though the very foundation of my life was built on shifting sands, constantly changing and unstable. This instability made it challenging to feel grounded or secure in any aspect of my life. It also hindered my ability to form healthy attachment with others; I found myself wondering why I should get close to anyone or become attached to any place when it could all disappear by tomorrow. This mindset was a protective barrier, but it also isolated me from the connections that could have offered comfort.

To cope with this transitory lifestyle, I developed a rich, detailed imagination. I would immerse myself in the world of pretend, creating imaginary friends and characters with whom I could interact. These imagined companions became a source of comfort and stability, offering consistent presence in a world where everything else seemed temporary and unstable. This imaginative play not only provided solace but also nurtured my creativity, helping me navigate the uncertainties of my environment with a sense of wonder and possibility.

As a child, I rarely had the chance to connect deeply enough to understand what friendship meant; it wasn't until much later in life that I truly comprehended the concept. Being around adults more often than children, I developed a keen sense of observation, learning to navigate my surroundings in a way that many kids my age did not have to. This unique upbringing shaped me into a highly observant individual, always watching and learning from the behaviors and interactions of adults, yet longing for a stable place and lasting connections.

As a child, I had a quiet, observant nature, captivated by the smallest details of my surroundings. At my Godfather's mother's house, I would immerse myself in her array of knick-knacks, savoring each intricate detail while carefully maintaining the delicate balance of the space. There was a palpable energy in her home—the rich aroma of pasta and Italian dishes mingling with the fresh breeze wafting through open windows in Pacifica, the laughter of joyful people, and the soothing sounds of Frank Sinatra and oldies playing softly in the background. It was a sanctuary filled with warmth and love, leaving an indelible imprint on my young mind and heart. In those moments, I learned what love truly looks and feels like.

Spending much of my time alone, without other kids around to play with, I delved into the realm of imagination. Sesame Street and Mr. Rogers became not just shows, but gateways to worlds of make-believe, where I could play out endless scenarios. With my record player, I'd soundtrack my adventures with the whimsical tunes of my Mickey Mouse record. The gentle crackle of the needle meeting the vinyl was like music to my ears, while the faint scent of the record added another layer of nostalgia to my solitary playtime.

In my early childhood, I have fragmented memories of a sibling, born to my mother and another man. I was just two years old, small enough to wander around their house, taking in scenes that seemed both vivid and dreamlike. Whenever arguments erupted, the world appeared to fall silent around me, and I felt enclosed in a bubble, detached and observing the chaos among the adults. Nothing they said or did made any sense to me; I was an outsider in my own experience, watching but not understanding.

Recalling the moment I was taken from my mom by Child Protective Services and placed into foster care feels like revisiting a half-remembered nightmare, where reality and fragments of dreams merge confusingly. It's still hard to accept that this is a part of my story, my beginnings. The memories surrounding that time are hazy and disjointed, making it difficult to distinguish what was real from what might have been imagined. Even now, it remains a challenge to untangle the threads of truth woven into the fabric of this traumatic memory.

When I look at the photographs from that period, I see a two-year-old girl burdened by a depth of sorrow no child should bear. On the backs of these photos, court documents confirm the reality of those moments—the stark evidence of my early trials. These images vividly capture the scars of abandonment and fear that have followed me throughout my life. The loneliness and uncertainty of those months were etched into my soul, profoundly shaping my life in ways I am still unraveling. After my mother regained custody and we moved, I never again saw my baby sister from that time. I was only two when we were separated, leaving a void in my heart brimming with longing and unanswered questions about her.

After returning to my mom from foster care, my memories begin to sharpen and become more vivid. Perhaps it was because I was a year older, or maybe the traumatic experience of being taken from my mom had awakened something within me that hadn't been there before. From that point on, my memories are clearer. We moved into a vibrant house owned by Uncle Jose, bustling with my mom's female co-workers, along with their abuelita and Uncle Jose himself—my mom's closest friends, all of whom spoke Spanish.

During the days while my mom was at work, their abuelita would look after me. Together, we would become deeply engrossed in Spanish soap operas, a scene that echoed the times I spent sitting at my godmother's feet in her in-law unit while she knitted—a place I've always considered the safest on earth. Although my mom and I shared just a small room, there was a profound sense of safety and warmth in this home that reminded me of the love and security I felt with my godfamily. Here, I felt enveloped in genuine love and care.

Returning from foster care and reuniting with my mom seemed to ignite a spark of ambition within my three-year-old self. One day, filled with determination, I decided to embark on a mission to go to Toys R Us to buy Barbies. I honestly do not remember what sparked this inspiration I just know I was committed to making it happen.

On that sunny day, I carefully packed my purse with coins and brought along my trusty Cabbage Patch Doll. Despite my efforts to persuade the niece of our landlord to join me, she declined. Undeterred, I set out alone from the cramped house we shared with so many people. With my mom at work and the abuelita engrossed in her shows, I quietly slipped out the back door, through the backyard, and into the field beyond.

As I ventured through the field of South San Francisco, off of El Camino, I eventually found myself at a bus stop. There, a friendly woman on a bike struck up a conversation, and I eagerly shared my plans to visit the toy store. Time seemed to slip away until, suddenly, the arrival of the bus was accompanied by an unexpected presence: the police – and Jose. His stern expression told me I was in big trouble. I don't recall him being a man of many words, his face said everything.

The details of what followed are foggy. I'm unsure how I made it home or what transpired exactly, but I recall waking up after receiving the worst spanking of my life. My mom's stern reprimand made it abundantly clear: I had overstepped my bounds and ventured too far without permission. It was a lesson learned the hard way, and from that day forward, I understood the importance of seeking permission before embarking on any adventures alone because the world is not safe and something bad could happen to me.

My mom's friends introduced her to a man named Bobby, believing he would be a good match for her. Not long after they began seeing each other, our lives took a dramatic turn. We bid farewell to Jose's house, which was filled with my mom's close friends and their abuelita, and settled into a sprawling three-story home in San Francisco. This new space was a striking contrast to our previous cramped quarters; our new room was three times the size of the last one, and we even had our own bathroom. Initially, my mom and I still shared a room after moving in with Bobby, but the possibilities of this new home felt exciting.

Before long, I found myself in my own room with a massive king-sized waterbed—a luxury I had never experienced before. My mom had chosen to share a room with Bobby, and I was perfectly fine with this new arrangement. Having my own space was a thrilling change. I loved the sound the waterbed made as I moved, the gentle sloshing of water hitting the sides, and the soothing sensation of its motion. It became a source of comfort, a little haven where I felt at ease.

With the move came a new preschool, where I have vivid memories of nap time and a cherished cassette tape of old Christmas songs that I was gifted. I cherished this tape; it became a comforting presence in my life, something I turned to during moments of distress. Whenever I felt upset, I would play it on repeat, allowing its familiar melodies to soothe my spirit and restore my sense of peace.

Living with Bobby brought moments of joy and stability, a contrast to the uncertainty I had known before. I hadn't had a 'dad' figure before him since my mom left my biological father before I was born, and the other man she had been with was in my life for only a brief period. So Bobby was my first real experience of having someone step into that role. We enjoyed picnics at Stinson beach, and I loved spending time with him. I even started emulating my mom's hairstyle, wanting to be just like her. Bobby would sometimes take me to work with him, where I met all kinds of new people. He was a businessman, and I felt a sense of pride and belonging in those moments.

He appeared to be a good dad figure on the surface, and there were moments where he seemed protective. When a white pit bull we brought home bit my upper lip, causing it to gush blood, Bobby immediately got rid of the dog. This action made me feel like he was someone who cared about my safety, reinforcing the image of him as a good dad. At that time, it seemed like he was looking out for me, providing a sense of security that I had never experienced before.

Despite these positive experiences, a darker undercurrent ran through my young life. Nightmares began to plague me, and I started wetting the bed. Dark creatures lurked in the shadows of my room, instilling a profound fear of the dark and being alone. These fears crept in at night, casting a shadow over the joyful moments I experienced during the day. The sense of safety I felt with Bobby during our outings contrasted sharply with the dread that gripped me in the quiet hours of the night. I often wondered: Was this turmoil a result of all the moving around and being placed into foster care, or was there something else happening in the present that remained unknown?

Strangely, I never felt unsafe around Bobby during our time in that big house in San Francisco. In my young mind, he was a protective and safe figure, and the moments of joy and stability seemed to outweigh any underlying unease. How innocent and naive I was.

Looking back, I wonder if those ominous shadows and the nightmares were a forewarning of things to come. It's possible that, even at such a young age, my intuition and body were trying to alert me to something that wasn't quite right. However, I wasn't aware of these gifts or how to interpret them at that age. It's unsettling to realize that the very signals that might have been trying to protect me were ones I didn't yet know how to heed.

Bobby lost his job suddenly, and with that, our circumstances took a sharp turn. We found ourselves moving into a tiny, pale pink, run-down two-bedroom apartment on San Bruno Avenue, near the San Francisco International Airport (SFO) airport. It was a stark contrast to the grandeur of our previous three-story home, a shift that was unsettling and disorienting. Even at that young age, I quietly became aware that good things don't always last, and life could change in an instant. This new reality was a harsh reminder of how fragile stability could be, reinforcing the underlying sense of not being safe.

As I entered kindergarten, my mom's work commitments grew, leaving Bobby to care for me at home. Despite the upheaval, I found solace in attending school. I relished the opportunity to learn, to read, and to express myself through art. Most of all, I cherished the chance to interact with other children, a rarity in my previous experiences where adults had been my primary company. School became a place where I could embrace the joys of childhood alongside peers.

Life before this run-down apartment feels distant, existing in shattered moments of color and darkness amidst the fog of memory. However, living in this space and facing the trials that came with it left an indelible mark on my life. The memories from this point onward are crystal clear, filled with trauma that shattered my innocence. Up until then, I had navigated life with a sense of purity, but the challenges and hardships of this house stripped away that innocence, forcing me to confront the harsh realities of life. I had experienced trauma before this house, but what I endured within its walls and beyond profoundly impacted my entire life moving forward.

C-LOVE

Chapter 2
He's a Monster!

I heard yelling and commotion in the front room, so I peeked out from my bedroom through the sliding door. My mom and Bobby were in a heated argument. I was so young that I have no idea what they were fighting about; in my memory, there are no words or sounds, only visuals and the palpable tension in the air. This was the first time I recall them fighting.

I vividly remember Bobby's face and my mom, heavily pregnant with my sister. Then, I witnessed something that would forever be etched in my memory: Bobby kicked my mom in her pregnant stomach, sending her flying backward across the room into the white wicker chair we had. The shock of that moment still lingers within me. I couldn't believe a man would kick the pregnant mother of his baby! It's a cruelty I have never forgotten. I closed my door and then I think he left the house.

The next thing I remember is hearing my mom crying in the bathroom. This was the first time I saw and heard her cry. It was so painful that I went into the bathroom with her and just sat there with her. To this day, my mom still doesn't remember this moment, but I can't forget it or unsee it. Bobby wasn't the same person we had lived with for the past year and a half. He was a monster. The shock of this moment remained in my body for decades.

After my sister was born, I found myself taking on many responsibilities. I changed her diapers, gave her baths, fed her, and looked after her while my mom was at work. Bobby, although home all the time, didn't like to do the 'work' and would have me do it instead. With no other kids around to play with, I spent a lot of time alone, finding solace in the driveway, yard, and the little shack-like building in the back of the apartment complex. I pretended the plumbing pipes were monkey bars, played with the snails in the yard, and imagined I was running a household in the dilapidated shed. I definitely remember talking to myself a lot, creating imaginary friends and an imaginary world to escape to.

Despite the loneliness, I formed a friendship with the landlady, a warm woman in her 50s who always greeted me with a smile. I would often spend time in her unit, where she would share snacks with me. I quickly learned a valuable lesson about staplers after accidentally stapling my finger—definitely a mistake I never made again!

There was also an older man who occasionally took me on walks up San Bruno Avenue to the store and back. He was tall and quiet, but I appreciated his presence; he had a kind soul. These small interactions brought a glimmer of light to my otherwise solitary days.

Then the unspeakable began to unfold. With my mom at work and me home after school with Bobby, while my sister slept peacefully in her crib, it felt like just another ordinary day. However, that illusion was shattered when Bobby summoned me into the bathroom for the first time. This moment is forever etched in my mind, its details deeply ingrained as if carved into the very fabric of my soul.

I naively stepped into the bathroom and immediately was faced with a magazine out on the counter of women doing weird things with men. My child brain couldn't quite make sense of what I was seeing or looking at. They were naked or almost naked and Bobby was naked. I had never seen him naked until this moment. I had never seen a grown man naked until this moment, I was frozen and so confused. Shock again took over my being. I felt paralyzed.

I must have jumped out of my body, because when I revisit this memory, it's as if I am up on the ceiling witnessing everything that took place next. Trapped. I felt so trapped. Nowhere to go, no one to call for. He began to put jelly on his private and told me to lick it off. I really didn't want to, and it felt like I had no choice. The experience was repulsive—the smell, the texture, and the idea of using my mouth to lick it off his body part, which also felt unclean. I couldn't comprehend how this was real life; it felt like a nightmare. Why couldn't I just wake up from it?

Once the jelly was gone, he had me use my hands. Showing me the motion of rubbing up and down and guiding my pace until white stuff flew out of his private and went into the toilet. What in the world was that white stuff? Did he just pee? All of this was so confusing. What was that smell? While making me do this he was flipping through the pages of this magazine staring at all of these women.

It felt like an eternity in that bathroom, the smell of jelly lingering, the sticky texture clinging to my hands and mouth, making me want to vomit. When it was finally over, I don't remember where I went or what I did. The details blur, but the feelings remain etched in my memory—feeling wrong, dirty, scared, and deeply confused. And just like that, my innocence was shattered, never to return. Innocence isn't something you can reclaim or repair once it's taken; when it's shattered, it's gone forever.

He made it very clear that I better not tell anyone, or else. The threat lingered in the air, and I knew I couldn't confide in my mom. After witnessing him kick her in her pregnant tummy, I understood that he meant business—he was a monster, after all. To ensure my silence, he began bribing me with gifts. One of those gifts was a second piercing in my ears, a moment that should have been filled with joy. Instead, it was overshadowed by the heavy secret I was forced to keep.

This was only the beginning—three years of sexual abuse. Three years of being forced to do things that were repulsive, things I didn't want to do, with no choice in the matter. It was torture. The bathroom incident marked the start of a harrowing period that would continue in secret, filled with fear, shame, and confusion. Each day became a battle to navigate the horrors that unfolded, leaving me feeling trapped and isolated. These three years of suffering were a heavy burden, shaping my understanding of the world in ways I couldn't fully comprehend at the time. It was a darkness that would take decades to heal from, a journey that was only just beginning.

The abuse was relentless, casting a dark shadow over my childhood and distorting my sense of self. He would rotate what he did. Sometimes, he had me do things to him; sometimes, he would do things to me. I felt so much embarrassment and shame about my body, and towards my body's functions and holding in this secret. I felt trapped in this nightmare, and there was no way to escape it. He was never satiated; he always wanted and needed more, and for some reason, he kept coming to me for it even though I was only a kid. This wasn't fair. Why me?

One day my friend came home with me after school and I thought I would be safe from Bobby, I was so wrong. When we were in my room playing, he showed up in the doorway naked. No shame. He came in and he directed us to get naked and touch each other and hump my teddy bear and to touch him. This memory is such a blur. The only solace I got from this is at least then I wasn't all alone in the shame. Someone else knew the secret of what I was going through and experienced some of it too. I wasn't a good friend, I couldn't protect her from Bobby.

This incident really awoke something in my private area that I hadn't been aware of before, and caused me to start humping my teddy bear on my own without Bobby around. Nothing felt good with Bobby, so I would check out of my body while he did what he did until he was done and I was alone. He would make my private burn like fire to the point it would hurt to pee after and I couldn't tell him to stop. I had no say in anything he did to me or made me do to him. I would cry and shower after trying to scrape away the 'dirty' sensations and feelings. However, when I would hump my teddy bear on my own, it actually felt good. I experienced, what I now know of as an orgasm, at 5 years old.

I remember one of the times I was humping my teddy bear in the closet and my mom walked in on me. I felt so mortified, shocked, wrong, and worried about Bobby. I felt caught and in trouble. I felt trapped because I couldn't tell her why I was doing that or where I learned it from out of fear of Bobby. Being trapped is an experience I felt and found myself in a lot in life and has been a hard pattern to overcome.

I couldn't bring myself to tell my mom about the abuse, even after she caught me in the closet with my teddy bear. My fear of Bobby was overwhelming. He had a violent temper that became even more apparent after we moved into a run-down, tiny apartment. I once saw him kick my pregnant mom in the stomach. Another time, he spanked me until I peed for accidentally breaking a window with my skates. When I peed from the pain, he spanked me even harder. Bobby threatened me, saying if I ever told our secret, he would hurt my mom, and I believed him. He was terrifying, a monster adept at deception, like a wolf in sheep's clothing. I felt trapped, powerless, just a child with no escape. Whatever he decided to do, I had no choice but to endure it.

Bobby wasn't the only source of fear in my life at that time. One day, as I skated in the long driveway near the landlady's unit, a sense of impending danger washed over me. A stranger, a man, emerged from around the corner, heading straight toward me like a dark shadow. My instincts screamed at me to flee, so I skated as fast as I could toward the safety of the apartment.

I stumbled and fell, my heart pounding in my chest as I saw the man closing in on me. With adrenaline coursing through my veins, I scrambled to my feet, sprinted to the door, and burst inside, breathless and shaken. I immediately sought out Bobby and told him what had happened. Without hesitation, he grabbed a knife and rushed outside to confront the stranger.

It struck me as strange how I had run from one potential danger and monster, only to seek refuge with another. At that moment, the world felt like a terrifying place, filled with monsters lurking in every shadow. There was nowhere to turn - no one to trust - especially for a young girl like me. As if the very act of seeking safety led me straight into the arms of a familiar nightmare. The realization that danger was hidden behind familiar faces was a hard truth to swallow, leaving me feeling more isolated and vulnerable than ever before.

C-LOVE

Chapter 3
Life is a Never-Ending Nightmare

Home wasn't the only place where I was touched inappropriately by others. It was as if the abuse at home turned me into a magnet for more of the same. No matter where I went, these types of people and situations seemed to find me. I felt that this is how life is and it's what I deserve. I didn't know any better. At Belle Air Elementary, on the playground, a classmate's older brother would touch me on my body during recess out in the field. Other kids would gather around and hide us from the yard duty teachers. His younger brother would touch me during movie time in the classroom, when we would all sit on the floor and the lights were turned off.

There was this older girl (I believe she was a teenager or even older) who would touch me during movie time, at the Latchkey Daycare I went to during the summer and after school. By this point, I was used to being touched and I just kept checking out of my body and going into my safe imaginary world, disassociating from my body until it was done. None of these experiences of being touched by others ever felt good and just made my shame, disconnection and embarrassment increase.

My body didn't feel like it was mine, it felt like it was everyone else's; I hated my body and being in my body. I never felt clean no matter how much I showered. The dirty feeling was always there and wouldn't wash away no matter how hard I tried.

I even had a younger cousin hump my face once in his backyard. It hurt so bad! I never told anyone, but I can never forget it due to how bad it hurt. It made me feel like I was going to die due to not being able to breathe. This is when the screaming in my head began to happen. I didn't feel like I was ever allowed to say "No." probably conditioning from Bobby. So I would just scream in my head when the not-so-great things would happen to me with others. This has always made me wonder what happens in other people's families. Is it normal for cousins to hump you and dad figures to touch you?

I hated using the bathroom at school. The thought of it made my stomach churn with anxiety. It got so bad that I'd hold my pee in until I couldn't anymore, and I'd end up peeing my pants. My mom noticed and started asking questions. She knew this wasn't normal behavior for me, and she wanted to understand what was going on. But I couldn't bring myself to tell her the truth. I didn't feel safe in the bathroom, and I didn't know how to explain why. Eventually she got me to reveal everything about the boy who was touching me at movie time. I never told her about the older brother. My mom took action and went to the school to address the situation. She spoke to them about what was happening, and thankfully, that particular boy stopped. It was a small victory, it gave me a glimmer of hope. Maybe I wasn't as powerless as I had been made to believe.

"America's Most Wanted" and "Cops" were two of my favorite shows growing up. I loved seeing them capture the bad guys, perhaps because I was aware of so many in my own life. It was a weird and eerie experience the day one of my classmate's older sisters ended up on an episode as missing and having been kidnapped. She was in her 20s. The reality of her disappearance made me feel even more unsafe. If an adult could be taken, kids were certainly vulnerable too. It made things on TV feel incredibly real—it wasn't just make-believe anymore.

Then we heard about Polly Klaas being taken right down the street from my aunt's house in Hayward. This event struck a particularly deep chord, solidifying my belief that the world was inherently unsafe. How could I ever feel secure when both my home and the outside world were filled with monsters? It reinforced the sensation of being trapped in a never-ending nightmare. Life felt like a perpetual torment, and I was only seven. It made me question the purpose of life itself. Was there a point to it? Why would any of us want to be here in a seemingly unending nightmare?

We ended up moving to San Mateo and I had to transfer to a new school with new kids and a new babysitter. Bobby wasn't home as much as he had been before. He had gotten some kind of job so he wasn't spending infinite hours at home. I thought I was safe and that the touching and burning down there would stop. It didn't. He still found time and moments to keep up the sessions with me. He also started adding things to them like cooking oil and soap. I hated the way my private part felt, it made me want to chop it off to make the burning stop and him to go away.

I loved my babysitter in 2nd grade, and I loved her house. It was safe there. I would spend time in the hammock under the trees, rocking myself to sleep as the breeze gently caressed my skin. I would swim for hours in the pool in her backyard. I loved holding my breath and being under the water; it was as if it turned the whole world of nightmares off. I was a fish in the water, never wanting to get out. No one could touch me in there and the water helped me feel clean and made the burning down there stop.

There were other kids around, but I never fully connected with them. The secrets I was holding made it difficult to bond. I always felt inherently bad and wrong, as if everyone perceived me as a monster. Bobby was the real monster, yet somehow I felt like the monster whenever I was around others, especially when their eyes were upon me. It felt as if they could see all the bad things I was involved in with Bobby whenever they looked at me. The shame was overwhelming, and I couldn't bear it.

One day while walking home from school with a group of kids, an elderly couple offered us candy. Since it was close to Halloween, I didn't think twice about accepting it—they seemed so friendly and kind. Unfortunately, I never got to enjoy that candy. When my mom found out, the consequences were severe. She cut off my long, beautiful hair, leaving it barely touching my shoulders. I was forced to eat stew for dinner, which I despised and it made me throw up. On top of that, I was grounded. The whole experience was harsh and left a lasting impression on me.

It felt like such a harsh punishment when these were good people and we lived with a bona fide monster. I, of course, couldn't tell her about Bobby, and I didn't understand how she couldn't see what was happening under her own roof. This confused my ability to sense good people and trust myself. The mixed messages made me question my judgment and added to the already heavy burden of secrets I was carrying.

This was the year that Bloody Mary became a big scary thing. Everyone kept talking about it at school, and it terrified me. It made it hard for me to be in the bathroom, at home alone or in the dark. I was so scared of this woman who supposedly kills you through the mirror. It felt like she could kill you by just thinking or saying her name once.

Somehow, my babysitter found out, and she forced me into one of the bedrooms with a mirror, insisting that I say the name three times. It was yet another experience of being coerced into doing something I was terrified of, leaving me with no choice in the matter. I felt that adults shouldn't be in charge, as they never seemed to make anything better. I never overcame that fear, and to this day, I still feel anxious around mirrors, especially when I'm alone in front of them. I still sleep with a night light on.

Adults around me often seemed at a loss for how to make children feel safe or shield them from harm. This experience, among many others, reinforced my sense of powerlessness and persistent fear. It added to the already heavy load of trauma and confusion I was carrying. I found myself yearning to grow up and escape the control of the adults in my life, believing that adulthood would liberate me from their influence and the nightmares that haunted my childhood.

Since I was often busy with school and homework, I didn't see much of my sister during this time. She was five years younger than me, and I frequently find myself wondering how she coped with our circumstances. I'm curious about her perspective and experiences during that same period, pondering whether she felt the same fears or faced similar challenges.

I don't recall exactly what sparked the change, but at the age of eight, my mom finally left Bobby. We moved back to San Bruno, settling into another tiny one-bedroom apartment, astonishingly just around the corner from where all the distressing events with Bobby had begun. The likelihood of us ending up so close to our old place seemed almost beyond belief. I didn't know the details of why we left, but part of me wondered if my mom had discovered something that prompted the move. Despite everything, I found myself worrying about Bobby—was he alright with this separation? What would he do next? The uncertainty of it all left me anxious about what the future might hold.

Returning to Belle Aire Elementary for the third grade, and reuniting with my old friends, I hoped for a fresh start and better days ahead. Yet, even though Bobby was no longer a daily presence in our house, the fear of him lingered. It felt as if he was there, even in his absence. My sister and I continued to visit him at his new place in San Francisco and went on outings with him. Despite the physical distance, the shadow of his influence remained a constant in our lives, affecting our sense of security and peace.

I'll never forget the day he took my tiny three-year-old sister to the bathroom instead of me. I thought that by always doing as he wanted and not telling anyone, I could protect my little sister. I was so wrong. This man was never satisfied; nothing was ever enough for him. He was a bottomless pit of sexual needs and desires, all that mattered to him was himself.

The fear and trauma didn't end with our move or my mom leaving him. It felt like Bobby's presence loomed over us. A constant shadow, even in his absence. Due to him being the father of my sister, he wasn't going anywhere. His connection to my sister meant he remained a part of our daily lives.

After this incident, my school friend—who had experienced similar things with Bobby alongside me in kindergarten—insisted that I had to tell my mom. We were only in third grade, being forced to make such difficult choices. She said it was the only way to help my sister. I agreed, but I was paralyzed with fear as we approached my mom's car after school. My mom could see that something was wrong just by the look on our faces as we drew near.

I couldn't get any words out, so my friend told my mom instead. My mom was in shock. I was crying.

Everything felt like a whirlwind after that. The next thing I knew, we were at my mom's friend's house, and the police arrived. They asked me so many questions, but I couldn't verbally answer any of them. My voice felt like it was gone, so I asked if I could write out what had happened instead. They agreed. I sat there and wrote an essay describing all the things Bobby had done over the years. I was so scared; it took me forever to write out the words.

This didn't make Bobby disappear. Instead, it triggered a series of events that introduced me to the complexities of the court system. I learned how long it actually takes to get a predator away from a child; it's not instantaneous at all. I learned that what Bobby did was wrong and that he was a predator, an adult word for monster. I learned that my sister still had to see him due to visitation rights, and now she had to visit him all alone without me. This filled me with guilt, shame, and confusion. I questioned whether telling my mom was the right decision. Did I make it worse for my sister? Why couldn't Bobby just go away forever?

These events added to my sense of helplessness. Even though I had finally spoken out, the system seemed slow and ineffective. The fear and trauma persisted, casting a shadow over every aspect of my life. The weight of protecting my sister now felt even heavier, knowing that she had to face him all alone. Especially after he had started to take her to the bathroom instead of me. Why did it feel like Monsters have more rights than kids?

C-LOVE

Chapter 4
I Can't Wait to Grow Up

Christmas morning arrived, but there was no joy in our tiny one-bedroom apartment. The small tree was lit, and a few decorations adorned the space, but the atmosphere was heavy with sadness. Instead of enjoying Christmas together as a family, Bobby was there to take my sister. None of us wanted this to happen; my mom even refused to open the door when he arrived to pick her up. We sat together, holding each other and crying, the warmth of the holiday overshadowed by our pain.

Eventually, Bobby called the police, and due to the court orders on visitation, my mom had to hand over my sister, even though it was known that he wasn't a safe person for us kids to be around. My mom bravely told the police officer about the things Bobby had done to us, but it didn't matter because of the court-ordered visitation agreement. This moment has forever stuck in my memory with so much heartbreak, pain, and injustice. How could you make a mom let her little 3-year-old child go with someone who is touching them inappropriately? The powerlessness, the heartbreak, the hopelessness— the world is so unbelievably unfair. The police seemed to be helping the Monster, not us.

This wasn't the last time the system failed us, and Bobby won. Even after I came forward and gave written testimony about all the awful things he did, my sister was not immediately protected.

This made me lose trust in the police and the system— who was there to turn to for help? I had no idea.

We lived in this one-bedroom apartment, with a rundown motel behind it that was very active at night with yelling and raucous behavior. I slept on a mattress on the floor next to the window that overlooked the motel. I would peek out when I heard sounds that woke me up and scared me. It was a constant reminder of the chaos just beyond our walls. It's during these unsettling nights that I remember getting on my knees and praying for a better life, for some kind of help. I had been to church with my God-family, I was aware of God and hoped maybe he would help us, since humans didn't seem to.

People didn't seem to offer much assistance; many felt like monsters themselves or enablers of the monsters, lost in their own struggles. Perhaps there was something—or someone—out there who could provide the support I needed. That's when my Godfather stepped in, taking me for weekly swimming sessions at a large pool in Pacifica. I cherished these moments with him. My Godfather and his family provided the sense of safety and warmth that I had been missing and desperately needed. During those years with Bobby around, we hadn't spent time with them, and I'm not sure why. But in their presence, I could momentarily forget the darkness surrounding us and simply breathe. I felt safe.

Looking back, it seemed like during the years with Bobby around, the good people were nowhere to be seen. Or perhaps the darkness of Bobby's actions overshadowed any pleasant memories, rendering them difficult to recall. Regardless, my time with my Godfather and his family shone brightly amidst the darkness.

I began to shower multiple times a day, sometimes for long periods of time. The water cascading over me offered a temporary escape from the turmoil within. I felt deeply dirty, tainted by Bobby's actions, and I just wanted to rid myself of the unclean feeling that seemed to linger no matter what I did. Each time I stepped into the shower, it was as if I was trying to wash away Bobby and everything he had done to me, to cleanse myself of his presence. To cleanse myself of his touch. I couldn't escape the sensation his hands and mouth left on my body.

But no matter how hard I scrubbed, how long I stayed underwater, or how hot I made the water, it never worked. The memories clung to me like stubborn stains, refusing to wash away. The shower became a futile attempt to rid myself of the emotional and psychological weight that Bobby had imprinted on me.

My mom took me to a therapist, hoping it would help me cope with everything I had been through. But that first encounter with a professional turned out to be deeply traumatizing. I had barely met this woman when she began instructing me to use dolls to reenact exactly what had happened to me. In that moment, I felt trapped in that room, forced to relive the horrors I had endured. It was as if my voice didn't matter; all that mattered was satisfying her curiosity. It was yet another incident with an adult who only made things worse, not better.

Thankfully, I didn't go back to her after that session. I don't remember if I told my mom about how awful it was; all I knew was that I couldn't bear to go back. Instead, we started seeing another therapist, one who was further away but much kinder. I never spoke about what happened again in those sessions. Instead, I would distract myself by playing Chinese checkers or doing my homework.

That experience with the first therapist left me deeply scarred. Talking about what had happened made my body ache with pain, and each word shared felt like I was reliving the trauma all over again. It was as if the words were knives, cutting into me, and I couldn't bear the thought of reopening those wounds. The pain was so intense that it made me question whether life was worth living, especially since it felt like a never-ending nightmare.

To cope with all the pain, I found solace in school, especially reading, although I didn't realize it at the time. Looking back, it's clear that diving into my studies and immersing myself in books became my way of escaping from the turmoil of my life. I found refuge in the pages of stories, losing myself in the worlds created by authors.

One of my favorite series was the Boxcar Children. I was captivated by how the children created a home for themselves in the middle of nowhere, using their creativity and resourcefulness to survive. Their adventures made me daydream about escaping my own life and starting fresh somewhere else. I longed to grow up and become an adult, believing that adulthood would offer an escape from all the nightmares I was living through, and an escape from all the monsters and incompetent adults.

In addition to my academic pursuits, I also found joy in Mexican Folk Dancing. After school, I would join my friends in practicing routines, wearing flowing skirts and heeled shoes. The rhythmic movements, Spanish music and colorful costumes transported me to a world far away from my own. Performing at school, hotels, and the mall was exhilarating, providing me with moments of lightness amidst the heaviness of life. These activities became my refuge, offering another glimmer and escape from the pain that weighed me down

At ten years old, I became acutely aware of our financial struggles. The signs were everywhere—from our modest living conditions to the daily adjustments we made, like using powdered milk in my cereal. We didn't have cable, so I would get incredibly excited about any promotional free week or month of Disney Channel programming.

My mom often had to leave me home alone because we couldn't afford a babysitter, or she would drop me off at the library or in the lobby of her workplace. These experiences were a constant reminder of our tight budget and her efforts to make do while ensuring I was safe and occupied.

Despite our financial struggles, my mom always managed to make birthdays and Christmas feel abundant. She had a remarkable ability to create magic out of very little. Reflecting on those times, I'm still amazed at how my mom worked her magic to make those celebrations so memorable out of so little. Her creativity and resourcefulness knew no bounds. Those moments have stayed with me throughout my life, serving as a reminder that even in the toughest times, there can still be moments of joy and abundance.

An old friend of my mom's began to reappear in our lives. She had known him and his family for decades, which fostered a deep sense of familiarity and trust between them. They had grown up just down the street from each other in Pacifica and both attended Terra Nova High School, he also used to play with one of her brothers. As he started to spend more time with us, I noticed how he brought a sense of joy and warmth into our home.

One thing that stood out to me was how he would create custom cards for all of us, often featuring Disney characters. It was so cool! As an aspiring artist myself, I felt a strong connection with him through our shared love of art. Watching him express his creativity and share it with our family fostered a sense of kinship between us.

But more than anything, I cherished how he made my mom happy. It was a joy to see her smile and laugh in a way I hadn't witnessed before. All I wanted was for her to feel that happiness all the time, and he seemed to bring it effortlessly into our lives. Maybe good things can happen for us, and perhaps my prayers to God were finally being answered.

C-LOVE

Chapter 5
I Don't Trust Adults

You can't be a model. Your legs are too big." One of my best friends in elementary school told me this after I answered her question about what I wanted to be when I grew up. Looking down at my legs, I became aware of how different they were from hers and other girls my age. They were thick and hairy. For the first time, I felt embarrassed and full of hatred towards them because I was stuck with them. It's not like I could cut them off. I hadn't thought of my legs before this moment and from this moment on I hated them.

I don't know if it was due to coming forward about what Bobby did, on top of all the emotional rollercoasters, or if it was just normal for my age, but my body began to go through a lot of changes and growth when I hit fourth grade. I began to thicken up, and it made me self-conscious because I was also really tall for my age. My friend pointing my legs out made me want to run and hide! I felt so fat and ugly. Did other girls feel this way? I felt so embarrassed about my body.

The kids began to play weird games on the playground too, comparing who looked better and interviewing other boys to ask who was better in each category. I always felt so humiliated by the things boys would say about me. Their comments made me feel even more awkward and out of place, adding to the growing discomfort I had with my body. It was a challenging time, trying to navigate all these changes while dealing with the aftermath of everything that had happened.

One day, I reached my breaking point. The girl who was always picking on me started making comments again while we were in line waiting for hot lunch, and I snapped. In a moment of pure frustration, I shoved her against the fence. The shock on her face mirrored my own, as well as the reactions of everyone around us. I was astonished by the way that outburst erupted from me like an untamed wild animal. She had grown accustomed to bullying me while I remained silent, but I just couldn't take it anymore, especially with everything weighing down on me from home. After that moment, she never picked on me again, but I felt terrible about my actions. I often wonder how bullies and monsters can live with themselves after hurting innocent people. Even when I hurt someone who deserved it, the guilt lingered. They must be made of something entirely different.

School became more complicated as our home life began to improve. We moved into a two-story house with my mom's new boyfriend off Westborough Blvd in South San Francisco. It was a lovely neighborhood, complete with biking trails, trees, and plenty of grassy areas to run and play, with parks nestled behind the houses. For a kid, it was a dream come true, especially after being cooped up in tiny apartments in rough neighborhoods with no backyards. It felt like an escape from jail.

The move represented a significant shift in our lives—a new chapter. The spacious house and safe neighborhood stood in stark contrast to the cramped apartment next to a run-down motel. For the first time in a long while, it felt like we had room to breathe. There was space to play, explore, and just be kids without the looming tension that had hung over us before.

On that first day, I rollerbladed up and down the street until it got dark. Later, I found a tree on the island at the end of the cul-de-sac and sat there, absorbing the essence of this new neighborhood, yearning to settle into this new reality. Was this real? Would it last? I felt a glimmer of hope that this time, things would remain good. Yet, even as I tried to embrace this newfound sense of safety, a part of me feared it wouldn't last—that it, too, could be taken away like everything else had been in the past.

Despite the hopeful changes at home, school grew increasingly complicated. The social dynamics became more challenging to navigate, and I struggled to fit in. My insecurities about my body, combined with the lingering effects of my past experiences, added layers of difficulty to my school life. A couple of bullies seemed to take pleasure in picking on me, which caused me to shut down and retreat to my escape place outside of my body. I suppose Bobby inadvertently gave me something useful through all the things he did; I learned to use that coping mechanism whenever people weren't being nice.

The combination of feeling out of place and dealing with bullies made school a challenging environment. I often felt overwhelmed and isolated, retreating into myself, finding solace in books, schoolwork, art, and learning as coping mechanisms. I also loved the monkey bars, where I would twirl around and around during recess until the bell rang. The sensation of flying gave me a rush, making me feel like a superhero. I was particularly good at swinging around the bar, switching my hands, and launching myself off like they do in the Olympics.

Fortunately, I had a few amazing teachers who poured love and encouragement into me—something I desperately needed and lacked at home. As my home life began to find balance, school remained a battlefield, highlighting the stark divide between my external circumstances and the inner turmoil I was facing.

We still weren't completely out of the woods with Bobby either. One day, he showed up at Latchkey Daycare during our outdoor playtime and kidnapped my sister. Right off the playground! None of the teachers intervened, and I felt utterly powerless and terrified. I couldn't protect her or stop him. I was left feeling like it was somehow my fault. The time it took for my mom to get my sister back felt interminable, stretching into weeks that seemed like months. The helplessness and fear of that period were profound, further compounding the trauma we were already enduring.

Thankfully, because of this incident, the court system FINALLY enforced supervised visits, meaning he could no longer be alone with my sister. It was a small victory—a glimmer of justice finally served but I couldn't help but wonder why it had taken them so long to act in the first place.

I still couldn't understand how the system, fully aware of his past abuse, allowed him to take her unsupervised in the first place. It's a piece of the puzzle that confuses and haunts me to this day. How could they permit someone so perverted to have access to her, especially after everything that had happened? This lack of protection deepened the mistrust I developed for the systems that were supposed to safeguard children like us. It felt like they were failing in their duty, as if adults didn't know how to truly care for children and instead enabled the monsters among us.

The incident at Latchkey was a terrifying reminder of Bobby's looming presence in our lives. Even though we were trying to rebuild and find stability, he managed to disrupt our sense of security yet again. The playground, a place meant for fun and play, became a scene of fear and helplessness. How could someone just take a child without permission like that?

When my mom finally managed to get my sister back, it was a relief, but the emotional toll had already been taken. The decision to move Bobby to supervised visits was a long overdue measure. Knowing that he could no longer be alone with my sister provided a small sense of safety. It meant he couldn't take her to the 'bathroom' anymore. Whenever she had to go visit him my tummy was in knots and distress because I knew what he was doing to her more than anyone, having lived through it myself. It was torture to know and not be able to do anything. Why this took so long, when they had testimony to what he did to us, is mind-boggling. But finally, there was some protection happening for my three-year-old sister and our family.

This episode at daycare reinforced the fragility of our situation and the constant battle to safeguard our lives. It underscored the unpredictable and erratic nature of Bobby's actions and the lingering threat he posed, even as we tried to move forward. I just wished he would disappear and never come back. The delay in holding Bobby accountable was a relentless source of frustration and bewilderment. How could someone do such awful things and get away with it? How many other monsters were out there, inflicting harm on children without consequence? Who was truly protecting kids?

This experience emphasized the importance of perseverance and advocacy, even when the system seems slow to respond. It also enhanced the resilience of my family in navigating these challenges and striving for a safer, more stable future.

Moving into this new house, being physically away from Bobby, dealing with mean kids at school, and going through so many body changes caused me to have huge emotional breakdowns when I would get home from school. I would go into my room, blast some music, and tear everything apart. I would have full on tantrums in there; screaming, crying, and throwing things. Then, after getting the pain out, I would clean everything up and come out as if nothing had happened. This went on for months.

My mom and lawyer were trying to prepare me to speak up in court about Bobby to get all of his parental rights taken away completely, so my sister would never have to spend any time with him again. This meant I had to verbally talk to a lawyer and share what I went through. Ugh, I didn't want to. The amount of fear that came up in my system anytime I tried to use my words to explain what he did was overwhelming. The sensations that would flood and take over my body felt gross. I hated the feeling. It made me want to chop my private off to stop the sensations from happening down there. Death seemed like a better option than trying to talk about all the things I lived through. Writing about what I went through was one thing; I could manage that. But speaking it aloud felt like torture.

I remember being in a room with my mom, a cop, and the lawyer. It felt like they were holding me down because I couldn't sit still. I kept throwing fits, crying, and desperately trying to avoid the conversation. "Can't I just write it out instead?" I thought. But no, that wasn't an option...ugh. My mom recalls this moment a bit differently, but that's how trauma works. For me, as a child, it was incredibly traumatic. It was yet another instance of being trapped in a room, forced to confront something I didn't want to, flooding my body with pain. I was exhausted from carrying that pain all the time. Would the throbbing in my private ever go away? I hated it so much. What was the point of this life? Why was I here if this was all it had to offer? I didn't want it anymore. I felt torn, having to keep my focus on helping my sister while being tortured by how long the process was taking.

The experience of going to a doctor who had to examine our bodies was another nightmare. At that time, I didn't realize this doctor was called a gynecologist. It was my first experience of being penetrated inside my private, and it added to the feeling of my body not being mine. Of being trapped in situations. I felt so exposed and vulnerable as my legs were spread wide open on the bed and in the stirrups, with a stranger staring into my private area. By that point, my private area didn't feel private anymore. Too many people had seen and touched it, making it feel like public property that I didn't have any rights or ownership to. I can't even remember if it was a man or woman. This felt just as wrong as what Bobby did. I was eight, no one should ever penetrate a child's private, how was this legal?

The explanation of needing to go to the doctor to ensure Bobby didn't do damaging things to our bodies never made sense to me. The irony was that the doctor's visit itself felt damaging in its own way. I couldn't understand why it mattered if a stranger could or couldn't see the damage done. I felt it inside and shared it, so why was that never good enough? Why was my testimony not enough and why did I have to tell it so many times to so many people? The whole process of wanting to help my sister and bring justice, felt like it brought on more torture for us in other ways. It was all so confusing and added to the layers of trauma we were already experiencing.

I felt immense pressure and conflict. I wanted to help my sister and see Bobby pay for what he had done to us, but why did I have to keep talking about it over and over again? Why wasn't once enough? The repetitive recounting and reliving of my trauma was torture. Each time I spoke, it only seemed to reopen wounds that no one could heal. I longed for it all to end, for the justice system to recognize our pain without making me relive it repeatedly. Why couldn't the monster just be taken to jail? He's a monster—can't you see it? It felt as though the adults around me were enablers, dragging out the process unnecessarily. If I did something small that my mom didn't like, I was immediately punished and faced consequences. So why did this grown man get to commit heinous crimes against us kids and take years to be held accountable? None of this felt fair, and it fueled my growing distrust of adults.

Eventually, Bobby stopped showing up to his supervised visits with my sister. After missing several appointments in a row, it became apparent that these meetings were no longer justifiable, and we were no longer required to take her to see him. This change marked a significant shift, relieving us from the stress and uncertainty these visits brought, and allowing us to move forward with our lives without his presence close.

This is a poem I wrote years later around the emotional experience of going through all of this and the stages of it as I got older.

Mommy Where Are You?

Only five years of age
Sexual urges
10 million showers
I keep scrubbing
Can't get clean
Mommy Where Are You?
Look what He's Doing to me

Tears come rolling down her face...Someone's touching her sacred private place... It's burning like hell... As she is staring at the ceiling...Zoning out... At a young age she is learning to void out... Turn off physically... As someone touches and abuses her body... She's screaming in her head for him to stop...The only way to see her agony... Is to look at her in her eyes...Wounded so deeply...By such lewd acts...Her eyes are glass... You can see right through...To the heart of the pain...The wound...They are stained permanently...With the blood of the crimes that happened while mommy was gone...Not at home...At Work... Away...

Only five years of age
Sexual urges
10 million showers

I keep scrubbing
Can't get clean
Mommy Where Are You?
Look what He's Doing to me

Tearing her room apart... Can't get rid of these tantrums...Body so young and immature...With such strong emotional urges...Jaded toward adulthood...He took her childhood away...Perspective pushed beyond innocence...In the Middle of exploring the world...So much built up anger...She's gonna explode...She keeps feeling his hands touching her... And he's nowhere around...Every time she closes her eyes...She feels the burning sensation between her thighs...Causes her to sleep with a light...Scared of the dark...Scared to be left alone...She doesn't like to go anywhere... Away from home...

Only five years of age
Sexual urges
10 million showers
I keep scrubbing
Can't get clean
Mommy Where Are You?
Look what He's Doing to me

As puberty approaches...Signs of being a woman do too...She hates her body...The way it moves...The way it looks...She hates the way each step she takes feels...Cover it up...Wraps herself up...Hides behinds her books...Behind her grades...Pours her heart out...Into scholastic achievement...Any and all things creative...Avoids what happened...Avoids the topic...Acts as if...It never really happened...She doesn't want to talk about it...And yet it still exists...In the back of her mind...In her dreams...Her heart...Is proof...From all the shattered pieces...Her healing has went into remission...For the time being...But it will come pouring out...With a vengeance...The moment she boils over...Just can't take it anymore...It will all come rushing out...Vomit...

Only five years of age
Sexual urges
10 million showers
I keep scrubbing
Can't get clean
Mommy Where Are You?
Look what He's Doing to me

She's blossomed into a young lady...Still not comfortable with intimacy...Introverted...Doesn't like attention...Doesn't like anyone too close...Guys have come and gone...Reinstating the pain the hurt...All she knows of men...Is what she got taught at a young age...They only want one thing...They use...They abuse...Step all over your heart...She takes a look in the mirror...Stares deep within herself...Comes face to face with all her past wounds...One by one the grieving has begun...The pain...The losses...She buried...The tears come pouring out...Seems unending...Like they'll never let up...Vengeance...The healing process has now began...The numbness she's been living in...All these years...Is thawing out...It's hard to turn off...To zone out...The switch doesn't seem to work anymore...The faucet turns to a steady tinkle...She's fully present...And ALIVE...Taken her a quarter of her life...To find her center...Feel any peace and joy...Thought she'd never see or feel the light again...Now she can live the other three quarters lying in it...Absorbing it...And letting it shine through...We're all meant to shine...Just some cycles take longer than others...

Mommy
It's ok that you weren't there
I forgive you
And I'm not five anymore
I'm clean from the inside out now
And HE CAN'T HURT ME ANYMORE

I can't blame you
And I can't blame me
It was all him
And he got his...

Cassandra Love Lambert, Sept 16, 2007

C-LOVE

Chapter 6
Answered Prayers?

Having never had a real 'dad' before—since my mom left mine before I was born—and with the last two men bringing so much havoc into our lives, it seemed like a no-brainer when my mom and her childhood best friend sat us down to ask how we felt about them getting married. My sister and I gave a resounding "Yes!" We were thrilled at the thought of becoming flower girls and being a part of his big family. His parents even lived just up the street from my godfather's parents, making everything feel almost too perfect. It seemed like, finally, things were coming together. Maybe all those nights praying on the side of my bed at night were actually heard.

The idea of stability and a 'loving' father figure in our lives felt like a dream come true. We were burnt out from the chaos, trauma and fear that had marked our past. The prospect of being part of a larger, supportive family filled us with hope and excitement. It was a chance for a fresh start, a new chapter where happiness and safety were possible. My mom deserved to be happy, and it was a beautiful beginning for all of us.

Our first Christmas with my stepdad's family was magical—so many people, love, gifts, and yummy food and snacks. There was an abundance of everything. It was an absolute contrast to the Christmases we had known before, filled with a sense of warmth and belonging that felt almost surreal. I remember doing chores to have enough money to buy gifts for everyone from his family and my godfather's family. We went to this "$1 and up" store. I loved thinking of each person, finding something specifically for them, and then wrapping it. I especially loved watching them open it; it always made me feel so good inside to bring moments of joy to others in the form of gifts.

After celebrating with his family, we strolled down the street in the crisp night air, the stars shining above us, making our way to my godfather's parents' house. There, we joined another huge, loving family filled with all my favorite people. We would indulge in more delicious food, sing Christmas carols, and joyfully open presents together, creating cherished memories that would last a lifetime.

These moments were filled with laughter, joy, and the comforting feeling of being surrounded by people who genuinely cared. For the first time, Christmas felt like a true celebration of love and togetherness. It was a time of healing and hope, showing us that despite the darkness in our recent past, there could be light and happiness in our future.

I would sneak away from the Christmas caroling and sit at my older godmother's feet while she knitted in her little in-law unit. The atmosphere was always so peaceful despite the bustling activity of the Spanish-speaking soap operas playing in the background. I loved how her room smelled a combination of her perfume and the food she would eat; it always made me feel so safe.

My godmother, originally from Bolivia, didn't speak English, but we communicated in our own silent language of understanding. As she sat knitting, her hands moved with practiced skill, creating beautiful pieces of fabric with each delicate stitch. I would watch her intently, mesmerized by the rhythmic clicking of the needles and the intricate patterns that took shape before my eyes. She always had something she had made just for me, and it felt extraordinary knowing her time, energy, and love were woven into every stitch. When I wore the things she made, I felt held by her love and care. I still have some of those cherished items to this day and have passed them down to my daughter so she too can feel the warmth and connection that was knitted into every thread.

In those moments, I felt enveloped in a profound sense of security and tranquility. My godmother would often offer me sugar cookies from a tin and brew me a cup of tea, enhancing the cozy ambiance of her room. She made me feel truly cared for and loved, always gifting me something she had crafted with her own hands. These handmade treasures became precious keepsakes, tangible reminders of our bond and the love she infused into everything she did. She was one of my earth angels, and the language barrier never hindered the deep love we shared.

Despite the darkness that often loomed over my life, those moments with my godmother provided a much needed reprieve that I have always returned to in moments of distress. They offered me a sense of stability and warmth, grounding me in the present and filling my heart with gratitude for the quiet moments of connection. I love her so much, eternally. I feel her love to this day and have shared it with my daughter.

The day my mom and my new step-in 'dad' officially got married was a joyous occasion, filled with love and celebration. So many people we had never met before came and were in attendance. The air was buzzing with excitement and anticipation as friends, family, and neighbors gathered to witness their union. There was an abundance of laughter, music, and delicious food, creating a vibrant atmosphere of warmth and happiness.

For me, it was a moment of profound significance. Finally, I felt a sense of belonging, a connection to something greater than myself. Having someone to call "Dad" and a family to call my own was a dream come true. No longer did I feel alone or adrift in the world; I had a father—someone who genuinely wanted to care for me and protect me.

As I looked around at the smiling faces and felt the love and support radiating from everyone present, I realized that I was truly blessed to be surrounded by such wonderful people. It was a day I would never forget, a day that marked the beginning of a newfound sense of normalcy and happiness in my life. With this newfound confidence, I navigated the halls of my school with a sense of self-assurance. I no longer shrank away from the stares or whispers of my peers. Instead, I held my head high, knowing that I was worthy of love and belonging.

Being part of the wedding preparations felt like stepping into a fairy tale. I relished every moment, from getting my hair styled into a beautiful French braid to being fitted for a dress that my new dad's mom crafted from scratch. I have always loved handmade items—the time and energy poured into them, created specifically for you. For the first time ever, I felt like a princess, and I cherished that feeling deeply. I felt a profound connection to Cinderella, as if I had been living a lie and was finally beginning my real life. I wasn't just a worthless peasant; I was truly a valuable and worthy child.

Even more than that, I loved watching my mom being pampered and showered with love. Seeing her have a bridal shower, surrounded by friends and family celebrating her, felt truly magical. The thoughtful gifts she received lit up her face with happiness, and in those moments, I felt a profound sense of joy for her. All I ever wanted was for my mom to be happy, especially after witnessing the mistreatment she had endured from other men before. It was heartwarming to see her bask in the love and support she so richly deserved.

Watching her get fitted for her dress and then seeing her get her makeup done on the morning of the wedding, with everyone helping and supporting her, filled me with joy. It was a day I'll never forget, filled with so much love and happiness. She had finally found someone who could love her the way I felt she deserved. It was like she had found her happily ever after, and I couldn't have been happier for her.

I remember how my mom's soon-to-be husband, who was going to be a dad for us, made the cake topper from scratch. It depicted Beauty and the Beast, which was the theme of their wedding. She was the beauty, and he considered himself the beast.

Witnessing the care and effort he put into every detail, from hand-drawing cards to crafting things with his hands, filled me with warmth and gratitude. It was evident that he deeply loved my mom and wanted to be a part of our family. If I was going to say "Yes" to anyone coming into my life and being my dad, it was surely this guy.

I'll never forget the moment he stood at the altar, tears glistening in his eyes, as he watched my mom walk down the aisle. It was a powerful expression of his love and commitment, etched forever into my soul. "Ah, indeed, that's what love looks and feels like" — like coming home to a place you never knew you were missing. It felt like a scene from a movie it was so perfect.

Bike rides with him were like moments of pure freedom, where the worries of the world melted away with each pedal stroke. I relished the feeling of the breeze on my skin and the scent of nature all around us. It was a simple joy, but one that filled me with a sense of peace and happiness.

Our weekly outings to Discovery Zone and McDonald's became cherished weekly rituals, something to look forward to amidst the routine of daily life. I loved those fun dates with him, where we could let loose and enjoy each other's company. Being able to bring a friend along sometimes made those moments even more special, creating memories that we would cherish for years to come.

In the garage, he would patiently guide me as we worked on projects together, whether it was putting together model cars or crafting wooden bookends. His creativity and skills inspired me, and I loved the sense of accomplishment that came from creating something from nothing with my hands.

I cherished the routines and structure that were beginning to take shape, the traditions that brought us closer together as a family. Whether it was visiting his family's home or my godfather's for holidays, going on weekly dates with him, or embarking on yearly camping trips to Calistoga and Yosemite, each experience was filled with memorable moments that anchored gratitude in my heart. I never wanted any of it to end. This is a life worth living.

I thrived on the adventures and new experiences that our new family life brought. From exploring the great outdoors to trying new activities and pushing our boundaries, I loved every moment of it, especially with so much family around to share in the fun.

When my mom gave us his last name after they were married, it felt like a piece of the puzzle had finally fallen into place. After using Bobby's name for so long, it was a relief to shed that connection. Although the paperwork for his official adoption was never completed, at age eight, I finally had someone I could call "Dad." This filled a void in my life that I had lost hope around. Seeing my mom beaming with happiness and our home filled with laughter confirmed that my prayers had been answered.

Moving into a neighborhood full of kids was a game-changer for me. Finally, I had the opportunity to play and connect with other children outside of school. One of my closest friends I made was Italian, and her dad worked for Nabisco. I adored spending time at their house, where we would ride bikes, climb trees, and shoot hoops on their basketball court in the driveway. They were Catholic like my godfather's family, and she wore a uniform to attend private school. I felt a deep kinship and safety with her and her family, reminiscent of my beloved godfamily.

What made it even better was that her dad was always generous, letting us pick out delicious Nabisco snacks to take home. It felt like a weekly mini grocery shopping spree, and I loved it. But more than the snacks, I loved being around my friend and her family. We would have sleepovers, eat meals together, and even go on trips to their cabin in Clear Lake. It was like having a second home and family. They reminded me of my godfather's family and I felt safe with them.

My Italian friend was such a positive influence on me, and I cherished our friendship. It was a welcome contrast to the complexities of my relationship with another friend, whom I had known since kindergarten. She had helped me tell my mom about what had happened with Bobby, and while I appreciated her support, our friendship had its challenges.

It's fascinating how shared experiences, even negative ones, can forge deep connections between people. My friend from Livermore and I strengthened our bond through the shared trauma we both endured with Bobby. However, reflecting on it now, I see that the environment at her house wasn't conducive to either of our well-being. What I didn't realize back then, but now understand more clearly, is that this was a trauma-bonded friendship.

We weren't connecting out of a shared joy or healthy support, but rather through the mutual pain that intertwined our lives.

Her parents' lack of involvement and frequent absence meant we often found ourselves getting into trouble. We would sneak out at night to hang out with older boys, try cigarettes, and even experiment with alcohol. While I felt a kinship with her because of our shared history, I now understand that this wasn't a healthy influence or environment for me to be in. I felt torn—part of me enjoyed the thrill of trying new things and living dangerously at her house, but another part of me longed for more parental involvement and protection. There were moments when the situations we got ourselves into felt downright scary, and I wished there had been someone to set boundaries and keep us safe. But I felt too scared to tell anyone—afraid of betraying my friend or being labeled a tattletale. Keeping silent felt like the only way to maintain the friendship, even if it meant sacrificing my own sense of safety.

On the flip side, I'm grateful for the positive experiences we shared during family vacations and summer visits when she stayed with us for weeks at a time. Those moments provided a healthier environment for both of us, allowing us to just be kids without the pressure of danger or rebellion. I'm glad she had the opportunity to be part of those experiences too. She was like a sister to me. It's a reminder of how important our surroundings and environment can be in shaping our behaviors and experiences. In those times, it felt like we could escape the chaos and just enjoy being together, without the weight of the trauma that had bonded us.

At one point, my mom brought up the topic of my biological dad and asked if I would like to meet him. Curious about this unknown person who had helped create me yet had never been part of my life, I agreed. The first time I set eyes on him, I knew instantly that he was my real dad. It was surreal to see someone who looked exactly like me—his face was my face—he was the male version of myself. There was an instant recognition, a strange mix of familiarity and foreignness. For the first time, I saw someone who reflected my physical features back at me, and it stirred a flood of emotions I wasn't quite prepared for.

Throughout the nightmares and traumatic experiences, I sometimes felt like I had been switched at birth or kidnapped from my real family. It just didn't seem possible that this could be my family, or that people could treat one another the way mine did. I didn't look like my mom at all, and I often felt like I didn't quite belong, like an outsider in my own home. But meeting my biological dad for the first time gave me a small sense of relief, a feeling of being in the right place with the right people, even if just for that moment. Seeing someone physically resembling me made me feel like I wasn't entirely out of place.

From that moment on, he became a constant presence during holidays and birthdays, always bringing gifts and helping out where he could. Though he never shared stories about his own life or family, it felt reassuring just to have him around. His presence was like a quiet affirmation that my existence wasn't a mistake, and that I wasn't in the wrong place. Yet, I wish I had known to ask more questions about his life, his family, and his childhood. These are areas where I still feel a huge void till this day. There's so much I don't know, and it leaves me with a sense that something is missing—an important part of my identity that remains a mystery.

C-LOVE

Chapter 7

My Favorite Adventures

Living in this new life meant having BIG birthday parties and finally being able to invite friends over from school and the neighborhood for sleepovers—something I had never been able to do before. It was so fun to have a house full of people, playing music, and celebrating together.

Every week, I diligently cleaned my room. I was so grateful to have such a big, spacious room that I took great care of it. I would read, go outside to play, and do my chores. I loved our new house and our new life, and I wanted it to stay this way forever. So, I made sure to take care of all my responsibilities; I didn't want to ruin anything.

This new environment filled me with joy and a sense of normalcy that I had longed for. It was a dream come true to be able to share my home with friends, to laugh and play without the weight of past traumas constantly hanging over me. I cherished every moment, every bit of fun, and every celebration. Our new life was a breath of fresh air, and I was determined to enjoy every second of it.

Some of my all-time favorite experiences while living in this house include driving cross-country to Nebraska to meet my new stepdad's family, attending Outdoor Education in 5th grade, and periodically visiting my godfather's family cabin in Santa Cruz. I loved that place so much.

The family trip to Nebraska was an unforgettable adventure. Traveling in a Ford Aerostar Van with a bed created in the back, equipped with a TV and VCR for movies (my new dad and grandpa were Mr. Wire with business so they knew how to wire up anything), alongside my new stepdad's father—my new grandpa—was thrilling. The journey was filled with the sounds of The Judds, Elvis, Garth Brooks, and the Beach Boys, thanks to my stepdad's collection of tapes; yes, this was the age of cassette tapes. To this day, hearing that music brings a wave of nostalgia and wonder. Along the way, we made stops at quirky tourist spots, museums, and natural wonders like the Grand Canyon. Meeting extended family in Utah, Wyoming, and Nebraska made the trip even more special, creating lasting memories that left an indelible mark on my childhood.

We first stayed at my new dad's great aunt's house in Nebraska, and it was such a fun experience. She had a swing set in the backyard where we played for hours, and even a treadmill, which felt like such a novelty to us. Her husband was hilarious—he would take his teeth out and talk with just his gums, which had us laughing uncontrollably because the sight was so funny, with his mouth puckering inward and the smacking sounds. The summer heat was humid and sticky, something we weren't used to at all, prompting us to head inside more often to cool off and dry off.

This great aunt also introduced me to two romance movies that became core parts of my childhood memories: *Dirty Dancing* and *Gone with the Wind*. Both left a lasting impression on me, and to this day, they hold a special place in my heart. I became obsessed with the clothing and costumes from *Gone with the Wind*, developing a fascination for 'old' things and the elegance they embodied.

One not-so-great moment occurred when I wanted to help my little sister experience the treadmill. It turned out to be the worst idea ever. She climbed on but quickly fell, getting stuck between the treadmill and the wall. In my panic, I struggled to shut it off, and seeing her burned and bleeding because of my mistake left me feeling mortified. It was a family moment I could never quite live down, despite it being an accident. My mom still brings it up to this day as a way to shame me for the mistake. I often wish I could have made a different choice.

We went to my grandpa's 50th high school reunion at someone's house, and they had a boat we got to ride on the river. I remember having to wear earmuffs because the motor was so loud, but it didn't matter—I was so excited to be there. The best part of the day was discovering the longest rope swing from the tallest tree I had ever seen. When you swung on it, it felt like you were flying through the trees. It was pure magic, and in that moment, I wished time would pause so I could stay in that dreamy space forever.

From that day on, I've always loved rope swings on tall trees. There's something about them that brings me back to that magical feeling of flying, of freedom, and the sense that anything was possible. Every time I see a rope swing now, it's like being transported to that perfect moment where life felt like a dream.

We ended our time in Nebraska with an amazing school shopping spree at Walmart, thanks to my new grandma. She took us to pick out all new clothes and supplies for the school year. It was a luxury we had never experienced before, and we were over the moon. Trying on different outfits and showing them and getting to pick what we wanted. She loved shopping and I now understood why, it was so fun! It was the perfect way to wrap up our time in Nebraska.

As we headed back toward California, we stopped in Wyoming to visit a relative whose exact title in the family I can't recall. Still, I vividly remember her warmth and kindness. What truly stood out was her incredible Barbie collection—she had an impressive array on display, all still in their boxes and perfectly preserved. A fellow Barbie lover and collector, she had a special section for the "Barbies of the World," which particularly caught my attention. Her collection inspired me to expand my own, which, until that moment, mainly consisted of unique Barbies I loved and the Holiday Edition Barbie released each Christmas. After seeing her stunning display, I felt a strong urge to start collecting the Barbies of the World that I adored so much

What also left a lasting impression was how loving and affectionate she was. I vividly remember her stroking my hair and hugging me often, little gestures that meant the world to me. It was something I wished my mom would do but didn't. Feeling that kind of tenderness, even for a short time, filled a void I hadn't realized was so deep. As I was getting older, I became more aware of this lack of affection from my mom and it hurt deeply.

Our final stop was in Utah to visit more of my new dad's family, and this time, there were kids to play with. It felt exciting to have other kids around. It made the visit even more fun. We all went to a restaurant, and I noticed a woman dressed in a long dress that covered her from chin to ankles. My mom explained that she was Mormon and mentioned that my biological dad had been raised in that faith. I remember feeling bad for the woman, thinking it was unfair that she had to wear such heavy clothing in the heat, especially since she didn't look particularly happy. Without fully understanding what being Mormon meant, I made a mental note not to ever be one.

Back at their house, we spent hours playing with the kids in the backyard on a massive trampoline. The scorching heat made it the perfect time for them to set up sprinklers underneath, allowing us to jump and flip through the air while being sprayed with cool water. We had so much fun that we didn't want to leave.

One thing that stood out to me about that trip to Utah was the lack of fences between yards. It was easy to see into the neighbors' spaces, which felt like a strange contrast to what I was used to. While I appreciated the expansive feeling it created, I couldn't help but wonder about safety. I thought to myself, "Monsters could easily walk right into your yard and house." But maybe Utah didn't have monsters? My mind was always on high alert, constantly scanning my surroundings for signs of safety and assessing what was around me.

This trip was one of my all-time favorite childhood experiences. Heading back home came with a tinge of sadness because I didn't want any of these moments to end. It felt like a dream—a perfect blend of adventure, connection, and joy.

We went from having no family to suddenly being surrounded by so much family, it was hard to keep track of everyone. The shift was overwhelming yet heartwarming at the same time. After years of just me, my mom, and my sister, it felt like we had been folded into this large, loving network of people who genuinely cared about us. It was such a stark contrast from the loneliness I had often felt before. Now, there were new faces, names, stories, and connections—more than I could have ever imagined.

As summer unfortunately came to an end and I entered the 5th grade, I was thrilled to be presented with the opportunity to go on my first week-long field trip away from my family. I eagerly brought home the permission slip for Outdoor Ed, and to my surprise, my mom said yes! Given everything we had been through, I was shocked that she was comfortable with me leaving for an entire week. This field trip held special significance, as it was one my parents had also attended at my age, which I found incredibly cool.

Although I felt a mix of excitement and nervousness at the thought of being away from home for so long without familiar faces, Outdoor Ed turned out to be my first real taste of independence. The week was filled with unforgettable adventures, from exploring the majestic woods of Santa Cruz to visiting the fascinating Monterey Bay Aquarium and hiking through the stunning trails of Pebble Beach.

One of the highlights was the exhilarating night hikes, where our flashlights illuminated the forest and sparked a sense of wonder within me. We participated in skits, engaged in bunker cleanup competitions, and had the chance to meet students from other schools, making the experience even more unique. Getting up close with the big, sticky banana slug and other creatures of the Santa Cruz Mountains added a mix of fascination and excitement to the week, leaving me with cherished memories that I would hold onto forever.

However, not everything was perfect. I remember feeling embarrassed during shower time. Even though we wore swimsuits, I couldn't shake the discomfort about my body around the other girls. The showers were in a big open space, allowing everyone to see each other rather than having individual stalls, which I hadn't anticipated. It wasn't my favorite experience, but the thought of feeling dirty was even worse, so I forced myself to take the showers we were allowed, trying to balance my discomfort with the need to stay clean. These small, awkward moments stuck with me, but they didn't overshadow the overall joy of the trip. Thankfully, we only showered twice, so I only had to navigate this discomfort a couple of times.

My mom gave me her long rectangular camera to take along. I was so excited to capture memories from the trip, but I wasn't very good at aiming when taking the photos. I still have some of them to this day and looking at them now always makes me laugh. So many of the pictures are just the tops of things or only capture a portion of what I intended. Despite that, I love having these keepsakes from the trip. Even though being away from home was hard for me—I'd often get scared—having the camera helped me focus on the fun and excitement. I created memories I can still revisit, even if they're a little off-center.

Back in the day, with old-school phones and far less technology than we have today, it felt much harder to stay in touch with the kids I met from other schools. I had gotten one girl's number and attempted to call her a few times. We talked once, but our connection fizzled out because we lacked the in-person interactions needed to build consistency. Maintaining friendships outside of the people you saw every day or week felt challenging back then. I remember feeling a sense of grief for the newfound connections that I knew I would never see again.

I cherished the spontaneous calls from my godfather's mom inviting me on adventures to her cabin. Each invitation felt like a delightful surprise, and I eagerly said yes every time. I loved spending one-on-one time with her, whether it was running errands or simply enjoying each other's company. She would pick me up in South San Francisco, and we'd make a pit stop at her house in Pacifica before heading to the grocery store and the florist. The drive up the coast was a treat; with the windows down and the ocean breeze filling the car, I relished every moment. I'd gaze out the window, soaking in the beautiful views of the ocean while listening to her sing along to the oldies on the radio, creating memories that still warm my heart today.

As we approached the long, steep driveway to the cabin, a wave of safety and love washed over me, making it feel like a sacred sanctuary. Each time, it felt like the car might not make it up that steep hill, yet somehow, we always managed to reach the top. Visiting my godfather's family cabin was a treasured experience, nestled among towering redwoods. We indulged in delicious food, listened to classic oldies, and engaged in lively card games that brought everyone together.

What I cherished most was the time spent with my godfather's mom. She radiated sweetness and humor, and I found joy in simply watching her move about the cabin—cooking, cleaning, or dealing cards. Her vibrant energy and love enveloped the space, creating a comforting balm that made every moment feel special.

During those visits, I didn't fully understand why I sometimes longed to go home, even in such a haven of safety and warmth. Now I realize that the familiar often feels safer, even when it's not ideal. A healthier, more nurturing environment can seem unsettling simply because it's unfamiliar, which is a common aftermath of trauma. Additionally, our ability to accept love is often tied to our sense of self-worth. When someone or something offers us more than we feel we deserve, we may unconsciously sabotage it or retreat from it. The trauma and abuse I experienced had deeply ingrained feelings of inadequacy and unworthiness that I wasn't aware of as a child.

I couldn't grasp these complexities back then. I would just cry and plead to go home, despite being surrounded by one of the safest and most loving environments and people imaginable. The aftermath of my experiences with Bobby, the monster, seemed to shadow me, sabotaging moments of joy and comfort whenever good things were present. It wasn't fair how much pain a monster could inflict without facing the same or worse consequences in return.

C-LOVE

Chapter 8
Growing Pains

I was growing taller and thicker, developing faster than the other girls in my class. I found myself wearing my mom's clothes because kids' sizes no longer fit over my butt and thighs. This shift made me feel fat and disgusting. My mom often admonished me to slow down when eating and to avoid bread, warning that my butt would only get bigger. While I wasn't sure if that advice was entirely accurate, it felt like the family trait was unavoidable. This prominent backside was a legacy passed down from her mother and brother. Even in childhood photos, that infamous bubble butt was already evident, and it became a complicated love-hate relationship for me throughout my life. It was so hard to find clothes that would fit me comfortably.

As I became more aware of how different my body and size were from others, I grew increasingly self-conscious. My body became the focal point of attention and commentary, making me hyper-aware of every inch of it. This constant scrutiny made it difficult to feel comfortable in my own skin, and I often wished I could blend in and be like everyone else. Ironically, the more I longed to fit in, the more my body seemed to become curvaceous and stand out. Why wouldn't my body cooperate with me to help me feel safe?

The struggle with my self-image was a constant battle. On one hand, I wanted to embrace my body and the unique traits that came with it, but on the other hand, societal pressures to be 'skinny' and comments from others made it difficult to do so. It was a confusing time, trying to navigate the changes in my body while also dealing with the complexities of growing up.

As my body continued to change and I started needing a training bra, I also noticed hair growing in my armpits. To help me understand these developments, my mom handed me a book about a woman's body that was filled with graphic images. I remember feeling intensely embarrassed by the explicit nudity, finding them overwhelming and far too advanced for what I was experiencing. I would have preferred having an open conversation with her, where she could answer my questions and provide guidance. Unfortunately, my mom often grew impatient with my curiosity and was reluctant to discuss such topics, especially when I asked questions. As a result, I was frequently silenced and left to navigate these changes on my own. I still have that book today, and I haven't felt the timing is right to give it to my daughter, who is now 11. I sometimes wonder if I'll ever share it with her; I can't believe my mom gave it to me when I was only 9.

When Christmas came around that year, I was beyond ecstatic to receive a razor and shaving cream as a gift from my mom. I was so relieved—I couldn't stand how hairy my legs were. Dealing with legs that were already larger than everyone else's was hard enough, but the hair only made things worse. Even though it was blonde, there was so much of it that it shimmered in the sun! Kids would comment on it, adding to my embarrassment at school. Shaving my legs was a small, but significant step towards feeling more confident and comfortable in my own skin. While it didn't solve all my insecurities, it was a welcome relief to address something that made me so self-conscious. The physical changes - and the self-consciousness they brought - were challenging, but moments like receiving that razor helped me cope with the awkwardness of growing up.

As I got a little older, I started to develop crushes on boys. One of my crushes lived on my street, and we quickly became friends.

I would often go to his house to play, where we would watch movies, including very scary horror movies that we probably shouldn't have been watching. We also played a lot of video games like Street Fighter and Mortal Kombat. I learned really fast that if I just pushed all the buttons quickly, the character would do cool moves to beat the opponent. They also had a pool table, so we spent hours playing that as well.

I probably shouldn't have been allowed to go over to his house to play. Eventually during a scary movie, he held me and his hands started to wander under the blanket onto my body. I didn't say anything to anyone. I never felt violated by him because I actually liked him, and I thought we were good friends. This was so confusing. It didn't feel bad like with Bobby or the kids at school, but looking back, I realize I was too young to have experienced that kind of physical interaction. When he moved away, our playdates stopped, and this didn't happen with anyone else in the neighborhood.

One of my favorite activities with my Italian best friend across the street, whose dad worked for Nabisco, was walking to Longs Drugs or 7-11 to buy snacks and candy. Now that we were 9, our parents trusted us with the freedom and responsibility to walk six blocks to the store and back. It was exhilarating! I loved wandering the aisles at Longs, a treasure trove of delights, with her by my side. The thrill of exploring without adults made our outings feel like special adventures. After our shopping trips, we would always find a tree to climb, enjoying our snacks like a picnic in the branches.

Money wasn't always easy to come by, and my parents wouldn't just hand it over, so there were times when I couldn't join our candy runs. To earn money, I'd crush aluminum cans in the backyard and do chores around the house. I also got creative. I started saving the candy I didn't particularly like from holidays like Halloween and Easter, then sold it door-to-door in the neighborhood. Additionally, I'd accompany my mom to her job, where I'd sit in a cubicle and draw pictures. I'd make copies of those drawings, staple them together to create coloring books, and sell them around the neighborhood as well.

Even as a child, I was resourceful, creative, and possessed an entrepreneurial spirit. Those experiences instilled in me the value of hard work and ingenuity—traits that have accompanied me throughout my life. While I didn't always appreciate that my parents wouldn't simply hand me money for the things I wanted, I loved finding creative ways to earn it myself. I do wish there had been a better balance, as I missed out on opportunities like gymnastics and other activities I longed to pursue. The answer was always "No" due to costs and the harsh reality that money doesn't grow on trees. Deep down, whenever my mom reminded me of this, I hoped to prove her wrong one day by creating my own money tree. Little did I know, this dream would eventually blossom through my own business I'd create one day.

When our landlord decided to sell the house we were living in South San Francisco, it became clear that it was more than my parents could afford. They began searching for homes further out of the Bay Area, in places like Brentwood and French Camp. Being part of the house-hunting process was exhilarating; I loved exploring model homes, taking in the fresh scent of new construction, and admiring how beautifully decorated they were. It felt like we were embarking on a new adventure as a family, opening the door to another chapter in our lives. I couldn't help but wonder how life could possibly get any better than it had been.

They ended up choosing a brand-new home in French Camp, close to a long-time family friend of my new dad's family. Witnessing the construction of our new home from the ground up filled me with anticipation and wonder. It was amazing to see a dirt patch transform into our new house. I was fascinated by how something could be created from nothing; it was a testament to human creativity and also inspired my own.

One of the hardest parts of the transition was leaving my friend across the street behind when we moved to our new house in French Camp. We had shared so many memories and adventures, and the thought of leaving her deeply saddened me. I never imagined we would move or leave the house and neighborhood I loved so much. However, the prospect of a new home with a bigger room and a walk-in closet was exciting! This new area also had bike trails and parks, and our school was just down the street.

Despite my excitement for the new chapter ahead, saying goodbye to my dear friend and leaving my elementary school behind was bittersweet. I held onto the hope that this move was for the better and would lead to an even brighter future for our family. A new house, a new neighborhood, a new school, and new friends felt like an inspiring gift waiting to be unwrapped.

I also cherished the thought of moving further away from the monster, Bobby, leaving behind all the places that reminded me of him and the haunting energy that lingered in those areas. The prospect of a fresh start filled me with hope, allowing me to envision a life unburdened by the shadows of my past. The idea of starting anew in a different place brought a profound sense of relief, as if we could finally put the past behind us and embrace a brighter future.

C-LOVE

Chapter 9
Family Dynamics

Moving day had finally arrived, and while I was excited about our new home, I couldn't shake the sadness that washed over me as I said goodbye to my best friend across the street. Leaving behind the familiar streets, the bike trails, and the trees where I had spent countless hours felt like leaving a part of myself behind.

I hugged my friend tightly, not wanting to let go, tears welling in my eyes as we drove away from the house and neighborhood that had shaped my life for the past three years. I promised to call and plan visits, especially wanting her to come for a sleepover at our new house. It was a bittersweet moment, a whirlwind of sadness and excitement swirling within me as we set off toward our new beginning.

Once I stepped into our new house, with its spacious rooms and my walk-in closet, I felt like I was stepping into a dream come true.

Setting up my new room was a pleasant distraction from the bittersweet emotions of leaving. The fresh bedding and furniture my mom had chosen for me, along with the floral border and sponge-painted walls, made the room feel cozy and inviting. I took my time arranging my belongings, hanging up my awards, and decorating the walls with things that inspired me. It was a comforting process that helped ease me into the new surroundings. I loved the feeling of being in a brand-new house and the smells that accompanied it. There was something so refreshing and exciting about the fresh paint, new carpet, and the clean, crisp scent of a home built just for us. It was a new beginning, full of possibilities and hope.

The prospect of walking to school for the first time filled me with excitement. After years of commuting long distances, I had always longed for that quintessential 'real childhood' experience—walking to and from school like in the movies and TV shows I loved. The thought of accompanying my little sister added to my thrill; it felt like a shared adventure, a chance for both of us to embrace our independence together.

I was incredibly grateful that we would finally be attending the same school together. It felt like we were getting a gift to have some childhood normalcy. After Bobby had kidnapped her from Latchkey, my mom had enrolled her in a school two cities away, in Daly City, which was an hour and a half away from mine, just to ensure her safety. This distance meant I didn't get to see her much during the school week. Now, instead of relying on rides, we could simply stroll down the street to school side by side. I cherished those morning walks, savoring the warmth of the rising sun and the promise of a new day ahead.

That excitement for my new school quickly faded when I overheard some girls talking about how chubby I was behind my back. I thought I was making new friends, so it was a crushing blow to realize that those I believed to be kind actually held such hurtful opinions about me. It made me question why people care so much about appearances rather than who someone truly was or how they treated others. I missed my best friend from across the street at my old house even more because we never cared about such things with each other. At that moment, I decided to focus on my studies and grades instead of trying to make new friends.

To hide my body, I began wearing baggier clothes to school, opting for oversized pants and sweatshirts instead of the skirts and dresses my mom preferred. This change was my way of shielding myself from the hurtful comments and judgments of others, even if it meant sacrificing my sense of self-expression. These kids had no idea about the nightmares I had endured before crossing paths with them. Compared to my past, navigating their judgments felt like a walk in the park.

Despite their hurtful comments, I knew I had faced far worse challenges in my past. I was determined not to let their words break me. I resolved to keep the hurt they inflicted upon me hidden, shielding it from their view, but I never forgot what they said and the impact they made in my life. Their words lingered, adding to the growing sense of self-doubt and insecurity I felt about my appearance and my body. Yet, amidst this struggle, I found a small source of strength in my resilience. I knew I had survived much worse and could withstand their cruelty as well. I had faced terrible monsters, and they had no idea that they even existed.

We got a real inground pool in the backyard—a dream come true! After years of having a shallow, three-foot Doughboy pool, this was an exhilarating upgrade. I loved swimming and feeling like a fish, splashing around in the water all day long. My mom started babysitting the kids in the neighborhood, so our house was constantly bustling with little ones to play with, even if they were younger than me. At least they didn't make fun of me, which made me feel safe and allowed me to embrace the joy of childhood again.

Our pool became a sanctuary for me, a place where I could escape from the worries and frustrations of daily life. The laughter and splashing sounds of the neighborhood kids filled our backyard with a lively, joyful atmosphere, a stark contrast to the tension and conflict that often filled our home.

Having the pool meant I finally had a place where I could feel confident and carefree. The water was a great equalizer; it didn't matter if I felt self-conscious about my body. In the pool, I could simply be myself and enjoy the moment. The younger kids didn't judge or tease me. Instead, they offered a sense of acceptance and belonging that I desperately needed when I felt like an outsider at school with my peers. In those moments, surrounded by the warmth of the sun and the cool water, I found a small piece of happiness.

The relationship between my mom and my stepdad began to change, and it was hard not to notice. Their arguments and disagreements became more frequent, and sometimes he would yell at me. His loud voice terrified me, mainly because he was so tall—six feet, to be exact.

When he came home from work, he would head straight to his room and shut the door, demanding silence from everyone around. If we made any noise, he would yell and bang from inside, creating an atmosphere of tension and unease in the house. While it wasn't the same as what I had experienced with Bobby, this behavior still sparked a deep fear for our safety. I was terrified of returning to the chaotic, unstable life we had left behind. I didn't want to lose this house, my room, all the nice things we had, or the family we had built together. Each time I heard him yell or witnessed another fight, the weight of losing everything pressed heavily on my heart. If he wasn't a full-fledged monster, then what was he?

What happened to the loving guy who had tears in his eyes as my mom walked down the aisle? The man who once radiated warmth and affection seemed to fade into the background, replaced by someone distant and emotionally unavailable. It was as if the vows exchanged that day held no weight against the challenges that lay ahead. The moments of joy and connection became overshadowed by the struggles of everyday life, leaving me to wonder how a love so profound could transform into something so cold and disconnected. The contrast between that beautiful day and the reality that followed was stark, and it left me questioning the foundations of love and commitment.

My mom was changing too. She no longer seemed happy; in fact, she appeared increasingly bitter. Her style of dressing evolved—her shorts grew shorter, her tops more revealing, and her movements seemed to cry out for attention from men. This transformation was striking, especially since her husband no longer seemed to notice or offer the loving attention he once did. It was as if she was protesting with her behavior, yearning for the affection she had once received when they first got together.

I felt a deep sadness for her and couldn't comprehend why he wasn't giving her the attention or care he used to. Gone were the handmade cards and thoughtful gifts; he wasn't spending time with her anymore—he was avoiding her. Watching this unfold was heartbreaking, and feeling helpless to assist her was equally distressing. To add to the confusion, I often found myself being blamed or yelled at, as if it were my fault their adult relationship was crumbling. It made no sense to me—how could I possibly be responsible for their struggles? The weight of that blame felt heavy, compounding my confusion about love and relationships.

She had discovered something about my stepdad that filled her with deep resentment, making her feel deceived in their marriage. It was as if he had married her to mask his secret activities and preferences, and this realization explained why he had stopped giving her the attention she once craved. For years, this issue lingered like a white elephant in the room, unaddressed and unresolved, until she finally found the courage to confront him and set firm boundaries. Before that moment, she would uncover his secrets, vent her frustrations, and engage in protest behaviors, hoping that by expressing her discontent, she could inspire some form of change.

She had never been the affectionate type with us. Hugs and "I love yous" were rare, if they happened at all. That's part of why I loved going to my godfather's mom's house. It was one of the few places where I could sneak a hug from my mom, and she would actually give one. However, as I grew older, it started to feel like she didn't like me at all. The way she treated me and my sister became noticeably different. I would be punished for things while my sister wasn't, and I'd be denied things that she was allowed to do. The unfairness of how she treated us became increasingly apparent, and it felt like I was always on the losing side. This made me feel deeply hurt and angry. Now I realize I may have taken some of that frustration out on my sister, even though I didn't mean to and wasn't aware of that so young.

While I had always known that my mom wasn't overly affectionate, this shift felt more personal. It seemed like she was directing her frustration and unhappiness with her marriage at me. I couldn't understand why, and it hurt. The warmth and connection I had felt in our new life was starting to fade and was being replaced by a growing sense of tension and disconnection. This was not the new beginning I had thought and hoped we would have with our move.

My sister seemed to get away with so much, and often I found myself unfairly blamed for her actions. My mom would call me a liar, despite the fact that my emotions were always written on my face, making it impossible for me to lie convincingly. This constant accusation left me feeling deeply upset. Watching my sister when they left us home alone was incredibly challenging; she refused to listen to me. In a moment of desperation, I locked her in the closet until they returned. I got in so much trouble for that decision and have always regretted it. At the time, I felt helpless—she was out of control, and nothing I said seemed to make a difference. I didn't want to be left in charge of her when they went out, but as the oldest, I had no choice in the matter. I was tired of feeling powerless and lacking any control over my situation.

The frustration and helplessness I felt in those moments was overwhelming. Being blamed for things I didn't do and not being able to manage my sister's behavior made me feel powerless. Locking her in the closet was a desperate attempt to control a situation that felt entirely out of my control. I didn't have the tools or the emotional support to handle these conflicts successfully. My voice was always silenced, and I couldn't even ask questions.

Looking back, I wish I had known how to navigate these situations differently. I regret taking such drastic measures with my sister, but at just 11 years old, I didn't know how else to handle the chaos when she was throwing a fit and refusing to listen. Our mom's inconsistency in treating us fairly only deepened my sense of isolation and confusion. I wanted to be a good sister and daughter, yet I often felt set up to fail in those roles.

As my sister got older, I sometimes saw her dad in her face, and her toes, which made me feel not-so-great feelings towards her. It wasn't intentional; it was just what came up due to everything he had done and the resemblance. The resentment was hard to manage, and it added to the already complicated dynamics in our household.

My mom sometimes used our pain against us, unwittingly creating a wedge between my sister and me. I don't believe she intended to hurt us, but during arguments, she would accuse me of hating my sister simply because she resembled her dad. It felt deeply unfair for her to poke at such raw wounds, and it did nothing to strengthen the bond between us. I hated how she weaponized these issues to prove her point, which led my sister to believe I didn't love her—when, in reality, my love for her was profound. This dynamic was part of the aftermath of trauma and the lack of healing in our family, perpetuating further damage. It was an ongoing struggle to navigate the lingering effects of the monster, Bobby. It felt so unjust that someone could inflict so much pain and suffering yet escape without harsh legal consequences.

It's profoundly difficult to reconcile the lasting impact of abuse with the fact that Bobby was never held accountable in court. He simply vanished, avoiding the legal consequences of his actions by failing to show up for his supervised visits with my sister, and as a result, the trial never occurred. He was never convicted of child abuse or sexual abuse, and I never had the opportunity to testify against him.

Hearing about his death from a rare disease caused by pigeons, which led to the liquification of his internal organs, brought no sense of justice or closure. It felt as though he escaped the lifelong emotional pain and torment that he inflicted, leaving us to grapple with the repercussions of his actions. The aftermath of what we went through with him has exacted a high price, affecting us deeply and persistently.

The notion that his death might be seen as a form of punishment does little to alleviate the suffering he caused. It's a harsh reality that there seems to be no punishment truly commensurate with the damage inflicted by sexual abuse, especially when it involves a child. The lasting effects of such trauma are profound and enduring, and it often feels like justice is an elusive concept in these situations, leaving survivors to navigate the painful aftermath as best they can.

Years later, my mother employed a similar strategy with my daughter and me, and it never felt right. It seemed like she was using our vulnerabilities as leverage and weapons, rather than fostering healing or offering support. This method only drove the wedge deeper between us, complicating not only my relationship with my sister but eventually with my own daughter as well.

Words wield immense power, particularly in our formative years. They plant themselves at the heart of our being, shaping our inner dialogue and the filter through which we perceive ourselves and the world. My mother sowed seeds of doubt and insecurity with her words, influencing how we viewed ourselves and one another. Whether she was a deliberate manipulator or simply acting out of her own conditioned responses from her past, I'm not sure. What I am certain of is the profound impact and the ongoing harm her words have caused.

Her constant criticism and lack of affection planted seeds of doubt and insecurity that took root and grew within us. Instead of nurturing us with encouragement and love, her words often left us feeling small and inadequate. The phrases she used, meant to "toughen us up," only served to erode our self-esteem and create a cycle of self-doubt.

These negative words became the inner voice that echoed in my mind during moments of failure or vulnerability. They shaped how I saw myself and my abilities, often making me question my worth. It took years to recognize and begin to undo the damage her words had caused.

I loved my sister a lot; I just didn't like that we weren't treated the same. I got more severe punishments for everything. Some things I got in trouble for, she never got in trouble for. It was confusing and hard not to take out the resentment on her, even though I now know it wasn't her fault.

Navigating the love I felt for my mother while grappling with the unfairness of our treatment was an ongoing battle. The stark differences in discipline and the palpable favoritism cast a long shadow over our family dynamics. My sister was always the 'golden child,' bathed in my mother's approval, whereas I was cast as the 'black sheep,' often left in the cold.

With the benefit of hindsight, I recognize that the situation itself was inherently unjust, not necessarily my sister. Yet, during those tender years, distinguishing between my own feelings of frustration and the bond with my sister was nearly impossible. I lacked the understanding of how trauma could weave through a family, subtly encouraged by my mother's unconscious behaviors. No one was there to guide me through this; after all, I was just a child caught in the complexities of familial roles and emotional survival.

I've come to realize that the treatment we received was a mirror to the unresolved traumas and issues lingering within our family's history. My mother's behavior, probably not deliberate, significantly contributed to sustaining this toxic cycle. It seemed as though I lived under a microscope, where my every error was magnified, yet my achievements were invisible. The sense of being a perpetual disappointment, of never quite measuring up, was overwhelming.

No words of encouragement came my way; instead, my actions were met with criticism for not aligning with her methods, not being done 'her way' or up to her expectations. The labels—stupid, overly sensitive, lazy—stung deeply, and being instructed to "stop being a baby" when I expressed my emotions only added to the confusion. This was particularly baffling because, on paper, I excelled; maintaining a 4.0 GPA from the fourth grade and earning numerous awards. Yet, from my mother, there was only ever critique, never praise. It felt as if my efforts were invisible, unseen by her eyes, which led me to a haunting belief: perhaps there was something fundamentally defective about me. This notion that I might be the catalyst for turning people into monsters was a reflection of how profoundly flawed I felt, trapped in a narrative where my worth was perpetually questioned.

When I pointed out things that were unfair, she would tell me it was her job to make my life hard and that life was not fair. "Life's a bitch, and then you die," she would say. When I questioned why she didn't hug us or tell us she loved us, she simply told me, "I just don't give hugs—that's just not me."

This constant barrage of negativity and lack of affection left me feeling inadequate and unloved. Despite my academic achievements and relentless efforts, nothing I did seemed enough to earn my mom's approval or affection. The harsh and neglectful environment deeply impacted my self-esteem and led me to feel unworthy.

The lack of love at home drove me to search for affection and validation outside myself constantly. The seeds of doubt and insecurity planted by my mom's words and actions blossomed into a deep-seated need for external approval. I found myself seeking validation from friends, teachers, and later, romantic partners, always hoping they would fill the void left by my mom's absence of nurturing and support.

This need for validation from others often led me into situations and relationships that weren't healthy for me. I became overly concerned with pleasing others and afraid of rejection, often compromising my needs and desires. It took a long time to start recognizing and unlearning these patterns and build a sense of self-worth that wasn't dependent on external approval.

As I grew older, I'm unsure if my mom was changing or I was becoming more aware of her impact on me. Our relationship deteriorated, and the conflict between us intensified as time went on. I grew tired of feeling like her emotional punching bag, so I began to stand up for myself. However, this often led to intense arguments where she was always right and I was always wrong. She never apologized for anything and demanded respect even though she didn't offer any in return. She had never been the type to comfort me when I cried or help me soothe my emotions; sometimes, she even mocked me when I was upset. It appeared that my mother had a difficult relationship with emotions, particularly uncomfortable with the display of my own. This posed a significant challenge for me, being inherently empathetic and sensitive by nature. I was a child who felt deeply, navigating through a broad spectrum of emotions, which often seemed to be at odds with her comfort levels.

She would also spank and hit me, sometimes using a belt. I never agreed with this type of punishment; it always left me feeling deeply unloved and hated. Her tone would shift abruptly from a normal conversation to a harsh yell, making me feel so small and worthless. I had already endured countless traumatic experiences—the foster home, losing a sister, and being sexually abused—and my mom wasn't the nurturing figure I desperately needed. It felt like my life was cursed. Was my mom becoming a monster, or did I somehow deserve this treatment that seemed to follow me? Could it be everyone else, or maybe I was the monster?

As the years went by, our disagreements became more volatile, rapidly intensifying. My efforts to stand up for myself only invited further criticism and fury. I was stripped of my voice, denied any form of agency. "Her house, her rules," was the mantra, leaving no room for my input or feelings. She would cut me off, shout me down, and diminish my emotions, reinforcing my belief that in her eyes, I could do no right.

This relentless clash not only strained our bond but left me feeling profoundly alone and perpetually misunderstood. The absence of emotional backing, combined with the severity of her discipline, dismantled any semblance of a safe haven at home. Instead, I was left with a sense of being unloved, unwelcome, as though I simply didn't belong.

I have this vivid memory that encapsulates the dynamic I had with my mom. One day, while taking family pictures, we met a boy and his mom who were ahead of us in line. He was in his football uniform, capturing moments for the school year, while we were there for sibling photos as holiday gifts for our family. My mom struck up a conversation with his mom, and they hit it off; they were from Lathrop, which wasn't too far from where we lived. To my surprise, he became my boyfriend right after that. He was a bit older, played football, and we went to different schools. His mom would bring him over on weekends to spend time with me. This was back when communication was limited to house phones—cell phones weren't even a thing yet! (LOL!).

Everything was fine until he began pressuring me for a kiss—something MORE than a quick peck. He wanted to use our tongues, and I didn't want to. I felt scared and unsure, not knowing how it worked or how to do it properly. The idea of it made me anxious, and I didn't want to do it wrong. I had a lot of fears around this idea and process. His persistent pressure led me to consider breaking up with him. When I told my mom about wanting to end the relationship, she said that if I did, I wouldn't be allowed to have my 14th birthday party. I felt trapped, but I stayed in the relationship despite my discomfort, fearing the loss of my celebration and facing punishment. It felt incredibly unfair, especially given my past. I wished she could celebrate and support my decision to say "No." rather than use it as leverage to control me.

I had my 14th birthday party, and it was awesome! He came, but I spent most of my time connecting with my friends. When Valentine's Day arrived, he brought a bunch of gifts and once again tried to force kissing on me. I snapped—I just couldn't take it anymore. I broke up with him on the spot, and as a result, I was immediately grounded. My mom punished me by grounding me for a month, taking away my makeup, and restricting my phone use and outings. It felt like a harsh punishment for standing up for myself and asserting my boundaries. This response made no sense to me, leaving me incredibly angry and frustrated.

I absorbed this ordeal into a belief system where leaving relationships was taboo, compelling me to mend them at any cost, even when my heart wasn't in it. This ingrained pattern of persisting in toxic connections, rather than choosing to leave, has echoed through various facets of my life. It seemed as though my efforts to advocate for myself were met with punishment instead of support, etching a profound scar on my psyche.

I learned that asserting my boundaries or expressing my desires was not just unsupported; it was actively opposed and punishable. Even now, my mother remains blind to the impact of those experiences. She stands by her actions, feeling justified in her approach, thus she sees no reason to apologize. This steadfast refusal to acknowledge the harm done illustrates just how deeply entrenched unhealthy family patterns can become. Being the family's black sheep, the one who not only recognizes but also vocalizes the toxic cycles, is incredibly challenging. It often means standing alone, facing resistance or outright rejection, as you challenge the very fabric of familial norms that others might prefer to leave unexamined.

A poem I wrote back in January of 2001 about my experiences with my mom:

Hopeless

Have you ever felt the need,
To do something
But couldn't,
Because there's always someone there to stop you.
Even though they're shorter,
Even if they are wrong,
Because they 'supposedly' know better.
So no matter what you do,
They don't care.
No matter how hard you try,
They don't acknowledge you.
You're a speck of dust.
You're a piece of shit.
You fuss too much.
You want to hurt them,
That way they feel as much pain,
As you do!
You say you won't forgive.
They say they won't give in.
It goes back and forth until they win.
Because no matter how much you push and shove,
They won't budge.
So you go through thousands of tears,
And all they do is laugh at your fears.
And you look at your life,
And realize that you're
HOPELESS!

Cassandra Love Lambert, Jan 2001

C-LOVE

Chapter 10
Body Image

Middle school was awkward. My body kept changing, and my childhood friend, who had helped me tell my mom about Bobby, came to live with us and go to school with me. To get away from some not so great things that were happening at home with her family. I felt like finally I had someone at school I could call a real friend. She showed up with these cool-looking eyebrows, and I wanted to be like her, so I asked if she could make mine look like hers. She said yes, so I shaved mine off. What a mistake! I looked crazy, and she definitely could not draw mine the way she did hers. I cried because I couldn't draw them on either. Without eyebrows, I felt I finally looked like the alien I had always felt like on the inside.

This was the beginning of a few years of really funny-looking eyebrows in pictures. Sometimes they were too curved, making me look super happy; other times they were too straight, making me look concerned. Sometimes they would melt off in the 100-degree weather or wipe off in the pool. They took hours to do and never came out right, which often made me cry. It was so embarrassing. Let's just say I learned my lesson and didn't do that again. I was so grateful when they finally grew back.

During these years, house parties became a staple. It would always be in someone's garage, decked out with strobe lights, music, balloons, and food. Everyone would start off sitting around the edges, shy and chatting, until the older kids showed up and got things moving with a 'freak train' line. Once that ice was broken, everyone else would join in and dance too. Back then our neighborhood felt pretty safe, so we'd all walk home in the dark, alone, after the party. Those were the good old days—I really miss them.

As the years went by, this once vibrant 'new' suburban development began to decline. Shootings started happening, and people in the community lost their lives. It's strange and disheartening to witness something that once felt so new and full of promise, deteriorate into darkness. It's a distinct reminder of how something that begins with such hope and potential can unravel, much like the new beginning with my family - that seemed to falter over time.

Getting older meant going to more intimate get-togethers where games like spin the bottle or truth or dare often left me feeling embarrassed and like an ugly duckling. The teasing I endured from boys about my appearance and body scarred me deeply and made me incredibly insecure and self-conscious. It made me feel like no boy would actually ever love me or choose me. Why would they? I even wondered if maybe I shouldn't have left the boy who was pressuring me for kisses. Perhaps he was the best I would get, especially since he didn't pick apart my body or appearance like others did. Boys were so confusing!

All of that pressure and confusion made my trips to the skating rink with my mom, sister, and friend a cherished weekly ritual. Our girls' nights out, filled with oldies and disco tunes, were always a blast! Shopping for cute outfits before hitting the rink added to the excitement, and with my friend living with us, these outings felt even more special. Her presence seemed to soften my mom's demeanor and made the atmosphere more relaxed and enjoyable. It was nice to see my mom happy and confident while skating in her new outfits, and it felt like it lightened her mood towards me.

This weekly ritual together provided a peaceful break from the ongoing tension between my mom and my stepdad at home, allowing us to bond and create cherished memories. It was also a respite from feeling like a target for my mom's frustrations. Skating has always been a favorite activity of mine; it brought a sense of freedom and joy that uplifted my spirits. It served as a reminder that even in the darkest times, there are glimmers of light. Skating taught me to appreciate the simple joys of life, finding gratitude amidst challenges and adversity.

Since the neighbors liked to go out on weekends, I eventually became the teenage babysitter of our block (and the cul-de-sac behind us). Every weekend I would be babysitting for someone, I also started to deep clean some of their houses. I'd play music and spend hours deep cleaning. The money I earned allowed me to do stuff I loved like getting Chinese food or shopping at Mervyn's and Forever 21 for new outfits. I even loved saving it! The feeling of making money and being able to pay for what I wanted, when I wanted it, was incredibly satisfying.

Some of the neighbors eventually became like second parents to me. They would talk to me for hours, sharing their wisdom on various topics. I cherished the time and attention they gave me because my parents weren't talking to me in that way or teaching me the things my neighbors taught me. I often felt like I was on my own to figure life out, so it felt comforting when other adults took me under their wing and nurtured me with useful knowledge, tools, and resources.

School seemed manageable with my friend by my side, but everything changed when a kid I'd known since 6th grade started calling me "IHOS"—International House of Sausage—referring to my legs. This kid knew EVERYONE, so soon, EVERYONE in school was calling me that. The humiliation was unbearable. I wanted to hide and felt desperate not to go to school. I cried at home, feeling this was worse than the teasing from those girls in 6th grade, who only made comments amongst themselves. This bully turned the entire 8th grade against me, targeting the part of my body I'd been self-conscious about since my friend made me aware of it in elementary school.

I'm not sure if I told my mom or if my friend did, but she went to the school to try to stop it. By then, so much damage had been done that it couldn't be undone. Even after the kid apologized and everyone else stopped, the sting never went away. I hated my legs and my body even more than before. It felt like I didn't belong. Even people I thought were my friends had joined in on the bullying. Sometimes, during lunch, the bullying would erupt, and everyone would join in, making it impossible to escape the humiliation. I'd gather my things and run out, as the noise echoed through the cafeteria. I wanted to rip my body apart and despised my curves and thickness. Why couldn't I just look like everyone else?

Experiencing my period for the first time was like stepping into an emotional hurricane. I'm not sure if it came before or after the bullying, but they intertwined, amplifying the turmoil I felt inside. Wearing a pad all day at school was uncomfortable and awkward. It felt and sounded like a diaper whenever I walked. I felt exposed, as if everyone could hear or see it and knew I was on my period. The paranoia and discomfort were overwhelming! Becoming a woman and dealing with the bleeding felt like another burden and curse imposed upon me, something I had no choice over and was stuck with. In those moments, I couldn't help but agree with my mom—life wasn't fair.

The experience of menstruation felt bewildering and deeply unfair, especially when it seemed to demand so much from my body without taking my well-being into account. The sheer amount of bleeding, the exhaustion, and the nausea felt like an unjust penalty, particularly knowing that this was a burden not shared by everyone. The cramps were another level of torment, at times so intense that all I wanted was to retreat from the world, curl up in a ball and wait for the pain to pass.

As my body began to adapt to this new cycle, changes in my physique became evident. My waist slimmed, contributing to a more pronounced hourglass shape, while my legs remained robust, a constant source of self-consciousness. It was frustrating; if my body was going to change, why couldn't it change in ways I desired, like slimming my legs, instead of adding to my discomfort and self-image concerns?

The cravings during my period were overwhelming, transforming me into someone with an insatiable appetite for the greasiest, most indulgent foods. It was as if my body had its own will, demanding satisfaction through specific, often unhealthy, dietary choices. And it wasn't just the eating; my concentration suffered too.

During those days, school felt like navigating through a fog where nothing quite stuck, and clarity was a distant memory. The thought often crossed my mind that if menstruation was an ordeal girls had to endure but guys did not, there should be some form of compensation or acknowledgment, like perhaps a week off each month. It seemed only fair, given how significantly it impacted my ability to function normally.

As my silhouette took on more of an hourglass shape, I noticed a shift in how I was perceived, particularly by older men. Even simple acts like walking to the store via the trails became tinged with a sense of vulnerability, as the catcalls and whistles from passing cars would jolt me, leaving me feeling exposed and uneasy.

This type of attention didn't boost my confidence as perhaps some might think; instead, it enveloped me in a flush of embarrassment and discomfort. It felt predatory, reducing me to an object rather than recognizing me as a person. It begged the question, why couldn't guys understand how to genuinely respect and treat girls with dignity, rather than making them feel like mere commodities on display? Part of me entertained the thought that perhaps retaining a chubbier figure might have shielded me from the unwanted attention. It seemed like a twisted form of protection, where my body shape could deter the inappropriate behaviors of guys, making me less of a target in their eyes.

It felt like I was caught between two undesirable worlds: on one side, the potential for mockery and bullying at school for having a chubbier physique, and on the other, attracting unwelcome and degrading attention from older men because of a more developed body. Both options were steeped in unfairness, leaving me to ponder why, as a young girl, my choices seemed limited to which form of objectification I'd rather endure from the opposite sex. The pervasive focus on my physical form by guys made me wish I could just vanish, highlighting how deeply unjust and objectifying the world could be towards young ladies. I wondered how long women and girls have endured this type of behavior from the opposite sex regarding their bodies.

Ugh, I just wanted to go back to my body before my period ever came. I longed for the simplicity of that time, free from the emotional turmoil and physical discomfort that came with growing up. The changes felt overwhelming, and I wished I could escape the complexities of womanhood and the scrutiny that accompanied my developing body.

It was a tumultuous time when my mom began reconnecting with my biological dad while her current marriage was crumbling. The arguments between her and her husband escalated, and it became clear that my mom craved the intimate attention that he failed to provide. In contrast, my biological dad seemed to offer the connection and understanding she needed. I found myself fantasizing about their reunion, hoping it would resolve the issues at home. I believe all kids secretly long for their biological parents to be together; it creates an indescribable sense of belonging that feels essential to our understanding of family and love.

My mom and biological dad both attended my eighth-grade graduation trip to Great America and a wedding for one of my mom's friends. Little did I know that this would be the last time I saw him for years. Had I realized it at the time, I might have made an effort to connect with him more deeply. I didn't know that the next time I would see him, he'd be on his deathbed. Life is fleeting; we often believe we have all the time in the world, but it can slip away in an instant. You never know when someone's time is up or when you'll see them again, yet we frequently take those moments for granted. This has become a long-held regret of mine. I wish I had spent more time with my biological dad, cherished those moments more intensely, asked more questions, and learned about his life and family. The void left by those unanswered questions still resonates deeply within me.

In the years that followed, I reached out to him but received no response or callback. I felt a profound sense of abandonment from him. Looking back, I wish I had hugged him longer, taken the time to truly look at his face, and cherished every moment we spent together. Those fleeting instances now hold a weight of regret, and I realize how important it is to fully embrace the people we love while we still can.

My 8th grade graduation soon arrived and I somehow found myself in a relationship with someone I had always liked. However, it didn't last long. He was just as shy and reserved as me, so neither of us took the initiative to engage more deeply. Our time together consisted of him coming over, and we'd just sit there with a movie or show on, not even looking or talking to each other. It was boring and seemed to not be going anywhere.

Looking back, I realize that he was probably the safest and healthiest guy I have ever been with, yet I chose to leave the situation. This pattern of leaving something healthy and seeking out unhealthy relationships repeated in my life. Driven by the impact of trauma on my brain. I gravitated towards what was familiar, even if it wasn't the healthiest choice. I had to embark on a journey of deep healing to find myself no longer drawn to situations and people that mirrored past trauma and drama, especially in love and intimate relationships.

My godfather and his high school sweetheart ended up getting married, and we were there with his huge family. It was such a beautiful moment to witness and be a part of. I loved their love story—how long they had known each other and how they were deepening that bond with marriage. I wanted this same type of love story for my life so badly. It was part of what I prayed for since I was little, back when my mom and I lived in that one-bedroom apartment with the noisy motel behind us. But I wasn't sure how I would ever have this type of love story with all the insecurities I had about my body and how ugly I felt.

That summer, I got to go to the gym daily with a mom my mother babysat for. She taught me what machines to use and gave me a little routine to do. We went multiple times a week and I loved it. As a result, my body began to change too. A lot of the baby fat that I had on me began to melt away and, for once in my life, I started to feel comfortable in my body. This newfound confidence even allowed me to express myself with my clothes.

At one of the summer house parties, an older boy began to talk to me. He was one grade older than me and already in High School. He would call me on the house phone and we would talk for hours. He would come over and we would swim, watch movies or shows, and talk. He was not shy, and he made me feel seen and special. He was my first real kiss and it was the first time I became aware of energy, how it moves, and how it lights up your body. He began to really take up space in my heart. I felt a real connection and love for him I hadn't felt with anyone else before.

Starting high school brought a wave of new experiences, but nothing stung as sharply as the moment he passed me in the hallway, acting as if he didn't know me. My heart sank, engulfed by embarrassment and humiliation. I began to hear rumors about him talking to and kissing other girls, deepening the pain I already felt. It was my first real encounter with the manipulative nature of some guys, and unfortunately, it wouldn't be the last. Though this experience was relatively mild, it left a lasting impression, leading me to vow never to talk to or date anyone from the same school again. Were all guys like monsters?

C-LOVE

Chapter 11
Love, Sex and Relationships?

Even though he made me feel small and embarrassed at school by not acknowledging me, I couldn't say "no" to him or stop him from coming over after school. I don't even remember the words he used to explain things to me. I was young, naive, gullible, and honestly, already groomed to be used and abused anyway.

Freshman year was scary. From getting bused to a bigger campus further away from home, to walking down long hallways filled with so many new kids from different schools, and noticing all the different cliques, this new environment was overwhelming. I wasn't sure where I fit in or if I would fit in anywhere. I didn't belong with the popular kids, the jocks, or the preps - at all. I'd see them at lunch and feel curious about them, but I never felt at home or welcomed there.

I ended up migrating between groups—the eccentric artsy types, the smart ones, and a lot of Black and Asian friends. I felt most at home with them. With the way my body was shaped, I never felt accepted by the other kids who were the same color as me. We just weren't built the same!

During our lessons on the African Slave Trade, I started to deeply resent the color of my skin. I hated being White and associated with the actions of White people. I felt out of place with my classmates, who were White and preppy, because of how I looked and how different I felt. The White boys at school didn't seem interested in me; it was only the Black boys who showed any interest. I created a narrative in my head that this was due to my legs, my thickness, and my bubble butt. I'm not sure if this was true, but it became a belief I carried for years. This growing awareness of race in high school was both confusing and overwhelming.

My best friend from kindergarten, who was like a sister to me, began a romantic relationship with a close friend of the boy I hung out with after school. As their relationship intensified, she shared every intimate detail with me, unknowingly creating a silent tension in my life. This situation fostered a strange, unspoken peer pressure within me, so when the moment came and he—the boy who always came by after school—made his advance, I didn't resist. Physically, I was present, but my spirit had detached, much like my past experiences with Bobby. I was passive, removed from the moment, echoing the helplessness I had felt years earlier.

Bobby had never crossed that physical boundary of penetration and for me this was new territory. Yet, I found myself just as passive. I liked this guy, yearned for closeness, but there was an evident contrast in his demeanor; affectionate in the privacy of my home, yet distant with me at school. This dichotomy didn't foster feelings of love or care; instead, it stirred a maelstrom of conflicting emotions within me, leaving me feeling more used than cherished.

I grappled with the puzzle of sexual pleasure. I was not able to understand why this act, heralded by others, but completely devoid of joy for me. In those intimate moments, I would sever the connection with my body, drifting into a void to escape the discomfort. The word 'no' seemed locked away - inaccessible. As if my voice had been stripped of its power to object. My sense of agency had eroded. I felt like a bystander in my own experiences, compelled to accept whatever was imposed upon me. This cycle of detachment and acquiescence was an ongoing pattern I eventually had to heal and overcome.

My mom found out about what we were up to and immediately took us to Planned Parenthood to get us on birth control. She was upset, but she didn't try to stop us from doing what we were doing. She just wanted to make sure we didn't end up with any unexpected pregnancies, especially since we were still young. She even went as far as to give us permission to "do it" at home. This always felt weird to me. Part of me was hoping she would have been strict, so that it would have protected me and been the "No" I didn't seem to have the power to say on my own.

I remember going into Planned Parenthood. It was located in a run-down old office building that had this feeling of shame around it. It was so quiet in there! No one made eye contact with each other. You knew anyone in there was having sex and more than likely, was not married. Out of all the options for birth control, the shot seemed the easiest and most foolproof. I ended up being put on it, and it immediately changed my body. I started to rapidly gain weight and develop more curves, taking on a more womanly shape. It felt like the more I hated having curves, the more they seemed to grow.

Getting whistled at and "hollered" at while just walking down the street to go to a friend's house or to the store always left me feeling embarrassed and uncomfortable. It didn't feel great. I felt like a piece of meat rather than a respected girl. Strangely, it seemed like older guys liked me more than the ones my own age. Maybe it was because of the way I looked and all these curves? Oh how I hated these curves.

The infidelity of my mom exploded into chaos. The air was thick with shouts and the walls echoed with discord like never before. The fights were ugly, leading my mom to carve out her own sanctuary in a room downstairs, distancing herself from my stepdad. Amidst this turmoil, she gravitated towards a friendship with one of the mothers whose children she babysat. Unfortunately, this woman was not a good influence. She introduced my mom to a lifestyle punctuated by what I came to understand were swinger parties, steeped in drugs and alcohol. Many times, I was called over there to babysit and keep the kids downstairs while a carousel of strangers reveled above us, partying.

My mom, starved for the spotlight she no longer found in her marriage, sought the gaze and affection from any man who'd offer it. It must have been incredibly confusing and heartbreaking for my mom to experience this shift in her relationship with my stepdad, especially from the early days when my stepdad's love was all-encompassing. I couldn't blame her for seeking attention and affection elsewhere; it's human nature. Sometimes, after the kids went to bed, I would sneak upstairs and witness what was happening. Occasionally, I found myself in dialogue with these adults, being prematurely ushered into realms and topics far beyond the scope of my years.

Encountering strippers and swingers was like stepping through a hidden door into an alternate universe of human interaction and sexual expression. This exposure was both enlightening and overwhelming. It revealed a world where sex seemed to be the central orbit around which everything revolved. I was baffled and was left with a barrage of unanswered questions. I felt out of sync with this fervor. It planted a seed of doubt within me—perhaps something was amiss, for I couldn't resonate with this intense fixation that appeared so natural to everyone else.

Attending club events in high school was a different experience from the house parties we were accustomed to; these were arenas where the lines of decorum blurred into oblivion. These places weren't just for teens, they were melting pots for adults too, including men far older than us. The most unsettling part was the pervasive disregard for personal space. Merely navigating through the crowd felt like running a gauntlet of unwelcome hands, where your body was treated less like your own and more like public property. Consent, now a cornerstone of discourse, was then an afterthought - if considered at all. Reflecting on those times, I'm struck by anger and disbelief at the liberties taken with my autonomy. It begs the question, who instilled in these guys the notion that such behavior was acceptable? Who raised these men?

Meeting a guy at those events was unusual, but this one stood out from the other guys I bumped into. Despite the age gap—he was four years older—he treated me respectfully. He would ask for permission before dates and traditionally courted me. He had his own car and took me out for meals and movies. He was a church boy from the East side of Stockton, and we began dating while I was still underage.

Attending church with him was both intriguing and uncomfortable. Being the only White person there, I often felt out of place and judged, as if I didn't belong. The stares from others made me feel unwelcome, and I sensed that the other church members disapproved of him dating me. This only deepened my insecurities about my skin color and reinforced the negative narrative I had already believed about myself.

Despite the challenges, there was something refreshing about his respectful approach to dating. It provided a different perspective on companionship; he wanted to be seen in public with me and wasn't hiding me like the guy before. Maybe I was worthy? It felt validating to be treated with openness and respect. Like I mattered to him beyond just being a secret fling. This newfound attention gave me a glimmer of hope that maybe I was worthy of love and affection from a guy after all.

The first time he came over, it was uncomfortable. My mom casually strolled around the house just in her negligee. Her presence during our time together made me feel uneasy, like she was intruding on our privacy. Sometimes, she'd initiate conversations about sexual topics or make suggestive jokes, which only added to my discomfort. It seemed like she was competing with me for attention from my boyfriend, trying to divert it away from me and onto herself. My mom craved attention from men, and it felt like there was never enough for her. She prioritized her desires over spending quality time with my sister and me. She made her priorities clear. It was disheartening to feel like I came second or third to her need for validation and attention from men.

It was difficult for me to watch certain shows or movies, especially when there was kissing or sex scenes. I would instinctively turn away or mentally check out to avoid the discomfort. Instead of showing understanding or support, my mom ridiculed me for it. She'd say things like "just get over it" and insist it was "part of life." I never felt like she understood or cared about the lingering after effects of being sexually abused. She would tell me to stop being a victim and stop having a pity party.

It was deeply unsettling when my mom would play pornographic content openly on the television and then summon me into the room. My immediate reaction was to avert my gaze or retreat inward, a natural response to such exposure. Yet, she would brush off my unease, insisting that I should "get over it." Perhaps in her mind, she was attempting to help me confront my feelings, but it only layered more trauma upon me. Here was another moment where my boundaries were disregarded, where my discomfort was ignored and criticized. I felt defective for my reactions. I often questioned why I couldn't just 'deal with it' as effortlessly as it seemed others could, or at least as they appeared to. This recurring theme of invalidation left me feeling broken like I was somehow less than because my feelings didn't align with what was expected or normalized around me.

Amidst the chaos at home, my boyfriend became my refuge, my source of stability and love. He was what I had been longing for ever since witnessing my godfather and his wife's marriage—a genuine friend and partner. He provided rides to school functions when my parents couldn't, and he was there for me at all my dances and school events. We attended church together, and eventually, I even started joining him for family dinners. His family seemed nice, certainly more harmonious than my own. I appreciated how involved they were with their church and how much they did together. He was one of eight siblings, and the way they all looked out for each other was something I admired deeply. It felt good to be part of something that seemed so functional and loving.

With the newfound stability I felt from my boyfriend, I found the courage to confront my mom more fiercely. However, my attempts to stand up for myself seemed to escalate our fights rather than resolve them. No matter how hard I tried to express my truth, she silenced me with escalated threats of kicking me out or calling the police. It felt as though I had no voice in her house, and that nothing I said or needed truly mattered. She demanded respect but offered none in return, treating me like a child whose opinions were irrelevant. Conversations with her often spiraled into chaos, with her saying cruel and hurtful things one moment, only to deny them the next. I longed to record our conversations to prove to myself that I wasn't imagining things. Her behavior left me feeling utterly crazy, as if I was losing my grip on reality.

She would provoke my feelings until I reached a breaking point. In a particularly intense moment, she even called the police on me! When they arrived, she flipped her demeanor completely, claiming, "I don't know why she's behaving this way, officer." Naturally, they believed her and treated me like a rebellious child. The whole situation was both confusing and infuriating. I felt constantly silenced; nothing I said or needed ever mattered. She positioned herself as the 'queen of this castle,' while I was 'just another child.' In her eyes, children didn't deserve respect or a voice in anything. She felt more like a dictator than a mom.

Talking to her felt like stepping into a surreal nightmare, with her words cutting deep into my core. She would hurl insults like "You were an accident" and "I wish I never had you," only to later deny ever saying them when confronted. Living in a state of constant confusion, reality seemed to shift and warp with each passing moment. I found myself questioning why I didn't have a mother who genuinely loved and cared for me. The thought of treating my future children the way she treated me was unfathomable.

Witnessing the contrast between how sweet and kind she was to everyone else, especially men, only deepened the anger and hurt I felt inside. Her tone would shift from warmth to harshness in an instant when addressing me, making it seem as if she truly hated me. Being around her felt like a scene from *Dr. Jekyll and Mr. Hyde*—one moment she was a caring human, and the next, she transformed into a monster. Her reputation in our community—her name, the parties, and her numerous relationships—spread like wildfire, and I feared it would cast a shadow over me as well. Older men began approaching me, claiming to know my mom, often trying to compliment me and get too close for comfort. Yet, despite their advances, my heart belonged to my boyfriend. His love and support empowered me; for the first time in my life, I was finally able to assert myself and say "No."

The divide in the house between my mom and stepdad was immense, but there were times they would put their differences aside and join forces against me during arguments. These conflicts often escalated uncontrollably. I remember one experience where I held scissors or a knife to my wrist and threatened to cut myself, and instead of helping, they coaxed and antagonized me. It felt like a nightmare! At that moment I realized that this wasn't real love and this isn't what a normal household looks like. I knew I had to start looking into divorcing my family to get out of this toxic environment—what it would take to leave and how to make it happen. Babysitting and house cleaning wasn't enough to provide the means for escape, so I began looking for a 'real' job to support myself and find a way out.

C-LOVE

Chapter 12
Enough is Enough

I landed my first real job at Hometown Buffet during my sophomore year. After school I would hitch rides with a classmate who also worked there and was a year older than me. I was incredibly grateful for this support, especially since getting help from my mom or stepdad was a struggle. During my shift, my job was to keep my assigned area clean, which meant sweeping the carpets and bussing tables. Even though I'd come home smelling of mashed potatoes and gravy, I loved my job! It was a huge step towards freedom, and the tips were rolling in. Most days my boyfriend would pick me up after work and take me home - which was really helpful. Whenever I would ask my mom or stepdad, they didn't want to be bothered or burdened. I kept facing the absence of parental support, even though I was taking on a lot of responsibility.

At this point, my mom was hardly ever home; she was living at the other moms' house, where there was constant partying and drugs. Our house felt abandoned and neglected. I was juggling full-time school and honors classes, working 30+ hours a week, participating in theater and dance, and taking care of the house and our four cats. I even had to walk to the grocery store to buy groceries because no one else was getting them for the house.

My school days were grueling: I'd wake up at 5 a.m., catch the bus at 6:30 a.m. for school, get home at 4 p.m. to change, then catch another bus to get to work. I'd finally get home around 11 p.m. or midnight and do it all over again the next day.

I was so overwhelmed by everything that I began confiding in my school counselor. She became a safe space for me, offering support that I should have been getting from my parents at home. She helped me with things like creating a resume, looking at colleges, and navigating other life steps. At home, I had NO support for any of those life transitioning things, which fueled my anger toward my mom and stepdad for abandoning their parental responsibilities. Thankfully, my better-paying job helped cover my food, toiletries, and most of my school necessities.

Through it all, my boyfriend and I eventually celebrated our first anniversary. He gave me a huge bouquet of flowers and lots of gifts. I felt showered with love and appreciation! However, I soon found out he had saved the worst gift for last. He sat me down in front of him, and I could tell it was something serious. He looked scared and nervous. I was so confused. I kept thinking to myself, "Isn't this supposed to be a happy moment?" Then the words started coming out of his mouth and it was as if time stood still. I didn't feel like I was in my body. I felt like I was floating around the room, in complete shock.

He confessed to me that I was his angel, a beacon in his life, yet there was a confession he'd harbored for months, too burdened by guilt to speak it. He admired me to such an extent that my perceived perfection made his secret even heavier. He continued to reveal to me, "...at the beginning, when we were getting to know each other and taking it slow, I slept with someone else and cheated." This truth had been gnawing at him, a shadow over our relationship, and he couldn't step into another year without laying bare his conscience.

I wish I could delete this from my memory bank. I wish this wasn't my experience. I thought I had finally found the love I had always wanted, just like my godfather and his wife. Something pure, something real. I was so wrong. I felt gross all over. Ugh, I had been intimate with him willingly and loved him! I felt so violated. The overwhelming feeling of wanting to chop off my vagina returned. I hated the way I felt in receiving this information. He became a liar. A monster. At that moment, our relationship became a lie - nothing felt real. The value, confidence, and strength I had painstakingly built throughout the year, crumbled immediately. Of course he cheated on me, who was I to think someone could actually love me and be faithful when there were so many other girls better than me out there? I cried, and he cried. Then, he left. I had no words to speak, I just needed to be left alone.

I let his calls go unanswered for days; in the era of landlines, it was a simple act of avoidance. My mind was in a surreal limbo. I would get through my daily routines as if on autopilot, disconnected from my own body. At home, my family life had spiraled into chaos, transforming into a waking nightmare. The one sanctuary I thought I had, crumbled into just another source of pain. Life indeed was unfair. The echoes of my mother's harsh mantra resounded in my mind like an inevitable prophecy. Life was a relentless adversary, with death as the only certain escape.

My stint at Hometown Buffet eventually ended and I took a job at JC Penney. Oddly enough, I was placed in the men's underwear section. A placement that, in retrospect, felt disturbingly inappropriate as a teenage girl. My boyfriend, unable to reach me through ignored calls, appeared at my workplace with an enormous bouquet, his apologies spilling over. That evening, he drove me home, and there was a lot of crying and holding each other, an attempt to mend what was broken. We didn't break up, but this fractured the foundation of our relationship. I never felt the same towards him or our relationship. From that point on, my trust in him was overshadowed by doubt; I couldn't feel secure or entirely believe in his fidelity, especially when other girls were around. This event either awakened or reinforced a host of insecurities within me, which lingered, never fully receding.

I don't know how I got through High School. There were so many things I had to figure out on my own. The guidance and support that should have come from home and parents was absent; I was left to decipher life's complexities by myself. It seemed as though the deck was perpetually stacked against me, with no control over the hands I was dealt. High school, already a challenging time for many, was fraught with additional trials. I found myself turning to strangers and acquaintances for the help I couldn't get at home, where I was met with friction or outright hostility. My parents, mired in their own unhappiness, were unavailable to provide the support we needed as kids transitioning into teenagers and young adults.

There were instances when my stepdad promised to pick me up from work, only to completely forget, leaving me stranded with no answer when I called. I'd try to reach my mom, but she would hang up on me and refuse to answer again. Stuck downtown with home a 30-minute drive away, walking at 11 p.m. wasn't an option. I had no choice but to swallow my pride and ask for rides from my coworkers' parents, feeling both embarrassed and abandoned. These experiences brewed a deep resentment within me; my parents' neglect turned every aspect of life into a struggle. It felt like hurdles were constantly being placed in my path just to get through school. Would I ever get a break?

Whenever I mustered the courage to confront them or sought some accountability for their actions, the tables were swiftly turned back on me. How dare I challenge their reliability? How dare I expect them to honor their commitments? The narrative was always twisted to make me the culprit for having expectations, for believing that they might care enough to keep their word. My needs, my basic expectations of reliability and support, were painted as unreasonable demands. I felt as though my trust in them was my own folly.

I shouldn't have had to juggle all these worries on top of school; I just wanted what seemed to come so easily for my peers—focus on my education. No one taught me how to drive or got me a car. I was dependent on a patchwork of solutions: public transport, my boyfriend's kindness, or the goodwill of neighbors, classmates, and coworkers. This forced me to become adept at seeking help, at being resourceful. This led me to trying to contact my biological dad, hoping he could help me. I had fantasies of wanting to go live with him. It had to be better than this. Yet, he too became unreachable; his phone number changed, his job location unknown, he vanished like a ghost from my life. This repeated cycle of abandonment reinforced a harsh truth: it felt like no one stayed, no one truly cared about me or had my back. I was left feeling profoundly isolated, navigating life's turbulent waters alone as a teenager.

As senior graduation approached, I felt like I was at my breaking point. Desperate for help, I took a leap of faith and reached out to my godfather's mom. The fear of contacting her was palpable; my mom had always threatened me about revealing the truth of what was happening at home to ANYONE. She cared more about her image and how people perceived her than about our well-being as her kids. Any mention of our struggles that painted her in a negative light was met with swift condemnation and punishment. But I was beyond the point of silence. The pain had become too overwhelming, and I knew I couldn't continue suffering in silence. I needed support, and I was determined to seek it out.

She came over that same week, and I was astounded by how quickly she offered her support when it felt like pulling teeth to get any help from my parents. There was no need for me to fight for her attention; she instinctively stepped in with love and care. Together, we tackled the mess left by the cats and went grocery shopping to restock the kitchen. She was shocked by how much the house had deteriorated from its once pristine condition. Her encouraging words, warm hugs, and unwavering support felt like a lifeline during such a tumultuous time. She even helped me plan my graduation party, which made the occasion feel even more special. For the first time in a long while, I felt genuinely seen, cared for, and supported. I could feel her love deeply, and it meant the world to me.

The night before graduation, I needed to pick up a few things from Walmart, so my boyfriend drove us. Unfortunately, his car broke down on Charter Way in Stockton. We weren't too far from my house, but it was a sketchy area to be walking around at night. I called my mom and stepdad for help, but they hung up on me. I had had it! I was so angry and I had a right to be. Luckily, a police officer came by and offered to give us a ride to my house.

When I finally got home, I called her again to confront her about hanging up on me and showing no concern for our situation. She felt justified in her actions and claimed I was wrong for raising my voice, promptly hanging up on me again. I had school the next day, yet she showed no regard for how or if I got home safely after the car broke down. What kind of parent does that? What kind of mom was she? In that moment, it felt like she was a monster!

High school graduation had finally arrived, and I was eager to turn the page on this chapter of my life. I decided to attend San Francisco State University, considering the possibility of staying at my godfather's mom's house in Pacifica, or if needed, commuting from my mom's place in Stockton. I had thought about Irvine State, but it felt too distant, and I lacked connections there. I was navigating all of this on my own, financing my education without any help from my parents. Staying closer to home and within the community I knew made the most sense, given my circumstances.

The neighbor behind us braided my hair into singles, and I wore a dress I loved. Graduating with high honors, I was ready to walk across that stage with pride. I had faced numerous obstacles over the past four years and had overcome them all - earning high honors despite everything. But as I went up to receive my award and diploma, I noticed my mom and little sister were missing from the crowd. My heart sank.

My stepdad, all the neighbors, my boyfriend, and my godfather's mom and dad were there, but my mom and little sister were missing. I felt so defeated, angry, and deeply hurt. It was always about her winning, always 'her way.' She was the queen of one-upping and punishing you if you went against what she wanted or said. I hated her. I officially felt so much hate in my heart towards her.

With everything she put us through—the poor choices, the lack of love and support, the countless obstacles—she couldn't even be there to celebrate my achievement of high honors and graduation. At that moment, something in me broke. I was done with her excuses and bullshit. I was DONE being pushed around by her and her manipulative tactics.

C-LOVE

Chapter 13
Betrayals and Heartbreak

After a long period away, my mom and sister returned to live with me and my stepdad, bringing with them a woman my mom had been staying with. This woman had recently gone through a divorce and lost her home, so my mom invited her to stay with us. Amidst these changes, I was making plans for my own future. I decided to live with my godfather's mom in Pacifica, and began packing up many of my belongings in preparation.

My boyfriend helped me learn how to drive, and I eventually bought a car and passed my driving test. Initially, I intended to return home every weekend, but I soon realized that balancing visits with my new academic schedule and homework demands at college would be too challenging.

The summer before I headed to SF State, my boyfriend and I attended the local junior college, Delta College, together. He played for their football team. During this time, he made comments about my body, suggesting I needed to tone up my arms more and be careful with what I ate to avoid getting cellulite like other 'White' girls. His remarks made me increasingly self-conscious about both my body and my skin color. Despite the discomfort these comments caused, I wanted to improve myself, so I followed his advice and started going to the gym with him. This experience highlighted the complexities of our relationship and my own struggles with self-image and identity.

As I prepared to move out for college, my mom claimed my large room with the walk-in closet, and I was moved into the smaller room that had previously belonged to my sister. My mom and stepdad, though still legally married, had drifted apart over the years. Their relationship had devolved into a purely transactional arrangement, resembling that of roommates who merely tolerated each other's presence. Meanwhile, my sister was relocated to a makeshift room downstairs that wasn't fully enclosed, further shifting the dynamics within our household. This reorganization of our living spaces marked a significant change as I was stepping into a new chapter of my life at college.

Complicating matters further, the family room was now occupied by the 'toxic' woman my mom had become deeply involved with over the years. This woman had been a negative influence, and with her living in our home, the not-so-great crowd of random adults who frequented her place for drugs and partying began showing up at ours. This led to an accelerated decline in our home environment. The influx of drug addicts who neither cared for nor respected our space meant that many people came and went, contributing to the deterioration of our household.

Leaving for college, I felt a deep conflict about leaving my sister behind in such a precarious environment. Her new room downstairs was not only makeshift but also lacked lockable doors, a concerning detail given the dubious characters now frequenting our home. Additionally, I was struggling with the emotional challenge of separating from my boyfriend.

After starting my studies and initially staying at my godfather's mom's house in Pacifica—a nurturing and secure environment—I found myself drawn back to my family home more often than was wise. Eventually, I stopped returning to Pacifica altogether and chose to endure a grueling four-hour daily commute to and from college from my mom's house, plunging myself back into the very toxic dynamics I had initially escaped.

This decision weighed heavily on me, laden with regret and shame. I had been granted an opportunity to live in a healthy, loving household, yet I found myself slipping back into the unhealthy, dysfunctional patterns I had so desperately wanted to leave behind. This backslide was a harsh reminder of the potent hold that trauma can have, illustrating the immense challenge of breaking free from its grip.

Returning to my mom's house full-time intensified the tension between us dramatically. We fought incessantly, and she started hurling outrageous accusations at me, such as stealing her wedding ring and other items. She even accused my boyfriend of theft. The situation at home grew increasingly complicated as my mom and stepdad, though still legally married, began having intimate relationships with others.

The arrival of my mom's new boyfriend, who started living with us, raised serious concerns. He seemed to be involved in drug dealing or supplying, as he began providing my mom with crystal meth. This had a severe impact on her health. She stayed awake for days at a time, her weight plummeted, and her skin erupted in large cysts that she would incessantly pick at. Her behavior became erratic and volatile, especially when she was coming down from the drugs. Witnessing her in this state was both alarming and terrifying, complicating my ability to navigate my own life and studies amid such chaos.

One day, during a heated argument—I can't even remember the details—my mom rushed at me on the stairs, and I instinctively raised my arms to protect myself. Later that week, while I was sitting in the kitchen after getting home from SF State, a friend of hers served me with restraining order papers. My mom demanded that I leave immediately, leaving me with nowhere to go. In desperation, I turned to a neighbor and asked if I could stay there for the night, hoping things would blow over quickly. But the next day, my mom called the police, reporting that I was within the 500-yard limit specified in the restraining order.

I found myself officially homeless. With no notice or time to pack, I had to leave most of my belongings behind, taking only what I could fit in my car—just the essentials I needed for school and work. I was utterly lost, with no clear plan for what to do next. I felt too much shame to return to my godfather's mom's house, what would I tell her now. I didn't want to tell people my mom was on meth. To make matters worse, the restraining order papers were manipulated to falsely claim that I had attacked my mom and pushed her down the stairs, which I had never done.

My boyfriend and I ended up at a Motel 6 while we figured things out. After a week there, we decided to get an apartment together. It was a tiny studio. At first we had no furniture —just a blow-up mattress we eventually replaced with a futon. Despite the hardships, it felt like an improvement over living under my mom's roof, with her hypocrisy and the constant presence of drug addicts. I hated the thought of my sister being there.

But why didn't I just go back to my godfather's mom's house? Why did I stay in these awful situations? The pull of trauma and shame can be incredibly strong, keeping you anchored in less-than-ideal situations despite knowing a healthier path exists. It's like being caught in a gravitational force that you can't escape, even when you deeply want to. The weight of past experiences, coupled with the fear of judgment or rejection, can make it feel almost impossible to make choices that lead to healing and safety. It's a profound struggle, but understanding this can be the first step toward breaking free from those patterns.

During those traumatic years, I barely had time to be with my sister due to my mom's choice to leave home and bring back all those drug addicts. I deeply regret this. I always wished for her to have a better life than I did. I wanted to shield her from the chaos and pain that enveloped us. Yet, it felt like I was continuously being dragged away or shoved out by the madness.

Not being there for her during those crucial years weighed heavily on me. I hoped she would find a way to escape and experience a more stable, loving environment. The guilt of not being able to provide that for her gnawed at me constantly.

Court day finally arrived. I hadn't seen my mom or anyone else for months, and it was strange how cold she was towards me in court. It was agreed that the rest of my belongings would be delivered to my new home, but I was still barred from going near the house or my sister. Without cell phones or iPads, I couldn't even call her, as my mom would answer the phone and stand guard. This was the most painful part of all. I constantly worried about my sister, feeling helpless and guilty for not being there to support and protect her. It was a stark reminder of the harsh reality I was living in and the deep fractures in our family.

The stress of living with my boyfriend and managing everything on my own began to weigh heavily on me. Living with him was vastly different from dating him while living apart. My distrust and paranoia grew as his mannerisms, behavior, and the inconsistencies in his actions became more pronounced. I didn't feel safe anymore and this only heightened my sense of feeling trapped. I was scared to stay, yet scared to leave—caught in a state of paralysis that left me unable to move forward.

His family urged me to get baptized again, despite my insistence that I was already baptized. It felt like they saw me as a "White demon" in need of saving. The hypocrisy was hard to bear—he had cheated on me, yet they wanted me to undergo the ritual of holy water. The expectations placed on women, like wearing long dresses instead of pants, covering our hair, and avoiding makeup; while men were free to cheat and still hold power, never sat right with me. It felt like a double standard that was impossible to ignore. What kind of church or religion was this?

The pressure of conforming to their religious expectations (they were Pentecostal Christian) only added to the strain. It felt like I was constantly being judged and found lacking, all while dealing with the emotional turmoil of a relationship that had already been broken by betrayal. The double standards were infuriating and I found myself questioning not just my relationship, but the values and beliefs that were being imposed on me.

Living with my boyfriend exposed facets of him I hadn't noticed before. Little things began to accumulate, revealing patterns that made me uneasy. His way of speaking to me, his wandering gaze at other women, and the small lies all contributed to a growing sense of discomfort. I couldn't shake the feeling that there was a truth just beyond my grasp. My trust in him eroded gradually, replaced by a persistent state of vigilance and doubt.

Amidst all this, I felt profoundly isolated. The support I had hoped for from his family came with strings attached, while my own family was more a source of pain than solace. I was trapped between the effort to make the relationship work and the growing realization that I was losing myself in the process. The weight of it all became overwhelming, and I started to understand that I needed to find a way out—to reclaim my sense of self and take back control of my life.

He disliked taking on responsibilities and paying his share of the bills, often making comments about it. To make ends meet, he started stealing sneakers from stores for extra income and would involve me by having me distract the sales associates. It felt like a twisted version of Bonnie and Clyde, reminiscent of the Jay-Z and Beyoncé song that had come out. But despite the external thrill, it never sat right with me internally.

I left JC Penney and started working at a call center for Marriott Hotels, always on the lookout for additional ways to boost my income. One opportunity I came across was an MLM called Excell, where I helped people save money on their phone bills. Another venture I pursued was selling Cutco knives. I enjoyed this job because it was all referral-based and allowed me to visit people's homes for presentations, demonstrating the knives' quality before making a sale.

I felt optimistic about my job with Cutco knives until I had a deeply unsettling experience at one of my stepdad's friend's houses in San Bruno. He initially seemed enthusiastic about purchasing a set of knives, but everything changed when he discovered my boyfriend was 'Black.' He launched into a tirade, expressing his disdain and insisting that being involved with a 'Black' man was beneath me. Ironically, he wasn't even 'White' himself! Yet, he harbored racist views toward 'Black' men. Although he bought the set of knives in front of me, I later learned from my manager that he called to cancel the order after I left. This was my first encounter with such blatant racism, and it left me with a sour taste regarding both the job and people in general.

Despite these challenges, I continued to push forward, determined to build a better life for myself. However, with each setback and instance of discrimination, it became increasingly difficult to hold on to my optimism and belief in the goodness of people.

After work one day, I received a call from someone claiming to know my biological dad. They informed me that he was battling lung cancer and might not have much time left, hospitalized in

Contra Costa. A flood of emotions overwhelmed me—he had vanished when I needed him the most, and now I was being told he was on his deathbed. Despite the pain and resentment I felt toward him, I decided to visit. At the very least, I wanted to express my feelings and let him know how his absence had affected me.

As I entered his hospital room, I was struck by how much he had withered away. His skin was yellow and sickly, and he looked so fragile and thin - barely able to articulate words. Yet, I could see in his eyes that he recognized me. We embraced. In that moment, all the hurt and resentment I had been carrying melted away. Instead, I was overwhelmed by a deep sense of love and sadness for the time we had lost and the time we would never have. My heart felt heavy with grief. A week later, he passed away. Although I never had the chance to see or hug him again, that one embrace was enough to convey everything that needed to be said and felt.

The woman who had called me about my dad turned out to be the mother of another half-sister from his side of the family. We had different mothers, but we shared the same father. She invited me to her house for a ceremony to celebrate his life. Meeting my half-sister was a remarkable experience. She resembled an Asian version of both me and my dad, and we shared a strikingly similar facial structure.

Her mom was an amazing paid artist, and being in her presence inspired me. I had always loved drawing in my spare time, in addition to writing poetry. Seeing her artwork encouraged me to explore my creative side even further and that artists do and can make a living.

A monologue I wrote for my dad years after his passing:

My Very Own Daddy

May 5, 2007

...I know this song...I remember it when I was a kid... Before I ever met you. Mom gave me this tape...it was called...Air Supply ...and told me this song was sung at your wedding. I would sit and play it over and over again...all day long. Longing to know you, connect with you...imagine what you were like. And then I finally met you and I saw just how much I looked like you. It was amazing...my daddy... my very own daddy. All I ever knew before, were men my mom dated and some of them hurt me. But not you cuz you were my daddy. As I look back, I wish I could have spent more time with you...gotten to know you better... gotten to hear about your childhood...what your family was like. Now all I have is a shoe and a box filled with old credit cards...a money clip...some pictures and a song. But nothing substantial to let me know who you were... what you liked...didn't. I miss you so very much and I'd give anything to see you again...talk to you...just hug you. Because I don't feel I hugged you enough...hold you...I wouldn't want to let you go. I wish I never would have. The last time I saw you I didn't want to believe it was the end. I said I would come back but I never made it back before you passed. And I regret it so much daddy...My very own Daddy. I didn't get to have you in my life much and the last moments I did have you... I cut them short and I wish I would have stayed by your side and never left... never let go of your hand... Never take my arms from around your sickened body... I would never let go if I could go back. Go back to the last hug... where you used what strength you had left to hold me and tried with every breath you took to say my name. How much love I felt coming from you... how much time we had missed each other in this lifetime... That was now passing. My daddy you loved me just as much as I loved you. You felt the regret that day... knowing you are going ...knowing you are gonna pass... you know we didn't get enough time. And your hug... your hug has apologized for it... and tried to make it up in that moment... In that short lived time... That I will forever remember and cherish all my life. I love you daddy... My dear Daddy. I only wish I would have taken the time to show you and share it with you in this lifetime...

My boyfriend and I shared a lot of experiences together. We went to the gym, I'd watch him play basketball, and we even took a cross-country trip with his family to visit his relatives in Texas. But as time went on, the dynamic began to shift and we started fighting more frequently at home. While I was busy with work and school, he had much more free time and would often be at home. When I returned, I was expected to handle all the cleaning and cooking. It felt increasingly like I was shouldering all the responsibilities, and our relationship started to feel less like a partnership and more like a burden.

Things took a turn for the worse when I discovered he had cheated on me again. I was furious and felt deeply foolish. One night, we went to a club together, and as soon as we walked in, he abandoned me to dance with other women. His blatant disrespect was becoming increasingly apparent, and I found myself blaming myself for remaining in such a toxic situation.

That was the final straw for me. I decided to go out the following weekend without telling him where I was headed. I ended up at a club in Sacramento and met someone who seemed nice. But I got way too drunk and ended up driving home a complete mess. When I got back, my boyfriend wasn't there—he had gone out as well and didn't return for a couple of nights. Part of me hoped he would have cared enough to be worried, but he wasn't. When he finally came back, we had a huge argument. As he started packing his things to leave, he threw me down on the ground. It was a terrifying moment, especially given that this was my first serious and longest relationship.

That experience established a pattern for the types of men and relationships I continued to attract. Even though I was deeply in love with him, discovering his infidelity shattered my heart and eroded my trust in love. The pain of heartbreak was excruciating. He had been my rock during the chaos of my family life for so many years, and suddenly, it all came crashing down around me. With my biological dad's passing, the end of this relationship, and the ongoing estrangement from my mom and sister, I felt profoundly alone.

As my relationship was ending, my mom started coming back around, and I decided to move back into her house. Living alone while going to school would have been financially challenging. During this time, a new guy started showing interest, taking me on dates and providing a distraction from the heartache I felt inside. However, one date took a dark turn. He drove me into San Francisco under the pretense of picking up money, but we ended up at a strip club. It turned out he was a pimp who 'managed' the girls working for him. He also took me on rounds where he bought weed, and I suspected he was involved in drug dealing as well.

I saw firsthand how some people navigate survival and financial stability through means that felt deeply unsettling. He even tried to recruit me as one of his 'girls,' which was oddly tempting at first, but then he demanded my student financial aid money-claiming all my money was his. I stopped answering his calls, but one day he showed up at my door. Feeling 'cornered,' I confided in my mom, and she called him, threatening him to stay away from me. He backed off, but the whole experience left me with a profound distrust and repulsion toward men. Monsters come in so many shades, sizes and walks of life.

C-LOVE

Chapter 14
Monsters Are Made of Something Different

Being back at my mom's house took some adjusting. I had to get used to who was there, who was coming and going, and the activities of everyone in the house. I didn't feel safe leaving anything of value in my room or money without hiding it first. She was still with that drug-dealing boyfriend. I never liked him; he seemed so shady, and he always kept my mom so high.

When she wasn't high and manic, her paranoia led to erratic and frightening behavior. One day, after I had just stepped out of the shower wrapped in a towel, she charged at me with a pole. I quickly shut my door, but the pole punctured a hole in it as she forced her way in. In a fit of rage, she spat a loogie in my face, screaming at me for supposedly wasting toilet paper. I hadn't wasted anything, but even if I had, her reaction was completely unjustified. Her drug use, coupled with the presence of other users in our home, created an environment that felt anything but safe. I couldn't comprehend how this chaos could be called "home".

It became a recurring pattern in our household to offer refuge to those in need. When my sister's friend needed a place to stay, my mom welcomed her into our home. Before long, this girl began dating a boy who also needed shelter, and our house became a magnet for those seeking temporary refuge. Eventually, the girl moved out and ended her relationship, but the boy remained, becoming like a brother to me amidst the chaos. As more people shuffled through our home, it deteriorated further, transforming into a far cry from the brand-new house we had once moved into with high hopes for new beginnings. What had started as a fresh start had turned into a halfway house, filled with uncertainty and instability.

He had a unique flair about him, always immersed in music and crafting outfits that were both creative and stylish. His artistic spirit was evident in everything he did, from the way he expressed himself to his eccentric mannerisms. Weed was his constant companion, keeping him in a perpetual state of relaxation. Despite his unconventional lifestyle, he harbored grand dreams and aspirations for a better future. His humor was infectious, often indulging in playful antics and impersonations of various characters. Unlike me, he eschewed structure and traditional employment, preferring the freedom of being at home. We became confidants for each other, sharing our challenges and dreams openly.

I remember the day I walked into my mom's room, just like any other day, but this day felt different. There it was: her wedding ring, the very one she had accused me and my ex of stealing, lying in her drug-dealing boyfriend's satchel. In an instant, I saw red. Without a second thought, I yelled and charged at this towering figure, standing 6 feet 4 inches tall and weighing around 300 pounds. Pure rage coursed through me as I confronted him, ready to unleash the fury that had been building inside me for so long.

But then, in a terrifying twist, he pulled out a knife. Fear gripped me, but thankfully, my "brother" - the one who lived with us - stepped in. He got between us and managed to persuade him to put away the weapon. It was a moment of intense relief amidst the chaos.

Later, when my mom returned home, we had to tell her what had happened. It was a difficult conversation, but one that needed to be had.

My stepdad's presence in our home was more of an absence. He'd vanish early in the morning, heading off to work, and wouldn't return until late in the afternoon. When he did come back, he'd retreat straight to his room, locking himself away from the rest of us. Sometimes, he wouldn't even make it home, opting instead to spend his evenings at the bar, stumbling back in the dead of night drunk, only to catch a few hours of sleep before the cycle started anew.

I was filled with curiosity about the drug my mom and her friends were always using. I wanted to understand her experience, so I ventured into her room and took a hit from her pipe alongside her. The effect was immediate and intense. Suddenly, I felt wide awake and hyper-aware, unable to stop talking. The high was exhilarating, but the crash that followed was devastating. An overwhelming heaviness enveloped me, as if the weight of the world was crushing me. No amount of sleep seemed to alleviate the sensation. At that moment, I could understand why my mom kept taking more hits to avoid coming down and facing this awful feeling. I began to comprehend the irrational and erratic behavior she displayed during her comedowns, realizing just how deeply the drug affected her.

An unexpected but thrilling opportunity came my way when I was invited to join a group for a hip-hop dance performance at Hot August Nights in Reno. This event was linked to a performer my 'brother' knew, and it represented a welcome diversion from the challenges at home. We practiced diligently, coordinated matching outfits, and geared up for the big day. Returning to dance in a group setting four years after high school felt like a breath of fresh air. At nineteen, this was the first time since graduation that I engaged in an activity I truly loved, and it was rejuvenating to reconnect with this artistic passion.

However, when the time for our performance arrived, our plans unexpectedly shifted. Instead of performing on stage, we were swept up in the lively street festivities, partying and roaming the strip. The vibrant atmosphere, the sight of classic cars, and the music enveloping us created an unforgettable experience. Despite not performing as planned, the energy and excitement of the event left a lasting impression, reminding me of the joy and spontaneity that life can offer.

Out of the blue, a tall guy from Stockton approached me, asking for my name and number. We hit it off quickly and soon began dating. He had a two-year-old daughter from a previous relationship and lived with his mom on the East Side. He was a hard worker but had a penchant for drinking, which often colored our time together. Our outings consisted of gatherings with his friends, exploring new restaurants (he was a total foodie), visits to his mom's house, and trips to see his sister. While he made me feel cared for in some ways, there were moments when I couldn't shake the feeling of loneliness that lingered in the background.

I got accepted for a job as a Burns Security Guard, and I found myself posted at a warehouse in Lathrop and a winery in Lodi. I was genuinely excited about this job—not so much for the work itself, but for the uniform. It reminded me of my theater days, where I'd step into different roles and embody various characters. As an artist with a passion for acting, wearing that uniform felt like donning a costume in a theatrical production, allowing me to embrace a new persona and experience a sense of play in my daily life.

My ex-boyfriend reached out, asking if I could braid his hair. At that point, I had regular clients coming in and out of my mom's house for braiding, so allowing my ex to come over felt harmless—a friendly gesture. However, as our conversations evolved and he dropped subtle hints, I found myself in a situation I never intended. Before I knew it, I had cheated on my current boyfriend with my ex, and the guilt weighed heavily on my conscience. Unable to bear the burden of my secret, I confessed to my boyfriend immediately. Seeing him cry broke my heart, a painful reminder of the hurt I had caused him. From that moment on, I realized that any reactions he had were a direct result of the pain I had inflicted.

I had officially become a monster by doing something so hurtful to someone I cared about. The guilt and remorse were overwhelming; I couldn't hold it in or lie about what I had done. I vowed never to hurt anyone like that again. It baffled me how others, the true monsters, seemed to feel zero guilt for their actions, inflicting pain without a second thought. Their lack of remorse contrasted sharply with the deep sense of accountability I felt, highlighting the vast difference between us. Monsters were made of something different.

The disrespect and potential infidelity started to surface little by little. My boyfriend's behavior became increasingly erratic, with signs of cheating surfacing and his unabashed confessions only adding to the turmoil. Whether his admissions were meant to hurt me like knives or if they were genuine, the pain they caused was real. His stories of being sexual with other women left me feeling disgusted and belittled, while his anger- especially when fueled by alcohol- left me feeling controlled and powerless. Once again, I found myself in a situation I didn't know how to escape from.

My period hadn't come for a month or two, so I reluctantly decided to take a pregnancy test. When the results revealed that I was pregnant, it hit me like a ton of bricks. Just as I was on the verge of making a significant change by moving closer to SF State, the reality of bringing a child into the world with my current partner felt overwhelming. I found myself crying while sitting on the toilet, staring at the pregnancy test. What a curveball this was.

While I knew that leaving him and moving in with friends from school was the right decision, the news of my pregnancy tethered me to him in a way I wasn't prepared for. I wasn't ready for motherhood, especially not with someone I couldn't envision a future with. My mind was clouded with uncertainty as I grappled with this unexpected turn of events.

After an internal nudge, I decided to move in with my classmates near SF State, leaving both my mom's house and the dwindling relationship behind. He expressed that he didn't want to maintain a connection if I wasn't just a drive away, he didn't do 'long distance.'. While it was a tough choice, I knew it was the right one for my well-being.

Realizing the toll my past mistake and current relationship dynamics were taking on me, I reached a critical point of self-awareness. Although I regretted cheating on my boyfriend with my ex, his response was excessively malicious and spiteful. His actions escalated to continual cheating, followed by gloating about his exploits to torment me, which I came to recognize as abusive and unjustifiable.

I was at my breaking point, I understood that I didn't deserve to endure such treatment. The cycle of negativity and pain had become too much, and I knew I needed a change to break free. The opportunity to leave my mom's house and the toxic environment there presented itself as I decided to move in with friends near SF State. This move was not just a change in location; it was a crucial step toward reclaiming my peace and building a healthier, more positive life away from the destructive patterns I had been trapped in.

I loaded the bed of my truck with everything I was bringing, leaving behind a room full of belongings at my mom's house. As I set off for my new home, I felt a complex mix of emotions—excitement for the fresh chapter ahead, yet also fear about the difficult decisions looming, especially since I was pregnant and facing it alone.

Upon arrival, my roommates quickly stepped in to help me unpack and settle in. It was immensely comforting to be in a loving, creative environment surrounded by others my age who were all committed to their education and building their futures. This support and the positive atmosphere of my new home provided a much-needed sense of belonging and hope, reassuring me that I had made the right decision to move.

The condo I moved into was conveniently located above an Albertson's grocery store, making daily errands a breeze and only an 8-minute drive from my school. I immediately fell in love with the fresh ambiance of our new home. The smell of new paint and fresh carpet gave the space a clean and welcoming vibe. It was beautifully maintained both inside and out, a stark contrast to my mom's house, which had deteriorated over the years due to neglect and the constant traffic of people.

I shared the spacious master bedroom with another roommate, which offered ample space and comfort. Our room featured double doors with windows that we could open to let in the fresh San Francisco air. I cherished the moments spent by those windows, listening to the sounds of the city below. The feeling of starting anew in such a vibrant and well-kept environment was both uplifting and reassuring as I navigated this significant transition in my life.

As I settled into my new home, I faced the reality of the difficult choices ahead. Being pregnant added a pressing urgency to each decision, with time ticking relentlessly onward. Thankfully, the support of my roommates and the proximity of my new apartment to my school provided some comfort.

This transition taught me how a drastic change of scenery can significantly alter one's perspective. Moving into this fresh, new environment infused me with hope and a sense of renewal. It empowered me, making me feel better prepared to tackle the upcoming challenges and make the tough decisions that lay ahead. This sense of beginning anew was crucial in helping me feel more capable and optimistic about the future.

C-LOVE

Chapter 15
Circle of Life

It was a gloomy, overcast day in San Francisco, and the dreary weather seemed to mirror the storm of emotions raging within me. As I made my way to the clinic downtown, waves of nausea and fear gnawed at my insides; I knew I didn't want to go through with this choice. I didn't want to have an abortion. Desperate for reassurance, I called the father of the baby growing inside me, hoping he would talk me out of it. Instead, his words were cold and final: "You better go through with this. I don't want anything to do with you or any baby." He hung up, leaving me stunned and utterly alone.

In my despair, I reached out to an old neighbor from my mom's house who offered me a comforting presence. She helped me feel a little less alone. Despite my reluctance, I proceeded to park and go inside the building to my appointment to check in, overwhelmed by feelings of isolation and uncertainty about my future. My world felt like it was crumbling around me.

Shame pressed heavily on me as I sat in the waiting room, where an unsettling quietness hung in the air, palpable enough to cut through. Outside, protesters held up large picket signs depicting bloody images of fetal remains, making an already shame-ridden experience feel that much worse. To my surprise, I recognized a girl from a recent fashion show at SF State sitting among the faces in the waiting area. When my name was finally called for the painkiller meds, I obediently took them. Almost immediately, nausea overwhelmed me, and I rushed to the bathroom to vomit them out. My youth and naivety left me ill-prepared and uninformed about what was to come. After what felt like an eternity, I was finally ushered into a room.

So much of that day remains a haze, but certain moments are seared into my memory as if branded there for life. The machine hummed to life, revealing the silhouette of the life inside me. Why did they show me this? Then came the jarring sound of the vacuum—a haunting, mechanical noise accompanied by an excruciating pulling sensation within. The pain was unbearable; it felt as if a part of me was being violently ripped away right there on the table. I can never unhear that sound or unfeel the sensation of the life inside of me being sucked away. I cried out in agony, overwhelmed by both physical and emotional torment. A part of me died on that table that day

Once the procedure was over, which felt like an eternity, they rolled me into the recovery room. Alone and consumed by my suffering, shame enveloped me as I lay in the recovery bed, waiting to go home. I emerged from that experience irrevocably changed, feeling as though a piece of my soul had been lost forever, never to return. In the aftermath, a deep-seated hatred toward men began to take root within me, along with a profound distrust of love and romance. The beliefs that "men are monsters" and "love isn't real" took hold of my psyche, leaving me grappling with the emotional fallout for years to come.

Recovery was a slow, somber journey through one of the darkest periods of my life. As my dreams of motherhood dwindled and the romanticized vision of enduring love faded, I found myself yearning for the kind of lifelong commitment I had witnessed between my godfather and his high school sweetheart. Instead, I felt discarded, worthless, and unlovable, questioning whether anyone would ever want me or be willing to share a life and a child with me.

For weeks, my days blurred together in a haze of sleep, tears, and occasional meals, followed by more tears. I remained in bed, wrapped in my sadness, wrestling with the heavy burden of my emotions. It felt like an unbreakable cycle of despair, and I fought hard to find a way out, yearning for a glimmer of hope amidst the darkness that surrounded me. During this tumultuous time, my roommates became my saving grace, cooking for me and tending to my needs. Their support provided a lifeline, but soon, the harsh reality of financial pressures began to weigh heavily on us all. Our involvement in the MLM, Excell, proved insufficient to sustain our living expenses, leaving us to grapple with the uncertainty of our future together.

We were desperately scrambling for alternative sources of income and explored various avenues—from pursuing modeling gigs on Model Mayhem to diving headfirst into the MLM business. The camaraderie of being in a house full of girls, all working together to navigate the same challenges, felt comforting and empowering. I had never experienced such a strong sense of support and encouragement before.

Eventually, we stumbled upon the idea of working in the gentlemen's clubs of San Francisco. This concept had been planted a couple of years prior by a guy I briefly dated from Sacramento, who had turned out to be a pimp. Now, still reeling from the physical and emotional trauma of my recent abortion and the heartache of rejection from my ex, I found myself thrust into this new and daunting environment.

We all auditioned together at a small venue that welcomed those 18 and up, and to our surprise, we were all accepted right away. Soon, we found ourselves working long hours amidst the pulsating music and flashing lights, navigating a world that was both exhilarating and overwhelming.

Strangely, the constant hustle and noise provided a temporary escape, allowing me to momentarily distance myself from the relentless cycle of thoughts about the painful experiences I had just endured. The rhythm of the club, the interactions with customers, and the camaraderie with my coworkers created a surreal, yet comforting bubble. In this environment, I could lose myself in the dance, the vibrant lights, and the fleeting connections. It was a world so different from the one I had known, and in its own way, it offered a bizarre form of solace.

The gentlemen's clubs of San Francisco turned out to be a weird sort of therapy for me, a place where I could let out all that anger, frustration, and pure resentment I had bottled up against men. My life had been one long series of betrayals and abuses that scarred me deep. It started with Bobby's sexual abuse, then being tossed into the foster system at just two years old. My first intimate partner pretending I was nobody at school. And love? My first stab at it ended with me being cheated on, not once but multiple times, setting a pattern for every relationship that followed.

It seemed like every guy I encountered only reinforced my belief that there were no good men—just individuals driven by wild, uncontrollable lust and a relentless sex drive. They felt like monsters to me, acting purely on their desires. Yet, within the walls of those clubs, I discovered a twist in the narrative. Here, I could turn their very desires against them. For the first time, I wasn't the one being taken advantage of; I was in control. I transformed their weakness into my strength, finding a way to benefit from the very aspects of masculinity that had victimized me for so long. This newfound power provided a sense of agency I had desperately craved.

In the club, I found a paradoxical sense of power and control. As I danced and interacted with the patrons, I could dictate the terms of engagement and set boundaries that had been violated in the past. It was a way for me to reclaim agency over my body and my interactions, even if only for a fleeting moment. Despite the superficial allure of the environment, it served as a battleground where I confronted my demons and sought to rewrite the narrative of victimhood that had defined so much of my life.

I finally found a way to turn my internal pain into profit, using men's weaknesses (the ones which had caused me so much pain) to my advantage. I believed that by taking their money, I was reclaiming my power, a counterbalance to the years of exploitation and lies I had endured. Initially, this approach seemed to work in my favor, providing me with financial stability and independence. I secured my own apartment, bought a brand new car, and transferred from SF State to the Fashion Institute of Design and Merchandising.

Having financial abundance allowed me to drive back home to see my sister and my 'brother.' I would spoil everyone and take them out to eat. I'd go on shopping sprees and treat my sister to all the things she wanted. Sometimes, I'd have her come spend weeks with me, and we'd go on adventures in SF together. I loved being able to take care of my sister and give her experiences we missed out on growing up.

The club was a revolving door of girls, each with their own schedules—some working the day shift, others the night shift, and some, like me, pulling doubles. Among them was a girl I befriended who seemed genuinely nice. She took me under her wing, showing me the ropes and teaching me how to maximize my earnings. Her guidance extended to what to say and how to navigate the ins-and-outs of the club. To top it off, she would sneak me drinks since I wasn't yet 21, which helped me unwind while I worked.

She even joined me for my 21st birthday celebration, along with her husband. We celebrated by going to Benihana's with my stepdad and my new neighbor from upstairs, who also attended SF State with me. To prepare for this special day, I treated myself to a fancy salon for a hair makeover and splurged on my first pair of Charles David shoes. It felt like a well-deserved pampering session for my milestone birthday.

This was my first experience at Benihana, and I was captivated by the way they cooked right in front of you, performing tricks with their utensils as they prepared the food. We indulged in sake bombs and shared laughs, creating unforgettable memories that stood out amidst the chaos of my life.

When I came back to work, all the girls were acting strangely toward me. They were mean, and making comments as if I had done something wrong. It was so confusing and scary because these girls were aggressive and quick to fight physically, much more so than the girls I knew from school or outside this job. They were 'harder' - tougher. They lived in reactive survival-of-the-fittest mode and were very territorial. These were not the kind of girls you wanted to get on the wrong side of.

The girl I thought was my friend suddenly turned cold, giving me the silent treatment. No matter how many times I approached her, she would just walk away, ignoring me completely. I would catch her glancing at me, pointing, and whispering with the other girls, making faces and sounds that made me want to shrink and hide. Confusion washed over me; I couldn't understand what I had done wrong or why she had gone from being warm and welcoming to so distant and unkind.

This sudden shift left me feeling sad, hurt, and perplexed. The atmosphere became increasingly uncomfortable, making me dread going to work. I longed for the camaraderie and support I had initially felt in this environment, but now it felt like I was navigating a minefield of mixed signals and unspoken tensions.

Eventually, one of the girls explained what was happening. My so-called friend had returned to work a day before I did and started spreading lies, claiming that I had talked "shit" about the other girls. She fabricated stories about things I supposedly said regarding their bodies and the ways they made money with clients. When I denied her accusations, she doubled down, insisting that I had indeed said those things.

With no proof to back me up, it became a frustrating battle of her word against mine and since she had been at the club longer, the other girls naturally took her side. The betrayal cut deep, and I felt completely isolated, thrust into a hostile environment where trust had evaporated overnight.

I learned the hard way not to befriend girls working in this industry and to keep my personal life separate from my professional one. After the betrayal, I decided to leave that club and start dancing at a different venue an hour and a half away. The toxic atmosphere and animosity among the girls had become unbearable, and I knew I needed a fresh start.

However, this experience left a lasting mark on me. It made it difficult to open up and befriend new people, and it took a long time before I could trust another dancer. Even then, I kept them at arm's length, never allowing anyone to get as close as that one had. The lessons learned from that betrayal made me cautious and wary about women, reshaping my interactions in ways I hadn't anticipated.

In retrospect, I can clearly see that this girl exhibited classic narcissistic behavior. She showered me with warmth and attention, making me feel special by taking me under her wing and teaching me the ropes. Then, just as quickly, she discarded me and turned the entire club against me after celebrating my 21st birthday.

This was an eye-opening experience. I was naive to the manipulations and betrayals that could occur among women in this industry, and it forced me to confront the reality of the environment I was in. It made me acutely aware of the caliber of people I was surrounded by and helped me become more cautious moving forward. This was not a typical workplace like Starbucks; it was a different world, and I needed to adapt to survive.

After I started working at the new club an hour and a half away, an unexpected opportunity presented itself: the chance to donate my eggs to couples struggling with infertility. Burdened by the shame, guilt, and grief from my abortion, I eagerly embraced this opportunity to help someone else have a child. While I couldn't erase or take back what I had done, I saw this as a way to contribute positively to the world and assist families in bringing life into their homes. Over the course of two years, I successfully donated between 20 to 30 eggs, finding a sense of purpose and redemption through this meaningful act.

The process involved numerous medical tests to ensure I was a healthy candidate, followed by daily hormone injections. As a result, I gained weight, my tummy protruded, and my chest felt tender and fuller, mimicking the physical changes of pregnancy. Once I reached a certain stage, they scheduled the retrieval, where I would be put under anesthesia to have the eggs collected. The recovery period afterward took time and was not particularly comfortable, but I was surprised by my ability to administer the shots daily, despite my aversion to seeing blood. This journey, while challenging, was a testament to my resilience and willingness to help others.

During the second round of egg donations, I faced a medical error that led to my hospitalization. My ovaries had been overstimulated and were overly sensitive; this, combined with severe constipation from being put under, created immense pressure inside me. Suddenly, something burst, and I experienced the worst pain of my life. Getting to the hospital felt like an eternity, and it took far too long for them to provide relief.

Enduring such unbearable agony, I was eventually connected to a machine that allowed me to self-administer morphine at the press of a button. I was immensely grateful for the drug as it alleviated the pain, but a part of me feared that this experience might jeopardize my dream of having children in the future. Deep down, I wondered if perhaps this was a punishment I deserved for all the mistakes I had made—cheating on my boyfriend, having an abortion, and exploiting men's weaknesses for my own gain in the name of justice. Dancing no longer felt empowering - it was a trap tying me to my past.

Dancing, which once felt empowering, now felt like an anchor, tying me to a past I desperately wanted to escape. The illusion had faded, replaced by a haunting reminder of the choices I had made and the pain I had endured. In that hospital room, as I wrestled with my thoughts, I realized I needed to reclaim my life in a way that honored my true self, not the monster I had feared becoming.

The guilt and shame surrounding all of my life choices weighed heavily on me. Part of me recognized that this wasn't the solution I had been searching for, nor was it the retribution I craved. I realized there could be no true justice if I became a monster like the ones I sought to hold accountable. I couldn't stoop to their level.

After this harrowing experience, I decided never to donate eggs again. However, I learned that both couples I assisted were successful in having babies, and the thought that little ones with my DNA are thriving in loving homes filled my heart with joy. Knowing I could help others build their families, despite my own challenges, brought me a tiny sense of fulfillment and peace.

Humanities Balance

One person lives
Another one dies
A baby is born
Someone is given a chance at life

A heart is broken
A tear is shed
Another crime is committed
Against humanities very being
Someone is smiling
Someone is sad
Someone is joyful
Another very mad
A war is progressing
Peace is reached
Someone is hungry
Another is being fed
Someone is all alone
Another is buried in a crowd
All of this is happening
Every fleeting moment
All around the world
Nothing stands still
Nothing remains the same
Constantly in forward motion
Never to come back again
There is no stop/pause button
No rewind either
We are all connected
In the yin and yang balance
In this intricate tapestry of life
For every cause there is an effect
In this intricate tapestry of life
For every cause there is an effect
What you do trickles through the whole system
And comes up somewhere else
All part of a whole
All One
Connected.

Cassandra Love Lambert, March 2008

C-LOVE

Chapter 16
'Brother/Friend' Boyfriend?

Continuing to work at a club, now closer to my mom's house, enabled me to see my sister and family more frequently. Despite the changes in my living situation, leaving the world of dancing proved challenging, primarily due to my financial obligations and the lifestyle I had become accustomed to. The flexibility and income that dancing provided seemed irreplaceable, and I wasn't sure what other job could offer similar benefits, which left me feeling trapped. Driven by a need to find a solution, I became focused on discovering a path to a more aligned life.

To manage these feelings and explore new possibilities, I decided to try working in a different environment. I transitioned to a new club in a city closer to my mom's house, hoping that this change of venue might provide a fresh perspective and potentially facilitate a smoother transition should I find a viable alternative to dancing. This move was a proactive step towards balancing my immediate needs with my longer-term aspirations for change.

As I kept reconnecting with my sister, my friend who was like a 'brother' had been living at my mom's house and started to get closer and closer to me. One day, in a heated moment, he made a 'move' on me, and the line was crossed. At that moment, we became more than just friends, marking the beginning of a profoundly heart-wrenching journey. It was the start of a path that would test the depths of my heart and resilience in ways I had never anticipated.

In retrospect, I now realize I was caught up in the heat of the moment, and wasn't able to think with the logical side of my brain. I also wish trauma hadn't been pulling me back to the same familiar abuse and monsters I was used to. As soon as we crossed that line, he became paranoid about me and would constantly accuse me of things I would never do. His jealousy and mistrust were relentless, turning our once supportive friendship into a toxic and painful ordeal. The bond that had felt so strong and safe started to unravel, replaced by suspicion and emotional turmoil.

It was difficult to reconcile the love and care I felt for him with the reality of his behavior. His accusations and paranoia ate away at me, making me question myself and the foundation of our friendship. This period served as a harsh reminder of how quickly things could change. "Good things never last" became an ingrained belief; I had witnessed happiness blossom only to see it crumble too many times throughout my life. The cycle of hope followed by disappointment left me feeling emotionally exhausted, longing for stability, yet bracing myself for the inevitable fall.

We found ourselves in a cycle of non-stop fights and arguments over trivial matters, draining my mental clarity and energy. When it was just the two of us hanging out, things felt slightly better than when we ventured out into public together. He didn't have a job, which meant I was the one footing the bill for EVERYTHING. I couldn't quite understand why I accepted this arrangement; perhaps it was because he had been around as a 'friend' and like a 'brother' for so long that I felt it was normal.

It was a pattern I recognized in my relationships with my sister and mom as well—I was always the one financially providing for everyone. I had the money, so why not help? Back then, red flags weren't something anyone discussed, and I was oblivious to the fact that I had a choice. I felt like my ability to advocate for myself had been stripped away. The experience of being grounded for breaking up with a boyfriend who pressured me to kiss him at 14 still lingered. It left me with a distorted belief that if someone showed interest, it meant I was obligated to be with them and I couldn't leave or I'd be punished. I still battled the remnants of that mindset, feeling trapped by the memories of my past experiences.

I felt ensnared in this pattern, unable to envision a way out. The idea of "red flags" or setting boundaries was foreign to me. It was as if I had been conditioned and groomed to accept whatever came my way, convinced that it was my 'duty' to endure and adapt. I believed I deserved this turmoil after all I had been through. The constant drama and emotional upheaval had become my 'familiar,' and I was oblivious that I held the power to change it.

Reflecting back on it, I now see how these beliefs and experiences shaped my decisions and relationships. I understand now that I deserved better, but at the time, it felt like I was stuck in a pattern I couldn't break free from. The lack of awareness and guidance on healthy relationships and low self-worth kept me glued to situations that drained me and stifled my growth.

I had transferred from SF State to The Fashion Institute of Design and Merchandising (FIDM), working full-time to cover a significant portion of my expenses, which left me with little spare time to spend with him. With the advent of cell phones, our communication shifted dramatically, and he often entangled me in arguments via text. He accused me of lying, cheating, and a myriad of other things while I was busy in the computer lab or buried under mountains of homework. I simply didn't have the time or energy to engage in any of the actions he accused me of.

As the constant fighting took its toll, I struggled to maintain any semblance of connection with him. It became apparent that his accusations were more reflective of his own behaviors. Eventually, I found myself mirroring his suspicions, beginning to accuse him of infidelity. Given his history, it felt plausible. Was he projecting his guilt onto me, deflecting attention from his own actions? This rotation of mistrust and blame spiraled out of control, leaving me confused and emotionally drained daily. What happened to my 'brother,' confidant and friend?

The emotional toll was immense, and the constant escalating drama made it hard to focus on my studies or my job. I felt trapped. Once again in a situation draining my life force and spirit. Despite everything, I couldn't bring myself to end it. The familiarity, the history we shared, and my own insecurities kept me tethered to this destructive relationship. It was as if I was caught in a web of my own making, unable to break free despite knowing how damaging it was. That's when I learned that you can be aware of something being unhealthy and still feel stuck in it.

He would make me walk from the 6th Street parking garage on Mission to FIDM with my head down. If I dared to look up, even for a second, he would scream at me, "You whore, you want to fuck that guy, don't you?" In those moments, I felt stripped of my dignity, as my homework was tossed to the ground and spit on. I wished I could melt into the sidewalk and disappear. I felt so embarrassed. He shattered the belongings in my apartment, showing no respect for anything I valued, like a wild animal in a rage.

Despite his destructive behavior, he always returned with profuse apologies, tears, and gifts—flowers meant to placate me. Whenever I voiced my concerns about our relationship, he would twist my words, making me feel afraid to leave. His threats of self-harm, accompanied by cries and desperate pleas, made it hard to break free. Even when I tried to distance myself by ignoring his calls or avoiding his visits, he would show up at my front door. I was trapped and didn't know a way out. It felt as though I was suffocating, unable to escape the grip of someone who claimed to love me while simultaneously tearing me apart. This was not the true love relationship I had always dreamed of. This was a living nightmare.

One time our fight escalated to the point where he sat in the middle of the intersection on Skyline Blvd, just before heading into Pacifica. He refused to budge, causing a traffic standstill. Eventually, the police arrived, and in the chaos, I became upset when they grabbed him to take him away. To my shock, they handcuffed me and put me in the back of a cop car. I felt a wave of helplessness wash over me. He ended up in a straitjacket, and I was left to pick him up from the hospital once he had calmed down.

His dad, upon hearing us argue, blamed me for his behavior, pointing fingers at my "job." He would say, "Of course, he's acting this way; look at your job," leaving me as the guilty party in a situation I didn't know how to escape. Despite the turmoil, I tried to support him in his aspirations as a rapper, helping him sell his CDs at work and even using some of his music during my performances. I believed I was spreading awareness about him and showing my support. However, deep down I was torn between my desire to help him and a mounting pressure telling me to get out.

One night, he unexpectedly snuck into my apartment, climbing up to my second-story patio and slipping through the sliding glass door. I jolted awake to the sound of him rummaging through my things. When he saw me, he yelled for the money I had made from selling CDs. In a fit of rage, he threw me to the floor and began tossing my belongings around until I finally handed it over to him. That money was meant to be our savings, a foundation for the life we dreamed of building together. At that moment, I couldn't help but wonder if he was using something stronger than just weed. This cycle of volatile abuse, followed by hollow apologies filled with fear, had become my new normal, trapping me in a relentless whirlwind of emotional and physical torment.

Reflecting on these experiences, I've come to realize just how deeply ingrained the patterns of abuse and manipulation were. I felt powerless, constantly walking on eggshells and doubting my worth. The threats, the violence, and the emotional manipulation eroded my sense of self, making it nearly impossible to break free. The guilt, fear, and shame kept me tethered to a relationship that was destroying me from the inside out.

I now understand these experiences' profound impact on my life. They shaped my perceptions of love, trust, and self-worth and it's taken me years to unravel the damage to reclaim my voice and power. But acknowledging this painful chapter is a step towards healing and breaking the cycle of abuse that held me captive for so long.

In a desperate cry for help, I spiraled into self-destruction. I found myself in a series of back-to-back car accidents and accumulating speeding tickets. My reckless behavior became a form of escapism; I drove home drunk, almost wishing that I wouldn't make it back. Yet, somehow, I always did - often unsure how I had managed it. Each journey felt like a blur, a haze of confusion and chaos. I wrestled with the conflicting desire to live while feeling trapped in a suffocating bubble of depression. Life had descended into a hellish nightmare once more, and I felt utterly lost.

This relationship had a profound impact on my mental health. I felt an overwhelming desperation for an escape, yet I was trapped in destructive patterns that had become my reality. The burden of the abuse, coupled with unresolved trauma, left me questioning my very existence. I found myself spiraling out of control, unsure of how to halt the descent. Life felt suffocating, and I grappled with the haunting question of what it all meant—was there a purpose in the pain I endured?

My reckless behavior became an outward manifestation of the inner turmoil I was grappling with. It was my silent cry for help, though I struggled to articulate the depth of my pain. The car accidents and speeding tickets were merely symptoms of a deeper issue—a desperate longing for change, for relief, and for some semblance of control in a life that felt overwhelmingly chaotic. I kept hoping that someone would notice my struggle and come to my rescue, but the truth was, no one did.

It was a dark period, and I felt utterly alone. Moments of clarity were few and far between, yet they were enough to keep me going. I clung to the hope that things could improve and that I could find a way out of the darkness. Deep down, I knew I needed to make a change, but the path to healing was anything but clear. I had no idea where to begin.

It took me a while to realize how strong I was to survive those years. It wasn't easy, and there were many moments when I wanted to give up. But I didn't. I kept fighting, kept searching for a way to reclaim my life and my sense of self. The journey was far from over, but acknowledging the pain and the struggle was the first step towards healing and finding my way back to myself.

I began my search for answers and stumbled upon an intense Meisner acting class with Rachel Adler at Fort Mason in San Francisco. Unsure of what I was signing up for, I felt an undeniable pull when I spoke with her on the phone; my heart whispered

'YES.' So, I jumped right in. This decision opened the door to profound transformation and healing. I quickly grew to love my teacher and classmates; we shared a bond that felt both close and unique, reminiscent of the camaraderie I experienced in high school theater class, where we felt like a family. Working together and delving into the depths of each other's beings was profoundly transformative. The support and connection we fostered in that class created a safe space for genuine expression and growth, a refreshing contrast to the tumultuous dynamics I had faced within my family and romantic relationships.

In Rachel's class, I found a sense of belonging and acceptance that I desperately sought. The exercises pushed me to confront my emotions and vulnerabilities, allowing me to explore and express parts of myself that had long been buried. The safe environment encouraged me to shed the protective layers I had built up over the years and connect with others on a deeper, more authentic level.

The bond with my classmates was unlike anything I had experienced before. We were all there to delve into our inner worlds, and the mutual understanding and support created an atmosphere of trust and compassion. For the first time in my life I felt truly seen and heard, not judged or criticized. This nurturing environment fostered my growth and healing in ways I never imagined were possible.

The class contrasted my experiences with family dynamics and past relationships. At home, I often felt silenced, misunderstood, and attacked. I had encountered betrayal, manipulation, and a profound lack of genuine connection in previous relationships. However, the acting class became my sanctuary—a space to reclaim my voice and rediscover my sense of self. It breathed new life into me, illuminating how lifeless I had felt.

I also found the class to be a powerful outlet for my emotions, a way to channel my pain and experiences into something meaningful and constructive. The Meisner technique focused on emotional truth and vulnerability. It forced me to confront my inner turmoil and brought me back into my body and the present moment. I had been disassociated before coming to this class. It was a raw and often painful process, but it was also profoundly healing. Through this class, I began to understand the depths of my trauma and started to find ways to express it and process it. This period marked the beginning of a journey toward self-discovery, recovery and rebirth. A journey where I started to piece together the fragments of my shattered self.

As I navigated through the exercises, I found a new understanding of my experiences. Repeating phrases and reacting in the moment to my scene partners' emotions mirrored the unpredictability of my life, but in a controlled and safe environment. It was a way to relive and, more importantly, reframe those moments of helplessness and pain. The class became a sanctuary - a place where I could explore these feelings without fear of judgment or 'real' repercussions.

The support from my classmates and Rachel was invaluable. They witnessed my struggles and breakthroughs, offering encouragement and empathy that I had rarely ever experienced. This sense of community helped me realize that I was not alone in my pain, and it was possible to heal and grow despite the scars of the past.

This class was a crucial step in my healing process. It gave me the tools to navigate my emotions, communicate effectively using my voice, and build healthier relationships. It was a reminder that I was capable of growth and transformation, even after all the pain and trauma I had endured.

The volatile relationship with my "brother/boyfriend" reached a critical point during one of our in-person practice sessions. He barged in, screaming at me and my classmates, got in their faces, threatened violence, and even threw a cup of ice at them. The shock and fear in the room were palpable. His behavior had escalated to physical violence, and now, my peers were directly witnessing the dangers that had become a part of my daily life.

Despite enduring repeated physical, verbal, and emotional abuse, I inexplicably found myself returning to him. I had become numb to the abuse, yet I felt a misplaced sympathy for him, interpreting his violent outbursts as a loss of control over his erratic emotions, thoughts, and paranoia. In a desperate attempt to find solutions, I even researched ways to improve myself, wrongly believing that I could somehow influence his behavior.

The immense stress from this toxic relationship manifested physically; my face broke out with large, painful cysts, a visible sign of the emotional turmoil I was experiencing. This physical reaction became another undeniable indication of the severe impact the relationship was having on me, making it impossible to conceal the truth of my situation from the outside world. My body was echoing the distress of my circumstances, signaling the urgent need for change.

The incident during the practice session served as a harsh wake-up call. It was not only humiliating and terrifying for me but also for my classmates, who were previously unaware of the extent of the chaos I endured. Their concern after witnessing the outburst reflected the fear I had been suppressing. This external acknowledgment made it impossible to hide the severity of my situation anymore.

My sister tried her best to pull me away from him, but it was complicated because he was still living with her at my mom's house. Her continual support and reminders of my worth were a beacon of hope. She emphasized how unhealthy the relationship was, yet the emotional ties and our complicated living arrangements made it difficult to fully sever the connection. Each time he showed remorse or vulnerability, I forgave him, clinging to the fleeting glimpses of the person I had once cared for, hoping they would fully reemerge. However, he never reverted to the person I remembered; instead, his abusive behavior only intensified, and my self-worth continued to diminish under his relentless manipulation and abuse.

Breaking free from such a toxic relationship felt almost like paralysis. The emotional entanglements and a lingering hope for change kept me trapped in a destructive cycle. Facing the reality that the occasional glimpses of kindness were overshadowed by a much darker reality—that defined who he truly was—was a harrowing realization. I was experiencing firsthand the complex layers of difficulty that arise in an abusive relationship, which I came to understand was akin to a drug addiction. No matter how harmful the relationship was, and despite others pointing out its toxicity, the challenge of walking away felt insurmountable. This understanding highlighted the profound struggle and internal conflict faced by those caught in similar cycles of abuse.

Rachel's confrontation in class was a pivotal moment for me. "I can't work with you any longer unless you get therapy," she declared, highlighting the complexity of my defense mechanisms as the most intricate she had ever encountered. Her words cut deep, resonating within me with an intensity that felt like a sharp blade to my core. It was a stark reality check, and I understood her message with crystal clarity. This marked the beginning of my journey toward healing and recovery.

The class had already been profoundly transformative for me, and the thought of being removed from it was unthinkable. Rachel's direct approach and the way she delivered her message managed to reach me in a way that others had not been able to. Her words not only highlighted the issues I needed to address but also motivated me to take the necessary steps towards personal growth and healing. It was a crucial turning point, pushing me to seek the help I needed to continue my path of self-improvement and to remain in the program that had already changed so much for me.

This moment broke me out of the constant dissociation I had been living in to survive for so long. Her words landed and caused an interruption in the pattern of my being. I needed to delve deep into my past, confront my traumas, and find ways to heal from them genuinely.

Rachel's callout served as both a challenge and a lifeline. It compelled me to seek therapy and other forms of healing that I had long avoided. This journey was not without its struggles, but it was essential. It marked the beginning of my reclamation of life and self, transitioning from mere survival to genuine living and healing. The combination of the acting class, therapy, and the new connections I forged became the bedrock of my recovery, enabling me to rebuild from within. I can honestly say that Rachel and her Meisner acting class saved my life.

During this period, I started to piece together the fragments of my shattered self. I began to see that my worth was not defined by the men who had hurt me or by the trauma I had endured. Through the Meisner technique, I learned to embrace my emotions, to find strength in my vulnerability, and to believe in my capacity for resilience and transformation.

I began to find the strength and resolve to distance myself from my "brother/boyfriend," redirecting my focus toward my acting class and the supportive community it offered. I leaned on my sister and friends, gradually rebuilding my confidence and sense of self. The journey was undeniably painful and HARD, but it was essential. I had to learn to value myself and set boundaries, even if it meant confronting the fear of being alone.

My sister was facing challenges at our mom's house too and had not graduated high school yet. So, I made the decision to move into a three-bedroom apartment in Pleasanton and invited her to join me. It felt incredibly rewarding to provide her with a fresh environment as she worked toward completing her GED. She tackled her studies with determination, and before long, she earned her GED and landed her first job at Safeway. I took immense pride in helping her get on her feet, nurturing her confidence, and encouraging her to embrace new responsibilities. It was such a relief to get her out of our mom's house and into a safe, supportive neighborhood where she could thrive.

We were doing well until I made the mistake of letting my "brother/boyfriend" come over. After a couple of months apart, I thought it would be okay, but I still struggled with saying "No." to him or completely cutting him out of my life without feeling guilty. Almost immediately, he began stirring up trouble, and before long, our neighbors were calling the cops on us. Looking back, I can't help but wonder if he was dealing with some form of mental illness, as his reactions and the things that triggered him were often far removed from reality. However, no matter what he did, I couldn't deny that he was my kryptonite.

One night, exhaustion weighed heavily on me after a long drive back from work. At that time, I was commuting all the way to Fresno while living in Pleasanton, which meant I spent hours in my car every day. My "brother/boyfriend" was at his dad's place in Lathrop, so I picked him up, expecting him to help me get home safely after driving for hours. However, he fell asleep at the wheel, and I woke up just in time to see us heading straight for a tall light pole. The airbags deployed with a jarring force, and as I stumbled out of the car. Still dazed, I reached into the trunk for my bags, accidentally slicing my hand on something sharp. We were just two blocks from my apartment, yet my brand-new car was now totaled. To make matters worse, he didn't have insurance, leaving me with a total loss that he never took responsibility for. It was my fault I shouldn't have trusted him to drive.

My stepdad's dad bailed me out of the situation with my car, and I didn't see my "brother/boyfriend" for a while after this. He never paid a dollar towards any of the damage he caused. He never apologized either.

The last straw came months later when I encountered him again. He started hurling insults, and in a moment of sheer frustration, I snapped and slapped him across the face. I had finally had enough of his verbal abuse and toxic behavior. He grabbed my thumb and broke it in retaliation while locking eyes with me. He was a monster. It was chilling to think that the only limb I had ever broken in my life was done by someone who claimed to love me. Thankfully, he eventually left for another state to pursue schooling. There was a toxic glue that had kept us circling back to each other, but our combination was never harmonious. His departure was the blessing I had been praying for to end his cycle of abuse. For the first time in a while, I felt a sense of relief and the possibility of moving forward without the constant turmoil he had brought into my life.

Ultimately, I came to understand that true healing necessitated the courage to let go of the monsters who perpetuated toxic cycles in my life. This was not just a step; it was a bold leap toward rebirthing my identity and my worth. I had to break free from the patterns of abuse that had long dictated my existence. In making this decision, I turned the page to a new chapter, one filled with the promise of healing and the exhilarating possibility of rebirth on the horizon.

A poem I wrote back in 2006:

Who You Are

A dented microwave
A pain in my thumb
It comes occasionally
A reminder of who you are.
The broken gas tank on the car
The piece of wood that always falls off
The coffee table
The taped up coat hanger
A totaled car
All reminders of who you are.
Shall I go on
How much damage you left me
And this is only on the outside
Dig deeper
What else did you leave broken
Not caring to fix a thing at all
It's a shame that everywhere I look
I am constantly reminded of you
And who you are
I want you to just disappear
As if you never existed
Never were here
But everywhere I look are reminders of who you are
Even if I close my eyes
To shut out the exterior world
There I see you too
Memories play back like a broken record
Over and over again
There's nowhere I can go to escape the damage you have caused
No matter what I try to do to cover you up
The reminders of who you are
Your existence
Are everywhere
Images memories
Visions interior and exterior
All evidence of who you are.

C-LOVE

Chapter 17
Unalignment is PAINFUL

With the toxic relationship with my "brother/friend" finally behind me, I embarked on a period of detoxification and healing. My sister and I found a charming two-bedroom condo in Martinez, complete with a garage. During this fresh start, she discovered a tiny golden chihuahua mix puppy that she simply had to have. We named her Cinnabuns. With her golden fur and playful spirit, she resembled a little baby fox. Whenever I took her out in public, people were so enamored that they often wanted to take her home, which led me to stop bringing her along for outings. Cinnabuns quickly became a beloved part of our new life together, bringing joy and warmth into our home.

After Rachel's class, I found myself in another transformative acting class at Seydways Theatre with Bobby Wineapple. I immersed myself in this ongoing stretch class for years, discovering a safe space to explore every facet of my being and range of emotions in a constructive manner. This environment was incredibly healing and transformational and allowed me to engage in stretch scenes that often mirrored my life. These scenarios helped me navigate situations differently than I might have in real life, empowering me to reclaim my strength and agency. It was an invaluable experience that nurtured my growth both as an artist and as a person.

Emerging from that abusive relationship and embracing the presence fostered by the Meisner class opened me up to a world of healthy new opportunities and connections I had previously overlooked. This transformative period in my life was characterized by newfound stability, a deep commitment to personal growth, and a dedication to healing. I began to see the beauty in the possibilities around me and was ready to embrace the change that was unfolding.

I cherished my new classmates; after class, we frequently found ourselves at one of the delightful 50's diners on Mason Street, indulging in fries and milkshakes. These outings became a cherished ritual. It was a place where we would share our thoughts on life, reflect on our lessons, and discuss anything that came to mind.

One classmate was particularly passionate about a life-changing personal development course he had taken, but we all brushed off his enthusiasm—until one day, I noticed a remarkable shift in his demeanor. He transformed from being socially awkward and fidgety to exuding a grounded, empowered presence. The change was evident not only in his body language, but also in his voice and energy. I was intrigued by what had facilitated this transformation. The course he had taken was the Basic Seminar through PSI Seminars, and after witnessing his change, I felt compelled to explore this for myself. Without hesitation, I went online and registered for their next class.

Attending this personal development class was both exhilarating and intimidating. Despite being surrounded by strangers, I felt an overwhelming sense of being in the right place at the right time, doing exactly what I needed to do. I've learned to trust that feeling instinctively when it arises. The people around me felt kind, and I found myself held in a safe and supportive environment. Our facilitator, who bore a striking resemblance to Bill Clinton and was a lawyer by trade, created an engaging atmosphere that drew us in. Meanwhile, my small group leader seemed like he could be a star on a daytime soap opera—funny, charismatic, and truly inspiring.

I made so many new friends in this class and absorbed a wealth of information. The experience was transformative, and I immediately wanted my sister and mom to experience the healing I gained from this first class. I invited them to my graduation night, but my mom, however, was not into it at all. She insisted her life was perfect and that she didn't need to work on anything, but my sister was timidly open to it, and I signed her up.

I was thrilled to volunteer and staff my sister's class, eager to immerse myself in another dose of the transformative experience from a leadership role. During the class, we engaged in a couple of intimate experiential exercises that fostered a new bond between us. After my sister completed the first class, I enrolled both of us for the next round, PSI7, which took place at High Valley Ranch in wine country.

This setting provided a unique backdrop for high ropes courses and other experiential exercises with participants from all over the world. The experience was profoundly powerful for both of us. I got to witness my sister accomplish things she had never attempted before, breaking out of her comfort zone and facing some of her greatest fears—especially her fear of heights. It was a joy to see her open up, let her guard down, and become more vulnerable. That experience was truly beautiful to witness.

Watching my sister grow and push her boundaries truly inspired me. Our shared experiences deepened our bond and instilled in us both a profound sense of accomplishment. This journey was more than just a personal development course; it was a collective exploration of growth and discovery, a testament to our resilience and strength. Our time at High Valley Ranch not only helped us overcome personal barriers, but also brought us closer together and fostered growth and healing that would resonate throughout our lives.

I continued my journey by enrolling in the Women's Leadership class, although my sister chose not to join me for this one. I respected her decision since I understood she was on her own journey. My passion for this transformative work led me to volunteer as staff for the Basic class—nine times, to be exact. I couldn't get enough of the deep connections and the supportive community that surrounded this experience. The more I participated, the better I felt. The change began internally, but gradually, my external circumstances began to shift as well.

Each class brought new insights, helping me peel back the layers of past trauma and limiting beliefs. The sense of empowerment and self-awareness I gained from these experiences was profound. I found myself stepping into new opportunities, building healthier relationships, and feeling a renewed sense of purpose. This community became a vital part of my healing journey, providing a consistent source of encouragement and accountability.

Being deeply immersed in these positive classes and experiences intensified the pull on my soul and heart from the misalignment with my work. I loathed my job and the way I was making money. It filled me with shame. Especially since now I was in a new environment surrounded by so many inspiring, healthy people. What initially felt like I was reclaiming my power from the monsters of my past, gradually morphed into a suffocating trap. The very avenue that had allowed me to transform my pain into profit began to erode my soul, reinforcing the traumas of my childhood. I felt like work was slowly killing me from the inside out, and I desperately needed an escape. No amount of alcohol could numb the feeling of being trapped in a place I didn't want to be.

As the contrast between my work and these transformative classes grew more pronounced, my skin began to rebel against me with a vengeance. I started experiencing the worst acne of my life, which left me feeling utterly defeated. I would spend hours picking at my skin, desperate to make it better, but all I succeeded in doing was creating oozing sores that took forever to cover up with makeup. It was excruciatingly awful. I felt hideous and would often find myself crying, especially on days when it was impossible to conceal the damage. Some of the blemishes were so large and deep! I later learned that they were cysts and my futile attempts to pick them only made things worse. This turmoil caused me to socially withdraw and I started declining invitations and calling in sick to work. I was overwhelmed by shame and embarrassment. I felt as if the turmoil I felt inside was vividly displayed on my face for everyone to see. I felt completely powerless, unable to hide what was happening within me.

I began visiting a local esthetician I knew of, someone I had previously gone to with a coworker. Initially, I hoped she could help me improve my skin. However, I quickly realized I had been taken for a ride. We scheduled sessions every other week, and I found myself spending $1,000 each time on services and products. Instead of seeing improvement, my skin seemed to worsen. Frustrated, I finally made an appointment with a dermatologist, who initially dismissed my concerns. It wasn't until I washed my face in front of her that her demeanor changed: "Oh yes, I see," she acknowledged. She prescribed a specific birth control and other medications, believing they would solve my issues. Unfortunately, they only made me nauseous, so I decided to stop taking them altogether. I realized money cannot buy everything.

The journey with cystic acne dragged on for years, becoming a barrier that kept people at arm's length. It affected my ability to form intimate relationships with men, led to countless canceled dates, and prevented me from enjoying sleepovers with friends. I avoided swimming and water activities, mortified at the thought of anyone seeing just how ugly my face was underneath my makeup. This struggle steadily eroded the little self-esteem I had begun to build.

I vividly remember a moment when I was walking down the street and two grown men began laughing and mocking my face, scrutinizing the makeup I wore. It was one of those days when I struggled to cover the damage I had inflicted on my skin, and their ridicule cut deep. At that moment, I wanted nothing more than to melt into the sidewalk, wishing I could disappear altogether. The humiliation was overwhelming.

After four long years of struggle, I was referred to a magical woman in Burlingame named Mimi. She transformed my skincare journey with her expertise, performing various procedures on my face, shaping my eyebrows, and tinting my eyelashes. What set her apart was the way she conducted extractions—she really got to the roots of each pimple, ensuring it wouldn't return to that same spot.

But it wasn't just her skills that captivated me; Mimi was deeply spiritually connected and would perform Reiki on me while I lay on her table. With each visit, my skin gradually became clearer - a true blessing after wasting so much money and enduring the pain and humiliation of ineffective treatments.

As my skin began to clear, the disparity between how I felt at work and in the rest of my life became increasingly pronounced. My job started to feel unbearable, and I found myself judging my worth more harshly with each personal development session. I longed for a way out, a path that aligned with the healthier, more empowered version of myself that was emerging.

The sense of empowerment I gained from those programs made the disempowerment I experienced at work completely intolerable. I cherished the feeling of being valued for more than just my body. Deep down, I knew I needed to make a change, but I was at a loss for how to break free from the job and lifestyle that felt so confining.

I started encouraging other dancers I had grown close to, as well as a few managers at work, to enroll in the Basic Seminar. I thought that if more people in our environment embraced the same principles of learning and growth, we could collectively foster a positive change in the workplace. Perhaps this would also help me carve out a new path for myself and find a way out of this industry. My hope was that I could make a meaningful difference in what often felt like a dark and challenging environment while I was still there.

Introducing the seminar to my coworkers and seeing their interest sparked a glimmer of hope. If we could bring some of the positivity and transformation we were experiencing into the club, perhaps it could start to change. Perhaps we could uplift each other and create a healthier environment, even if just a little bit. This thought became my anchor, giving me a renewed sense of purpose and a way to cope with the growing internal conflict.

Seeing my colleagues and managers attend the seminar and begin their own journeys of self-improvement felt like a small victory. It was reassuring to know I wasn't alone in seeking a better path, and it gave me the strength to keep pushing forward. I hoped that together, we could create a ripple effect, transforming not just our personal lives, but also the space we occupied. This was my attempt to find light in a dark place and build a bridge to a brighter future.

Any sense of victory I felt was quickly overshadowed by the harsh reality of my work environment and the relentless objectification from male clients. The industry's focus was solely on lust, sex appeal, and objectification - attracting men who thrived on that energy. Unfortunately, there was not enough positivity to counterbalance the negativity permeating this job, the industry, or this particular venue.

One of the most humiliating aspects of the job was being required to go downtown for promotions, where we would pass out cards and invite men to come to the club later. We did this at the ballpark, downtown during conventions, and at any large gatherings where potential customers could be found. It felt degrading to stand there, pushing ourselves on strangers, and it served as a painful reminder of the unaligned nature of our work.

The way men looked at us as we handed out cards made me feel incredibly small, like dirt beneath their feet. I vividly remember one instance at the ballpark when I approached a guy with a card, and he shouted, "What are you doing? You're too good for this!" before tossing the card on the ground. It was a moment that struck deep, and unfortunately, it wasn't the last time I'd hear something like that. Each comment pierced my heart, igniting a fire within me to find a way out of this life.

Maybe not all men were monsters. Maybe I did deserve more. However, the thought of transitioning my entire life felt overwhelming, and I had no idea how to begin or where to start. The desire for change clashed with my uncertainty, leaving me in a constant state of turmoil.

Each interaction and every look of disdain or pity chipped away at my already fragile self-esteem. The fleeting moments of empowerment I experienced inside the club were constantly overshadowed by the harsh reality of how the outside world perceived me. This external validation of my worthlessness starkly contrasted with the inner work I was doing through the seminars. It served as a brutal reminder that I was living a double life—torn between the person I was striving to become and the person I felt I had to be to survive.

These experiences fueled my determination to escape this life. The disconnect between my internal growth and my external reality became unbearable. Living an unaligned life is PAINFUL. I knew I had to find a way to align my life with the newfound sense of self-worth and empowerment I was discovering. It wasn't just about surviving anymore; it was about finding a way to truly live and thrive.

Don't Come Near Me

A runner
A hider
That's what I've been all my life
Hiding from my fears
My feelings
People I care about
I ran at the slightest inclination of attachment
Of caring
Of the feelings of quicksand
I don't want to lose myself again
Not to another
I've been there, done that
Don't want to do it again
I hide physically
Under lots of clothes
Makeup
I hide emotionally
By never being near anyone
Never bringing anyone close
I don't want someone so close
That they know all the things I hate about myself
I don't want them to see these imperfections for themself
I'd rather be an illusion of perfection
That doesn't exist
From a distance
I seem to have no flaws
But the closer you come towards me
The worse the picture becomes
Even though it is still a masterpiece of artwork

With all its scars, flaws, bleeding sores
It is not the picture I want anyone else to see
So I push away
I run
I hide
Prevent anyone from stepping past a certain line
Keep intimacy at bay
Keep all intricate delicacies that come with it away
Even though I long for them in my heart
Dream about them in my mind
I've learned that dreams are better than reality
Illusions and fantasies beat the stone cold truth
So why bother letting anyone else figure that out about me

Cassandra Love Lambert, October, 2007

C-LOVE

Chapter 18
This Job is a TRAP

Tears streamed down my face as I drove home each night, and I would toss the money I had earned onto the floor, treating it as if it were tainted. It felt like blood money, a contribution to the wounding of my soul and I despised it due to feeling like a slave to it. At work, I often found myself sobbing in the bathroom, seeking solace in alcohol to numb the pain. I'd drink a whole bottle of vodka and then some more, hoping to dull the internal turmoil of being in a place that felt so wrong to my soul. I would cry on the phone to my sister and her boyfriend driving to work, desperately praying for a way out of this job. As time went on, I realized no amount of alcohol could drown out the overwhelming emotions and the toxic environment that mirrored the very characteristics of the men I had come to loathe. The ones that had caused me so much anguish.

The constant objectification and degradation I faced felt suffocating. The more I sought escape through substances, the more trapped I became by my emotions. What was once a space where I thought I could reclaim my power had turned into a prison. The men who frequented the club embodied the very worst of my past experiences, and every interaction served as a painful reminder of the betrayal I had endured.

As I engaged in healing and personal growth, I found myself becoming more vulnerable at work, making it increasingly difficult to maintain any protective shield or wall. Being vulnerable in a gentlemen's club was like mixing oil and water; the two simply didn't mix. The dissonance between my internal journey and the harsh external environment only amplified my feelings of entrapment.

Each night after work, I arrived home emotionally exhausted, tears streaming down my face. Overwhelmed by conflicting emotions, I would toss the money I earned onto the floor, unable to reconcile my feelings about it. No amount of money seemed worth the internal pain and degradation I felt from this job. The resentment toward the money was profound—I hated it, yet I was entirely dependent on it for survival.

This painful experience was teaching me a harsh reality: not all money is good money. The cost to my inner peace and self-respect was too high a price to pay. It was a bitter lesson in the true value of personal well-being over financial gain, and it forced me to confront the impact of my choices on my mental and emotional health.

I felt trapped, torn between my need for financial security and the soul-crushing reality of the job. Despite earning more than my stepdad at a young age, this wasn't the life I had envisioned. The chasm between the life I longed for and the one I was living felt unbearable. The emotional toll was immense, blurring the line between mere survival and the edges of self-destruction.

I craved change, but felt lost. I became stuck in perpetually cycling through classes and programs in search of guidance from mentors and coaches. Despite my efforts, it felt as though I was trapped in a loop of unfulfilling experiences, going in circles without making any real progress. I had built my life around this income, and the thought of finding something else that could provide the same financial stability and time flexibility felt daunting. This job had become a cage, with the key to my freedom seemingly out of reach.

Deep down, I began to wonder if something was wrong with me. I was committed. I kept showing up and investing in the classes, courses, and programs, devouring the learning opportunities presented to me for my personal development and entrepreneurship. Yet, despite my dedication, I struggled to transform my outer reality. It left me questioning why others seemed to achieve their goals while I remained stuck in place. This never ending experience was so frustrating.

Conversations with my sister and her boyfriend became my lifeline, offering solace amidst the ongoing conflict of my life. They served as my sounding board, providing comfort and perspective when I felt lost and hopeless. Their unwavering support illuminated moments of clarity, reminding me that there was a way out, even if it wasn't immediately visible. I clung to those glimmers of light, fueled by a determination to find a way out of the industry and lifestyle I had found myself entangled in.

Even God found me at work in the club. One day, a group of people came in and spent a significant amount of time talking to me, inquiring about my life and dreams. They tipped generously, showering me with money as they engaged in heartfelt conversation. The woman in the group asked for a dance, and when we reached the private area, she handed me a substantial amount of cash. I thought it was for a dance, but instead, she looked me in the eyes and said, "You don't belong in this job or this place. God has much bigger and better things in store for you."

Her words resonated deeply within me, sending goosebumps coursing over my entire body. It was as if a light had flickered on in the darkness I had been navigating. After that encounter, returning to work felt unbearable. I gathered my things and went home that day, the weight of her message echoing in my heart.

Once again, I felt trapped, worn down by this relentless cycle repeating in my life. It seemed that if I wasn't battling monsters, I was ensnared in some kind of trap—and sometimes, it was both. I was weary of thinking I'd found freedom, only to realize I was still confined. Here I was, caught between the life I was living and the job that kept it afloat. As degrading as it was, this job's income allowed me to pursue my education, care for my sister, and escape the poverty of my past. I was determined never to return to that life of struggle. Yet, the weight of relying on something that drained my spirit was a bitter pill to swallow.

Deep down, I knew I had the ability to figure things out, but the more I efforted, the more elusive the answers became. It was utterly defeating to crave change, to yearn for something different, and yet have no clear direction or understanding of what steps to take. It felt like I had my foot on the gas, full throttle, yet something held the brakes tightly in place. I was ready for the adventure of a lifetime, only to find myself stuck in the driveway, unable to move. Each time I pressed the gas, the brakes would activate, leaving me trapped in the same place, yearning for forward motion that never came.

Despite the financial stability my job provided, the emotional and psychological toll was staggering. The club, with its flashing lights and pulsating music, morphed into a battleground for my soul. This atmosphere only exacerbated the wounds I carried regarding relationships and love, perpetuating the childhood traumas that haunted me. It became clear that while I remained entrenched in this lifestyle, I couldn't truly heal at a foundational level. The money I earned, which should have been a symbol of success, instead felt like a shackle, binding me to a life I desperately sought to escape.

I had initially thought that becoming a dancer would be my ticket to reclaiming the power that life's injustices had stripped from me—power lost through experiences of sexual abuse and betrayal. However, it soon became evident that this was not a path to true empowerment, but rather a snare that drew me deeper into a cycle I felt powerless to escape. The facade of blessings that accompanied this job came at a steep price, ensnaring me in a pattern that would take a decade to transcend.

I felt as though I was trapped in a relentless struggle between who I was, who I aspired to be, and the reality of my current situation. My engagement in personal development classes had provided me with glimpses of a brighter future, yet the weight of my present circumstances often felt overwhelming. The dissonance between my current life and the life I longed for became a wellspring of constant pain and suffering. I remained ensnared in the belief that life was unfair, happening to me rather than for me, stuck in a survival mentality rather than stepping into my power as a creator. I longed for someone or something to save me, yet no one came.

Causing Me to Drink

You cause me to drink to excess
To the point where I get sick to my stomach
The more I keep coming back to you
The more I become an alcoholic
If it weren't for you I'd be dry
I'd be sober all of the time
But you drive me to gulp down Greygoose by the shot
I get one
And I can't stop
I need another and another
Shit just give me the whole bottle on some rocks
I drink so much
The next day I wake up
Dizzy
Falling over all over the place
You aren't good for me or my health
Days keep rolling over
Smushing and mashing together
I can't tell when one day ends
And the next begins
It's so robotic
Systematic
Same thing just a different day
Yet this day is so much like the last
And will be like the next
So I lose track of how many days have passed
You consume so much time
So much energy
I hardly ever get time to spend with me
I don't get to relax and chill
Cuz you stress me out
Give me anxiety
I can't live with you
But I can't live without you

Not right now
But I can't figure out how to escape you
No matter how bad for me you are
You torture my spirit
My very essence of my being
You test my strength
You test my heart
My mind
Everyday
I get no peace of mind with you
You consume all of me
Leaving only crumbs to fend for what I love
You're killing me day by day
Minute by minute
I don't know how much longer I can handle this
I just want to be free
From your lethal attachment
From the codependence you've gotten me to crutch on
Cuz the side effects are deadly
And the casualty is my very spirit
And I refuse to sell it or give it to you
I know my worth
I know I'm better than you
Yet why am I still here returning
Time and time again
To get slapped in the face with your
Contradictive endeavors
Why when I don't want to ever come back
Do I feel this pulling sensation
Like I'm connected to a chain and shackles
Let me go peacefully
Let me be free
You aren't any good for me
I need to be without you
Only me

Cassandra Love Lambert, November 2007

I got into a really bad accident one night while driving home. It was my fault—I had glanced at my phone, and in that split second, I ran through a red light and t-boned another car. The driver emerged from their vehicle bleeding from the head, and a wave of guilt and horror crashed over me. My car was totaled, stranded in the middle of an intersection in downtown San Francisco. To add insult to injury, homeless people began emerging from the shadows of nearby alleyways, scavenging my car for anything valuable. It felt surreal, like watching cockroaches scurry out when the lights flick off, desperate for a treat. I didn't even care; I just observed the whole scene unfold in a detached haze.

At that moment, I realized my life had to change. The weight of what had happened, the harm I had inflicted on another person because I wasn't present, became too heavy to bear. I could no longer continue down the path I was on. I made the decision to move into a small studio apartment in San Francisco, a significant shift in my life. This change meant my sister had to return to our mom's house, a choice that filled me with guilt for separating from her and for her having to go back to that environment. I stopped driving altogether and didn't replace my totaled car; the guilt from the accident lingered, and I didn't trust myself behind the wheel anymore.

For years after the accident, I avoided having a car and avoided driving. The trauma of that night, the image of the injured person, and the realization of my carelessness haunted me. I felt an immense responsibility for the pain I had caused, and the thought of getting behind the wheel again was terrifying. This incident was a stark reminder of the importance of being present and the profound impact our actions can have on others. It forced me to confront my own behavior and the choices I was making, pushing me to seek more healing and accountability.

I immersed myself in a series of business workshops with a woman I met in one of my PSI programs. We became inseparable, relishing the thrill of attending these events together, even though we hadn't yet launched a business of our own. I saw these workshops as my ticket out of dancing. However, the thought of finding a job that could match the financial security and flexibility

I had in my current role felt daunting—especially without a degree. The income I earned from dancing had become the foundation of my life and lifestyle, making it all the more challenging to consider walking away.

After completing a transformative 90-day goal-setting program with PSI, I was over the moon when my peers unanimously voted me as the team leader. Being the second youngest in a group of 20, I felt a surge of pride and purpose, knowing that my commitment to service and leadership had resonated with others. This experience breathed new life into my belief that I could break free from the life I had been living.

Shortly after this empowering moment, a close friend from Rachel's acting class reached out with an exhilarating proposition: she wanted to plan a once-in-a-lifetime trip to Europe and asked if I would join her. With my life undergoing such positive transformations, the idea of traveling to Europe for the first time felt like the perfect opportunity to embrace my newfound freedom and adventure. It was a no-brainer for me; I was all in!

I stepped way out of my comfort zone for this epic three-week odyssey, having never taken more than a week off or ventured outside the US. Our journey ignited in the dynamic city of Barcelona, then we soared to Rome, rode the rails to the enchanting Florence and Venice, and concluded in the love-filled air of Paris. Each city was a burst of new experiences, sprinkled with unforgettable moments and a few mishaps.

Barcelona captivated me instantly with its gorgeous coastlines. I was spellbound by Antoni Gaudí's masterpieces—my favorite artist. From Park Güell to the monumental Sagrada Família and his distinctive home, Gaudí's artistry, with its flowing curves and intricate details, deepened my passion for art and creativity.

As we wandered the vibrant streets of Barcelona, the kaleidoscope of colors, sounds, and scents enveloped me, serving as a reminder that there was so much more to life than the confines of my past. Each day unfolded with new adventures, from savoring delectable tapas and refreshing glasses of sangria to exploring bustling markets brimming with local treasures. I cherished our mid-afternoon siestas, which revitalized us for evenings spent beneath the stars, discovering the city in a whole new light.

Barcelona felt like a safe haven. I loved watching the older residents play chess at the small tables dotting the streets, their laughter and camaraderie creating a warm, inviting atmosphere. The city's energy was infectious, inspiring us to buy roses and share them as random gifts with strangers. Their faces lit up with gratitude and joy, creating a beautiful ripple effect of happiness. In those moments, I felt a profound connection to the world around me, and for the first time in a long while, I truly felt alive.

After our time in Barcelona, we flew to Rome, where history whispered from every corner. However, our arrival was less than ideal, as we were greeted by a shady taxi driver who kept changing the fare, increasing it as we approached our hotel. He was a muscular guy covered in tattoos, and his intimidating demeanor made us reluctant to argue, so we paid him rather than risk a confrontation in unfamiliar territory.

Rome seemed rife with swindlers and hustlers, but one of the most memorable experiences of our trip was joining a pub crawl. There, we met a diverse group of guys from all over the world who quickly became lifelong acquaintances. They spent several nights with us, exploring various restaurants and attractions, making the experience even more enjoyable as we shared our adventures together.

The Colosseum stood as a majestic testament to a bygone era, its ancient walls echoing stories of the past. Our trip continued with a visit to the Trevi Fountain, where we tossed coins and I made a wish for a brighter future. It was a moment filled with light and joy.

However, the atmosphere shifted dramatically when we visited the Vatican. Despite its rich connections to art, culture, and spirituality, the energy there felt heavy and dark, which was perplexing and contrary to the inspiring and sacred aura I had expected. I found myself uncomfortable and out of place.

Years later, I learned of the over 200,000 cases of sexual abuse reported within the Roman Catholic Church. This revelation cast a shadow over my memories of the Vatican, suggesting a possible explanation for the unsettling energy I had sensed. It was a stark reminder of the complexities and contradictions that often lie beneath the surface of historical and religious institutions.

Next, we hopped on a train to Florence, where the art and culture radiated from every street. I relished the journey, gazing out the window at the picturesque countryside, each passing landscape more beautiful than the last. Upon arriving, I was left speechless by the grandeur of the Duomo, its intricate details captivating me. I lost myself in the masterpieces of Michelangelo and Botticelli at the Uffizi Gallery, each brushstroke telling a story that resonated deep within my soul.

However, by the time we reached Florence, tensions had risen, and my friend and I decided to go our separate ways. I explored charming little restaurants, indulging in delectable local cuisine, and enjoyed the enchanting sounds of street performers serenading under the stars. There was something profoundly empowering about navigating a foreign city on my own, armed with nothing but a map and no cell service. This journey was not just a trip; it was a much-needed balm for my spirit, filling me with a renewed sense of purpose and freedom.

In Venice, we reunited and embarked on an adventure through the labyrinthine streets, crossing charming bridges and soaking in the enchanting atmosphere of the canals. It felt surreal to be surrounded by such beauty. We rode a gondola, gliding through the tranquil waters, and took a water bus to the iconic shopping center I had admired in countless movies. The water surrounding Venice was nothing short of mesmerizing, its vibrant hues sparkling under the sun like a sea of diamonds. Every moment felt like a scene from a dream, capturing my heart and igniting my wanderlust.

Finally, we arrived in Paris, the City of Light. The Eiffel Tower sparkled against the night sky, and I felt as if I were living in a dream. To explore the city, we opted for a nighttime Segway tour, gliding past many of the iconic landmarks. It was exhilarating and so much fun! One of my favorite indulgences in Paris was visiting the local bakery to grab fresh bread, slathering it with butter for a simple yet delightful meal.

However, Paris also had its quirks. Despite its reputation for elegance, I was surprised by the dirtiness of the streets, with dog poop littering the sidewalks. It struck me as ironic how the seemingly stuck-up locals could overlook such a mess, as if they believed their pets' waste didn't stink. We even visited the Louvre, where I had my first glimpse of the Mona Lisa—so small in person, yet still captivating. The contrast between the grandeur of the city and the little imperfections added to its charm.

Our final night in Barcelona, meant to be a fun farewell, took an unexpected turn when my friend slipped in the shower and busted her lip open. Instead of dancing the night away, we found ourselves in the ER, where doctors stitched her up. As I sat there, the reality of heading home sank in, leaving a bittersweet ache in my heart. I didn't want to leave this enchanting world or the adventure we had shared; I was reluctant to return to the life I was constantly at odds with.

This trip had been eye-opening, infusing me with new life and inspiration. I held onto the hope that these experiences would help guide me toward the solutions I had been desperately seeking for so long.

Each moment on this journey served as a powerful reminder that I was capable of so much more than I had ever allowed myself to believe. This trip became a pivotal point in my journey—illuminating the vast possibilities that lay ahead and the inner strength I possessed to forge my own path. It opened my eyes to the world and allowed me to step into my leadership, especially during those solitary walks along the cobblestone streets of Europe. For the first time in a long while, I felt vibrantly alive, filled with possibilities, and dared to dream again after this transformative experience.

C-LOVE

Chapter 19
God Doesn't Send Traps or Red Flags

After enduring such an extremely abusive relationship, I had built walls around myself, consciously avoiding men and keeping them at a significant distance. Emotionally, I was particularly guarded. While I had come to realize that not all men were monsters, my past experiences made me wary. I couldn't shake the fear that I might attract another toxic individual instead of a genuinely good guy. Trusting my luck felt futile, especially when it came to relationships. My primary focus became learning, working, healing, and dreaming of a better future.

Then, during a business event in Las Vegas, something unexpected happened. A man approached me with a confidence that was both refreshing and intriguing. He was articulate and spoke both Russian and English, and I noticed that one of his hands was missing fingers. He shared with me about his business with a friend, where they taught personal development classes. His passion for his work piqued my curiosity and sparked a sense of inspiration within me. He seemed different.

We spent the entire night together, enjoying each other's company until it was time to catch our flight back home. I had my doubts about whether he would reach out after returning to LA, but to my surprise, he did. He planned a visit to see me in San Francisco, and from there, we went on countless dates, strolling through the city and sharing our dreams and visions.

His passion for his business and his genuine desire to help people resonated deeply with me, aligning perfectly with the future I had been envisioning and dreaming about. Our conversations flowed effortlessly, and I found myself captivated by his enthusiasm and ambition. For the first time in a long while, I felt a spark of hope and possibility blooming within me.

As we spent more time together, his unique blend of confidence, vision, and genuine interest in personal development began to shift my perspective on relationships. His presence felt like a refreshing breeze in my life, and I started to entertain the possibility that not all men were the same. Perhaps, just maybe, there was a chance for a healthy and inspiring connection—a partnership where my dream of building a fulfilling life with someone could finally come to fruition.

He was so captivating when he spoke that I found myself overlooking the red flags—like his habit of asking me to pay for things and promising to reimburse me, but never following through. At that time, my shyness prevented me from speaking up and holding him accountable, so the amount of money I was fronting kept adding up. He also fed me lines I desperately wanted to hear, like how he wanted me to move to LA with him, assuring me he would take care of everything. He painted a picture where I could quit the job I loathed and help him with his business. All of this resonated deeply with the dreams and desires I harbored, but I failed to realize I was giving away my power in the process. I didn't see that I was leaving one trap for another.

I chose to believe him, even though a part of me was becoming aware of the inconsistencies regarding money. In an impulsive decision, I decided to let go of most of my belongings—mostly handing them over to my mom—and packed up my essentials, including Cinnabuns, to move to LA with him. He shared an apartment with his roommate, who was also his business partner. Despite my lingering doubts, the excitement of embarking on this new journey and the prospect of leaving behind a job that had suffocated my spirit filled me with hope.

The excitement of stepping into a fresh chapter overshadowed my apprehensions. I was eager to embrace the possibilities of a new city, a new job, and the potential for a meaningful relationship. The thought of leaving behind the toxic environment of my previous job and starting anew was incredibly appealing. I saw this move as a chance to rebuild, to focus on personal growth, and to align myself with a vision that resonated with my aspirations. Little did I know, this decision would come with its own set of challenges and invaluable lessons.

It's no surprise that I found myself entangled with someone who deceived me at every turn. I ignored the warning signs, convinced that I could overlook the red flags, only to unravel the tangled web of lies he had woven. Far from being the successful businessman he claimed to be, he relied on his mother and friends for financial support—and now he expected me to join the ranks of those propping him up.

Once I arrived, it became clear that my small savings would be the new source of funding for the responsibilities he had assured me he would handle. Little by little, I ended up paying for everything—from his portion of the rent to our groceries and utilities. He had no steady income, no real business. His dreams were nothing more than unfulfilled fantasies, with no concrete plans or actions to bring them to life. I was so angry and embarrassed with myself when realized I had been duped once again.

My trust was shattered even more when I stumbled upon pornographic images he had taken with his own camera at an event, revealing a side of him I hadn't known existed. He was an undercover monster. To make matters worse, he abused my dog to the point where she developed severe anxiety and began urinating indoors. Trapped in this toxic relationship, I endured his gaslighting and manipulation, forced to mask my emotions whenever we were around his family and friends. Ashamed of my impulsive decision to move, I felt too embarrassed to seek help.

Living in a constant state of fear and humiliation, I felt more isolated than ever. I had no car and I was in a town where I didn't have any community or friends. The man who had promised me a new life was now the source of my greatest pain. His deceit and abuse left me questioning my judgment and self-worth. I was trapped, not just physically, but emotionally and psychologically too. Stuck in a situation that seemed impossible to escape.

The toll on my mental health was immense. I became increasingly withdrawn, afraid to confide in anyone about the reality of my situation. I was terrified of the judgment and the "I told you so's" from those who might have seen through his façade from the beginning. Each day was a battle to maintain some semblance of normalcy while I felt my spirit breaking under the weight of his lies and abuse.

After enduring eight grueling months, I finally reached out to my family for help. My savings were depleted, I had gained weight, and I had given away all my belongings. Feeling utterly shattered and lost, I found myself starting life anew from square one. Returning to my mother's house, I focused on eating healthy, crying a lot, and exercising. The weight I gained came off and then some. I began to get in the best shape of my life. After realizing that this relationship was completely over, I reluctantly stepped back into the familiar - yet dreaded - role of a dancer, but this time at a more upscale club. Despite my attempts to break free from this line of work, it felt as though the more I resisted, the tighter its grip became.

Faced with this reality, I surrendered to my circumstances, embracing my role at this luxurious club with its showgirl ambiance. After experiencing eight months of hell in that relationship, I was grateful to get out and become independent again. This newfound feeling associated with this line of work ultimately helped me to transcend this job and close this chapter for good. By using it as the vehicle and tool it was to move forward in life, it lost its weight and power over me.

The upscale club, with its glamorous environment and showgirl style, offered a different perspective on dancing. I began to see it less as a trap and more as a means to an end. This shift in mindset was crucial in helping me regain a sense of control and purpose. I was no longer dancing out of desperation, but as a strategic move to secure my future and move beyond the past.

I was also embracing a unique skill I had picked up from all my dancing days—the ability to shake my butt in very creative ways. One night, during an all-girl sleepover with some of my closest girlfriends from the PSI community, I decided to share this talent with them. We had good food, wine, and lots of laughter. I started teaching them the moves, trying to get them to tic toc their hips and drop their butts into what I called the "hydraulics."

They would try so hard and laugh at how hard it actually was. We were all laughing so hard, and in that moment, an idea was born. The concept of transforming these fun, energetic moves into a class to teach others started to take shape. The name ABunnDance was born. It was a perfect blend of fun, fitness, and empowerment—everything I wanted to bring to others. The tag line became, "Work it Out, Shake it Off & Laugh it Out the Fun Way!"

The sleepover with my friends evolved into a vibrant brainstorming session, and their enthusiasm and support for my idea were incredibly uplifting. We discussed how ABunnDance could transcend the concept of a mere dance class. We envisioned it as a sanctuary where women could feel confident, have fun, and embrace their bodies without fear of judgment. This idea planted a seed that I was eager to see flourish in the near future.

I had finally stumbled upon a business idea that resonated deeply with me. The most beautiful part was that I would be transforming a job that had brought me so much pain into something beautiful and impactful. Additionally, ABunnDance would be a vehicle for transforming my own struggles with body image into something empowering and offering the same transformation to other women. It was a profound alignment of my personal journey with my professional aspirations, promising to create a space of healing and joy. And it was so damn fun; we laughed so hard we cried and then laughed some more, which was such good medicine for our hearts and souls. I knew it would be good medicine for other's too.

As I embraced this new role, I found a renewed sense of confidence and determination. I set clear goals for myself, both financially and personally, and used my time at the club to work towards achieving them. Slowly but surely, I began to rebuild my life, reclaiming my sense of self-worth and independence.

Hard lessons were learned in this chapter of my life: prayers don't show up as traps, and God doesn't send red flags. Through the pain and deception of this boyfriend, I came to understand that true answers to my prayers would not come wrapped in deceit and betrayal. This realization became a cornerstone in my journey, teaching me to trust my instincts and recognize the warning signs that I had previously ignored.

I learned that genuine blessings align with my well-being and growth, not with manipulation or exploitation. This chapter taught me to distinguish between the false promises of those who would take advantage of me and the true opportunities that would lead me toward healing and fulfillment. It was a harsh but necessary awakening, one that reinforced the importance of listening to my inner voice and seeking out the paths that genuinely resonated with my higher self.

Understanding these lessons was pivotal in breaking free from the cycles of abuse and self-doubt that had haunted my life. They empowered me to set boundaries, make healthier choices, and move toward a life that resonated more deeply with my true desires and values. I realized that someone meant for me wouldn't embody the traits of a monster, and the opportunities that came my way would align with my vision, rather than conflict with it.

Chapter 20
Playa Initiation & Magic

My friend from PSI Seminars, who had also been attending all the business courses with me, was facing challenges covering her expenses and debt. In an effort to help, I introduced her to the world of dancing as a viable source of income. She embraced it wholeheartedly, diving in with enthusiasm. In return, she opened my eyes to a completely new world: Burning Man. She spoke about this annual event with such fervor that it ignited my curiosity. However, it took me a couple of years to feel ready to attend this intriguing, yet terrifying experience. It wasn't until I left behind another abusive relationship and returned from LA, focusing on rebuilding myself, that I found the courage to embrace this new opportunity.

We dove into one seminar after another, fueled by our shared hunger for knowledge and our desperate search for a way out of dancing into something more fulfilling. It became addictive, a shared passion that we both embraced wholeheartedly. We yearned to be of service and make a difference in the world, yet we struggled to figure out how to transform that desire into a sustainable business.

I found myself irresistibly drawn to invest in the next class, workshop, retreat, or seminar, and to work with the next coach or mentor that came along. Each new opportunity fueled my endless quest for something more—something better, something different—within the realms of healing and personal development. Deep down, I was craving a new life, one that aligned with the values I was discovering in myself.

Each seminar and workshop experience opened new doors, offering glimpses of the person I could become. I was determined to transform my pain into purpose, to turn my suffering into a story of resilience and empowerment. The more I immersed myself in these learning experiences, the more I began to see the possibilities for a future unbound by the chains of my past.

When the opportunity to support an art installation at EDC for one of her "burner" friends presented itself, I eagerly accepted. This experience introduced me to the world of music festivals, the use of substances like "Molly," and a new level of consciousness I had never encountered before. I met artists and individuals who were unlike anyone I had ever known—more spiritual, more magical, and more aligned with a different way of thinking.

We arrived in Vegas at night and immediately got involved in setting up an art installation called "Wish," a huge, intricate dandelion sculpture. We were greeted by the artist, who welcomed us with warmth and enthusiasm. It was exhilarating to be part of a group and contribute to the behind-the-scenes work before the event even began the next day. This group was so full of magic, with everyone coming together from different parts of the world to support the artist and his vision. The experience of working together, sharing ideas, and physically constructing something so beautiful was incredibly rewarding.

During setup, everyone was in practical, work-ready functional clothing, focused on the tasks at hand. There was a sense of anticipation in the air, an excitement bubbling just beneath the surface. We were all strangers, brought together by a shared purpose, each contributing our skills and energy to bring the sculpture to life.

The transformation from setup to the actual event was nothing short of astonishing. Before the festivities began, the grounds resembled a blank canvas, a vast desert backdrop teeming with potential, yet awaiting its moment to burst into life. As the event unfolded, the energy shifted dramatically. Meeting the group beforehand felt like catching a glimpse of raw potential; they were still somewhat reserved, their true essence yet to be unveiled. But once the doors opened to the public, they blossomed into vibrant expressions of creativity and spirit, adorned in their eclectic attire that mirrored the energy of the event. It was as if the entire space breathed in anticipation, ready to come alive with color, sound, and connection.

This hands-on experience of bringing an art piece to life, and then witnessing it become a part of a larger community's experience, was profoundly moving. It underscored the power of collaboration and creativity, and it deepened my appreciation for the role of art in connecting people and evoking emotion. It also highlighted the beauty of transformation—how something can start as a mere idea and, through collective effort and vision, become a source of inspiration and delight for many.

Once the event began, it was as if we all stepped into a different world. The festival atmosphere was electric. Everyone was decked out with vibrant, imaginative outfits, embodying a sense of freedom and expression that was truly inspiring. The dandelion sculpture, which we had meticulously assembled, now stood tall and radiant, illuminated by the festival lights and surrounded by awe-struck attendees.

Dressing up in cute costumes was an absolute delight. I had always loved playing dress-up, and now, after finally getting into the best shape of my life, I felt confident in my body for the first time. The costumes, the pulsating music, and the vibrant festival atmosphere created an exhilarating experience! In that moment, I felt liberated, unburdened by the weight of past traumas and current struggles. The sense of community and acceptance enveloped me, disarming any lingering insecurities.

With our VIP wristbands, we gained access to behind-the-scenes areas, getting up close and personal with the performers. We danced the night away under a canopy of stars, losing ourselves in the rhythm until the sunrise painted the sky with hues of orange and pink. It was a breathtaking sight, and for the first time in ages, I felt like a child playing freely. Life felt lighter, filled with joy and possibility.

Experiencing 'Molly' was truly eye-opening. It amplified my dormant intuitive gifts, igniting a clarity that was both startling and liberating. Insights about my recent relationship came rushing in, illuminating the chaos I had endured. It felt as if a veil had been lifted, revealing the harsh truth about my ex—a pathological liar and sociopath. I received profound realizations that his deceit had physically manifested as sores around his mouth. Witnessing this vision was a powerful reminder of the darkness I had successfully left behind. In that moment, I felt a surge of empowerment, finally grasping the full extent of the toxicity I had escaped.

Music festivals became a sanctuary where I could heal and rediscover joy. It felt like I had stepped into a world where anything was possible, where the weight of my past could no longer hold me down and I was able to PLAY. The nights were filled with music that seemed to sync with the rhythm of my newfound freedom. As the beats pulsed through the air, I danced with abandon, losing myself in the moment. The sunrise brought a sense of renewal, a reminder that every day was a chance to start anew. Surrounded by people who accepted me for who I was, I felt a deep sense of belonging.

This experience was transformative, another significant step in my journey of healing and self-discovery. It reminded me that despite the darkness I had faced, there was still light and beauty in the world. I was learning to trust myself, to embrace my intuition and the gifts that had been dormant for so long. The festival was more than just an event; it was a turning point, a reminder that I could reclaim my life and create a future filled with possibilities.

The newfound clarity and sense of liberation I experienced at EDC marked the dawn of a profound rebirth. My last toxic relationship had drained me, but this experience reignited my spirit, filling me with renewed energy. It became a pivotal moment—a turning point where I began to reclaim my power and sense of self. I felt as though I was in the right place, at the right time, surrounded by the right people, all engaged in the right activities. I knew deep down to trust this feeling. I was finally ready for Burning Man!

We started off by meeting up with this same group of individuals in Reno to help set up the art installation at Burning Man. It was a lot of fun. We would eat, talk, joke around, and play horseshoes. This was going to be the group we camped with for my first Burning Man, and getting to spend more time with them made the adventure to Black Rock City seem not as intimidating.

In preparation for "the burn", I was given lists upon lists of things to make sure I had. You can never be too prepared out there; you need to be ready for anything and be self-reliant. For my first year going, we chose to rent an RV from one of the guys in the group.

Spending time with everyone in Reno helped to build a sense of intimacy and trust. We shared meals, swapped stories, and bonded over our shared excitement and nervousness about the upcoming adventure. The camaraderie eased my anxieties about the unknowns of Burning Man. The meticulous planning and advice from seasoned "burners" was invaluable. They emphasized the importance of being prepared for the harsh desert conditions and the need for self-reliance.

Deciding to rent an RV was a practical and comforting decision for my first "burn". It provided a sense of security and a place to retreat to when needed. The preparation and planning turned into a ritual of its own, building anticipation and excitement. We gathered supplies, packed thoughtfully, and ensured we had everything from hydration packs and solar showers to costumes and goggles. Each item checked off the list was a step closer to the adventure of a lifetime.

The artist in the group had a room in a shared home with roommates in San Francisco and offered me the chance to sublet it, knowing I was trying to get back on my feet and start anew. I eagerly jumped at the opportunity. It provided a way out of my mom's house, brought me closer to work, and connected me with this inspiring community. The house was nestled in one of my favorite parts of San Francisco, characterized by its hilly, quiet streets - yet just a quick jog down to the Ferry Building and back.

In the following month, I immersed myself in thrift and costume shopping all over San Francisco, collecting anything that spoke to me, regardless of whether it matched anything else I owned. I embraced my inner child, artist, and intuition, reveling in the joy of gathering playful and unique pieces. The city transformed into my playground, and I delighted in the newfound freedom to explore and express myself fully.

Moving into this new space felt like a breath of fresh air. The house exuded a unique charm, brimming with creative energy and the constant buzz of artistic endeavors. My roommates were equally inspiring, each carrying their own stories and passions. Together, we shared meals and ideas, cultivating a supportive and vibrant home that felt like a true sanctuary for all of us.

The journey to Burning Man, along with the preparations alongside my new friends, marked the beginning of an exciting new chapter—one filled with creativity, connection, and the promise of transformation. As the departure day drew closer, my anticipation intensified. I felt ready to embrace the unknown, bolstered by the support of my newfound community and the thoughtful preparations we had made. The trek to Black Rock City felt like a rite of passage into a new life, and deep down, I sensed that I wouldn't emerge unchanged from this experience. The desert awaited, and with it, the potential for profound discovery.

I met up with my friend in Sacramento as she wrapped up her packing, and together we prepped food and loaded her car. We then headed to Reno to pick up the RV we had arranged to rent, only to discover it was far from ready for us. This setback meant we had to stay an extra night and a half while the owner finished getting it into shape. It was during this time that I realized the moment you decide to go to "the burn", you're already on the journey; it's all part of the experience. The ups and downs, the unexpected obstacles—they're all integral to the adventure. "The burn" has a way of giving you exactly what you needed, even if it's not what you initially wanted.

This unexpected delay marked my first real encounter with the unpredictable nature of the Burning Man experience. While the initial frustration lingered, it soon transformed into an opportunity to bond with my friend and the other fellow "burners" who were also waiting. We shared stories, laughter, and an increasing sense of anticipation for what lay ahead. The waiting game in

Reno, surrounded by like-minded individuals, became an experience in itself—a lesson in patience, adaptability, and the importance of going with the flow. One of the most profound lessons that Burning Man has to offer is the importance of flexibility and the acceptance that things may not always go according to plan, in fact most of the time they won't.

We spent our extra time exploring Reno, gathering last-minute supplies, and fine-tuning our plans. The energy of our group was infectious, filled with excitement and camaraderie. We played games, cooked meals together, and shared our hopes and expectations for the days ahead. It became clear that "the burn" had already begun and each moment was a meaningful part of the larger journey we were embarking on.

During our wait to leave, I experienced a couple of emotional breakdowns. It felt like we were never going to reach "the burn" because things kept going wrong with the RV. Finally, we hit the road, only for it to break down again, forcing us to call for help. However, when we finally arrived at the playa (the dried up lakebed where Burning Man takes place in Black Rock City, Nevada) we were met with warm welcomes. As a first-timer, I had to step out and ring the bell to signify my initiation into the dust. I rang that "virgin" bell with all my might and then followed the instructions to lay down in the dust and become one with it. Face down, I created a dust angel, fully embracing the moment.

As we pulled into our camp and parked the RV, we began to settle in and catch a nap, only to discover the RV was infested with beetles. We quickly set to work gathering them up and putting them in plastic baggies. Despite all these mishaps, I found myself handling everything surprisingly well. I realized that just two years prior, I would have struggled to cope with such chaos. In that moment, I felt a swell of pride for my growth and resilience, knowing I was capable of navigating so many curveballs.

We decorated our bikes and rode into the dust, soaking in the surreal environment. The first thing we stumbled upon was a random snow cone stand. We stopped to get a snow cone, made some new friends, and then continued our adventure. The sheer amount of art, creativity, and experiential activities was overwhelming in the best way possible. There was no way anyone could ever be bored here.

The energy and excitement of the playa was contagious. Every turn brought a new spectacle or interactive installation. We saw towering sculptures, intricate art pieces, and mobile art cars that defied imagination. The creativity and effort everyone put into their camps and costumes was astounding.

We participated in various activities, from meditation sessions to dance parties, each offering a unique experience and perspective. The sense of community was profound; everyone we met was open, kind, and eager to share their stories and experiences. It was a place where you could truly be yourself, without judgment or fear. The connections made here felt genuine and profound, transcending the superficial interactions of the outside world.

Riding our bikes through the dust, exploring the vastness of Black Rock City, felt liberating. In comparison to the confined, predictable default world we lived in. Here, spontaneity reigned, and every moment held the potential for discovery and connection.

The mishaps and delays we faced on the way to Burning Man now seemed like distant memories, overshadowed by the wonder and magic of the event itself. It was a reminder that the journey, with all its challenges and unexpected turns, is just as important as the destination. In the midst of the dust and art, I found a sense of freedom and possibility that I had never experienced before.

We arrived early, giving us the unique opportunity to witness the city being built around us. During the day, it looked vastly different than it did at night when the lights illuminated everything. The vibrant glow made Christmas seem like the little leagues. I had always felt a magical energy connected to Christmas, but Burning Man was a hundred times that. The magic was palpable, vibrating through my entire being. I was healing on so many levels simply by being immersed in this incredible vortex of energy and creativity.

As the sun set and the city came alive with lights and art installations, the transformation was breathtaking. The contrast between the daytime and nighttime experiences was lovely to experience. During the day, the playa was a vast expanse of creativity and construction. By night, it was an electrifying wonderland, with illuminated sculptures, art cars, and glowing costumes filling the landscape.

Being in this environment, surrounded by such positive energy and creativity, was transformative. It was a reminder that there was more to life than the pain and struggles I had endured. It was a place of possibility and hope, where I could begin to envision a future filled with joy, fulfillment and play.

Burning Man was not just an event; it was a catalyst for change, a turning point in my life. It gave me the space and the freedom to explore who I was and who I wanted to be. It was a place of healing, of magic, and of profound transformation.

The vibration of abundance on the playa was incredibly potent, amplifying the healing energy that surrounded us. As an artist, I began to see art as something sacred, shattering the myth of the "starving artist" that had clouded my reality.

Here, artists flourished, their work celebrated and nurtured by a community that truly valued their contributions. The playa was a realm where dreams weren't merely envisioned; they were brought to life. A place where the impossible transformed into reality. The intangible became tangible and manifested in vibrant forms that resonated deeply within me.

Instant manifestation also became a constant phenomenon at "the burn;" I would simply think of something, and it would materialize before my eyes within seconds. The immediacy of manifestation was astounding. I would wish for a connection, a conversation, or a specific item, and it would appear almost instantly. This synchronicity made me realize the power of intention and the abundant nature of the universe. It was as if the playa amplified every thought and desire, turning them into reality in real-time. If only I could carry this experience and magic back with me into the default world, I knew my life would never be the same.

This experience taught me that abundance is not just about material wealth, but also about the richness of experiences, connections, and opportunities. It showed me that living in a state of abundance is about being open to the endless possibilities that life offers, trusting that what we need will come to us when we need it.

Taking this mindset back to the default world felt like the key to transforming my life. If I could hold on to the belief in abundance, trust in the power of manifestation, and embrace the magic of everyday moments, I knew I could create a life that was not just about surviving but thriving.

Meeting people from all over the world at Burning Man felt like finding an instant soul family. Energetically, we connected in a way that made them feel like long-lost relatives, and they indeed became just that. This event became an annual sacred journey to see them, catch up, and play. Once you experience such profound expansion, there's no going back.

The expansion I experienced at Burning Man was immense, creating a momentum that propelled me toward a new chapter in my life. The transformative energy of the playa was palpable, igniting within me a renewed sense of purpose and possibility. At the heart of this event, I visited the temple—the sacred soul of Burning Man. This beautifully crafted art structure serves as a communal space for reflection, celebration, and remembrance.

There, I placed all my past experiences on the wall—the challenges with my mom, the sexual abuse I had suffered, and the tumultuous relationships I had endured. It was a deeply cathartic process, pouring out my pain, struggles, and heartache onto that wall, preparing for it to be released in the temple's burning fire. This act symbolized a powerful release of my past burdens, allowing me to let go and embrace the potential for healing and new beginnings.

Watching the temple burn at Burning Man was a profoundly moving experience. As the flames consumed the structure, it felt as though they were also consuming the burdens I had laid to rest within its walls. This act was a powerful, symbolic release—a purging of the old pains and traumas to make way for new beginnings. The sight of the temple burning, transforming all my past experiences into ash, filled me with an overwhelming sense of liberation and renewal. It was a visceral reminder that from the ashes of the old, new life can emerge, rejuvenated and free to explore uncharted paths.

This ritual marked a significant turning point in my life. It was a moment of profound healing, where I let go of the weight that had been holding me down. The act of releasing my past into the fire allowed me to reclaim my power and step into a future unburdened by old traumas. This opened up a whole new world of healing to me that I hadn't known before.

My journey onto the more "woo woo" healing path began, dipping into energetics, reiki, crystals, angel cards, and shamanic healing practices. I found myself exploring modalities that connected deeply with my soul, practices that resonated with the parts of me that had longed for a more holistic approach to healing. Each crystal, each card reading, each shamanic session opened new layers of understanding and self-awareness. I began to see the world through a lens of magic and possibility, where healing wasn't just about addressing the mind and body, but also the spirit.

The momentum from Burning Man flowed seamlessly into my everyday life, as if the dust from the playa had woven itself into the fabric of my 'default' reality. My inner child and inner artist were reawakened—life breathed back into these parts of me I hadn't realized were dormant. With their return came a lightness I hadn't felt in years. Life felt more like play, shedding its heaviness and density. The connections I forged, the profound lessons I absorbed, and the deep healing I experienced became central to my way of being. The sense of community and belonging I found was unparalleled, serving as an ongoing source of strength and inspiration. It fueled my creativity and propelled me forward with a renewed and vibrant sense of purpose.

Burning Man was more than just an event; it was a powerful reminder of the beauty and potential that exists within each of us. It was a lesson in living fully, embracing creativity, and believing in the magic of the universe. Carrying this experience with me meant living with an open heart, a creative spirit, and an unwavering belief in the abundance that surrounds us all.

Returning from my first "Burn," I was imbued with a profound sense of clarity and alignment. It was as though everything in my life had suddenly clicked into place. However, the time at my sublet was drawing to a close, and I found myself uncertain about my next steps. Serendipitously, I bumped into someone I had previously coached in a PSI program who mentioned having a room available in his home. Seeing this as a sign, I decided to move out of the sublet and into this new space with a roommate I trusted.

This move brought me to the vibrant Castro neighborhood of San Francisco, known for its dynamic energy and community spirit. My new living arrangement offered a cozy nook away from the busyness of city life, providing both comfort and inspiration. This transition seemed to perfectly embody the renewed path I was embarking on, surrounded by supportive energy.

With renewed enthusiasm, I began working with a business coach to explore turning my ABunnDance idea into an actual business and class. It was exhilarating to take concrete steps toward a dream I had been envisioning. I was finally on a path that felt true to myself, moving away from the shadows of my past and toward a future full of potential.

As I returned from the "burn" and settled into my new home in the Castro, it was also time to prepare for the yearly leadership PSI program, Principia. This time, I approached it with heightened enthusiasm and a clearer sense of purpose. I felt more aligned with my goals, ready to embrace the challenges and opportunities that awaited me. The experiences at "the Burn" had ignited a spark within me and I was eager to channel that energy into my personal and professional growth.

Still vibrating at a high frequency from "the Burn," the universe brought me face to face with a soul that felt incredibly kindred—a magnetic connection that was undeniable. We had been within the same community for years, orbiting the same events, but it wasn't until this year that we truly saw each other. Throughout the entire week, we kept synchronistically being brought together, as if our meeting was divinely orchestrated.

We spent a lot of time together at the retreat that year, sharing stories and experiences that resonated deeply within us. As we prepared to leave Principia and return to our respective homes—

me in San Francisco and him in Los Angeles—we exchanged totems that we had been wearing, marking the beginning of something special between us. I gifted him my magical sea glass ring, a cherished piece I had received from a mysterious, enchanting woman in San Francisco. In return, he presented me with a jade necklace on a simple string, a symbol of the connection and energy we had shared.

This was the beginning of something different, something that felt spiritually aligned. The energetic connection we shared was unlike any I had experienced before, and it filled me with a sense of hope for what lay ahead. It felt as though our paths had been leading us to this moment, and I was eager to see where this new journey would go. This meeting felt like a continuation of the magic I had experienced at "the burn", a sign that I was on the right path.

As I moved forward, I carried the energy of this new connection with me, allowing it to inspire and guide me. The jade necklace became a symbol of this new chapter, a reminder of the power of synchronicity and the beauty of divine timing. I felt more connected to myself and the world around me, ready to embrace whatever came next with an open heart and a sense of wonder.

C-LOVE

Chapter 21
Love Hurts, Relationships Are NOT Rainbows

Driving back home, I couldn't help but smile, feeling a sense of awe wash over me. I kept holding the jade necklace that hung around my neck, a tangible reminder that this was real, that I had connected with a real person. We communicated the old-school way, through our cell phones, and daily conversations became the norm. We shared texts that included each other in our daily adventures, swapping pictures of the places we visited and the people we met. He would send me inspiring quotes, which I cherished. I had always devoured positive quotes and memes, using them as fuel to stay focused on the life I was creating. Every night, he'd stay up just to ensure I got home safely and would talk me to sleep. We'd drift off on the phone together, and it felt like the sweet innocence of high school love, yet somehow, it was so much more.

Living six hours apart allowed us to see each other every other weekend, creating a rhythm that worked perfectly for both of us. I would make the trek down to LA, while he would venture to my neck of the woods in San Francisco. This arrangement suited me well, as I was busy working and pursuing the things I loved. It provided the space I needed to stay on track with my goals and aspirations, preventing me from getting swept away in a whirlwind of romance and losing sight of everything else that mattered. I knew I couldn't afford to let that happen if I truly wanted to transcend my job once and for all.

Our weekends together were filled with laughter, exploration, and deep conversations. Each visit felt like a mini-adventure, a break from the routine where we could fully immerse ourselves in each other's company. Whether we were discovering new spots in LA or enjoying the familiar charm of San Francisco, our time together was always so special.

This newfound sense of stability and emotional safety was a breath of fresh air. He understood me in ways I hadn't experienced before, offering comfort and reassurance during moments of uncertainty. With him, I could finally exhale, shedding the burdens of my past and embracing the potential for a brighter future. It felt like a beautiful blend of love and friendship, and for the first time, I believed I could have both.

Our relationship felt like a beautiful blend of independence and togetherness, a dance of two souls who had found each other at the right time. It was as if the universe had conspired to bring us together, aligning our paths in a way that allowed us to grow both individually and as a couple.

During my time on my own, I immersed myself in work and collaborated closely with my business coach to develop my ABunnDance class. We were creatively fusing elements of NLP (Neuro-Linguistic Programming)—a powerful set of techniques that use language to transform thoughts and behaviors—with booty-shaking lessons to help create a dynamic, fun and experiential goal-setting class. After the exhilarating experiences of Burning Man and Principia, I was ignited with passion for this project. The energy and insights I gained during those transformative moments fueled my determination to bring this vision to life.

I finally hosted my first ABunnDance class at Fort Mason in San Francisco, and the turnout was truly incredible. People from all areas of my life came together—my PSI community, Burning

Man family, and the club where I worked at—creating a beautiful blend of experiences.

As I looked around and saw familiar faces alongside newcomers, all eager to dive into what I had created, I felt a mix of humility and exhilaration wash over me. The class was an undeniable success, and the feedback was overwhelmingly positive. Participants left feeling inspired, moved, and buzzing with excitement about the new possibilities ABunnDance had to offer. In that moment, it felt like a dream had been realized—a testament to my journey of growth and transformation.

This event marked a pivotal milestone in my journey toward escaping the job that had long felt like a trap. It provided me with a tangible sense of progress and a clear direction for where to focus my energy. The dream of rendering my dancing job obsolete was finally beginning to feel attainable. Each class and every person impacted by ABunnDance brought me closer to that goal. It was incredibly fulfilling to take the very elements of the job that had caused me so much pain and transform them into a source of healing and joy for others. This reminded me that everything can be illuminated and transformed, paving the way for something beautiful to emerge.

Life felt truly magical with my business blossoming and a new relationship unfolding. I was vibing on such a high frequency. Whenever we were together, it felt like we were wrapped in a cocoon of healing energy and love. In many ways, he felt like the best friend I had always longed for in a guy. We shared so many bucket-list experiences that enriched my life in countless ways.

For the first time, I went horseback riding, feeling the exhilaration of connecting with such a powerful, majestic animal. We sailed into the ocean, the vastness of the sea mirroring the expansive depth of our connection. One of the most unforgettable moments was when I finally got to pet a penguin, fulfilling a cherished childhood dream. He also introduced me to yoga, and from the first class, I was hooked. It became a new avenue for inner peace and physical well-being, opening me up to even more growth.

We played dress-up and attended music shows, dancing under the stars and fully immersing ourselves in the rhythm and energy of live performances. Our adventures included experiencing Coachella, where we danced under the desert sky, with the music of Sia and Florence and the Machine resonating through our souls. We traveled to Hawaii, basking in the island's natural beauty and serenity. After that we ventured into Mexico, where the vibrant culture, stunning landscapes, and the ancient pyramids of Chichen Itza captivated us. Biking and stargazing from hammocks on the beaches of Tulum were moments of pure bliss. We engaged in shamanic breathing journeys with wolves and sampled a myriad of amazing restaurants, tasting a bit of every culture.

Our time together was enriched not just by the activities, but by the profound connection we shared. He was supportive, encouraging, and genuinely interested in my dreams and aspirations. With him, I felt safe and valued—like I truly mattered. He wasn't just my partner in adventure and play, but also my confidant and healer. Each moment we spent together strengthened our bond and deepened my appreciation for his kindness and the love he brought into my life. This relationship was a beautiful blend of friendship and romance, laying a foundation of mutual respect and understanding that was both healing and transformative.

As the journey with him continued, we encountered choppy waters. Issues began to surface, eroding the trust we had painstakingly built. He wasn't entirely forthcoming about certain aspects of his life, which ignited my fears and made me feel unsafe—a feeling all too familiar from my past. This erosion of trust began to unravel the fabric of our relationship, causing old wounds regarding trust and safety around men to resurface. Additionally, I discovered he regularly watched pornography, a revelation that I found deeply troubling and couldn't reconcile with my values. This issue, in particular, was something I couldn't tolerate and strained our relationship further, as it didn't align with the intimacy and connection I valued.

Discovering these issues not only triggered deep-seated insecurities and fears, but also shook the foundation of trust and transparency that I had so cherished in our relationship. The once solid ground we stood on began to feel unstable, as this new revelation intertwined my past traumas with present fears, clouding the future with uncertainty.

The gap between his actions and my core values created a rift that seemed increasingly difficult to bridge. I found myself questioning the sustainability of our relationship, weighing the profound connection and beautiful moments we shared against the looming shadows of these significant obstacles. What had begun as a journey marked by alignment and mutual understanding now faced turbulent waters. Torn between the love we shared and the values I held dear, I grappled with how to move forward, especially as his actions felt akin to a betrayal to my system.

After uncovering the depth of his addiction to porn, we decided to take a break, separating for several months to reflect on our relationship and what had transpired. This period was marked by a profound sadness for me, as I mourned the loss of what I had once believed was a magical and exceptional connection. What began as something dreamy and extraordinary had come crashing down into something that felt all too normal and typical. I had always aspired for a relationship filled with magic and passion, not willing to settle for mediocrity. However, learning about his long-standing issue had drained all the magic from our connection. I was left grappling with the reality of our situation and the stark difference between what I desired and what was unfolding.

During our time apart, I delved deep into introspection, questioning my values, boundaries, and what I truly sought in a relationship. Finding clarity amidst the confusion and hurt was challenging, yet crucial. I longed for the magic we initially experienced, yet I also recognized that trust and alignment in values were foundational for any relationship to thrive. This period of reflection was not just about evaluating our relationship, but also about understanding and affirming my own needs and standards for the future.

The time apart led me into a challenging situation with someone (another artist and creative) from my Burning Man community. We connected through my artist friend who created the installations. This experience was a harsh reality check, reminding me that not everyone associated with such a creative and open community necessarily holds good intentions. It was a painful lesson in discernment, teaching me the importance of being more cautious and less naive in my interactions, no matter how trustworthy the community might seem.

Meeting this artist, known for their collaborations with other creatives, filled me with excitement and anticipation. I was eager to be inspired and possibly forge a meaningful co-creative connection. The thought of working alongside someone who shared my passion for art and creativity was exhilarating, opening up new possibilities for artistic expression and collaboration.

However, as our interactions progressed, it became clear that his intentions were not as I had hoped. The initial admiration I felt quickly turned into discomfort as boundaries were crossed, making the situation increasingly unsettling. The trust I had placed in him due to our mutual connections was shattered, leaving me feeling vulnerable and deeply betrayed.

He grabbed me firmly, and in that instant, I froze—like a deer caught in headlights-I felt myself disconnecting from myself, leaving my body. He had his way with me while I was immobilized by fear, unable to say or do anything to stop him. His intense, frightening eyes haunted me even after he finished and fell asleep, snoring. He was a monster and raped me. It took an hour for me to come back into my body, to reconnect with the pain and terror I had been detached from. As soon as I could move, my soul screaming and crying, I gathered my things and fled. The tears didn't stop as I bawled my eyes out in the cab, racing away from the nightmare I had just endured to get back home.

I reached out to my sister, overwhelmed by tears, though I couldn't bring myself to tell her what had happened. I just needed to hear her voice, to tell her I loved her. After hanging up, I sobbed in the shower, trying to wash away the feeling of violation, then cried myself to sleep. My body ached, and I felt nauseous from the trauma. Overwhelmed with shame, I struggled to share the ordeal with anyone else. I blamed myself, agonizing over my inability to speak up or leave. "Why didn't I just get up and walk out? I'm an adult, not a child," I chastised myself repeatedly, unable to understand how I could have frozen in such a critical moment. The confusion and self-blame consumed me, as I replayed the incident in my mind, again and again. I couldn't erase the visual of his dark eyes out of my mind.

In the days following the assault, I was engulfed in a haze of pain and bewilderment. I felt tainted and abused, unable to rid myself of the visceral sense of violation. The trauma lingered, pervading every moment and disrupting my ability to engage with daily life. His face, his gaze, the feel of his touch—the memories invaded my mind relentlessly, especially in the quiet darkness of my room when I tried to sleep. Isolation deepened my torment, as I found myself locked in a suffocating spiral of self-blame and despair. I felt utterly alone with my anguish.

Confiding in my business coach, who practiced energy healing, marked a pivotal point in my recovery. She recognized the depth of my pain and guided me toward another energy healer, who helped me navigate the overwhelming grief and begin to reclaim my sense of safety. I started exploring different modalities of healing, each step representing a small victory in reclaiming my power. However, this violation had shaken my newfound confidence and self-esteem in ways I couldn't have imagined.

The experience reminded me of a quote by Maya Angelou: "I can be changed by what happens to me. But I refuse to be reduced by it." I clung to this sentiment, knowing that while this trauma had impacted me deeply, I was determined not to let it define or diminish me. Slowly, I began to rebuild, finding pieces of myself along the way.

Sharing my ordeal with my roommate brought an unexpected comfort. He disclosed a similar trauma from his past, which forged a deeper connection between us based on mutual understanding. Discussing the assault openly gradually loosened its grip on me. This exchange of vulnerabilities alleviated some of the burden I bore, reassuring me that I wasn't isolated in my experience. Understanding that I wasn't alone in freezing during such a moment helped me begin to forgive myself and diminish the relentless self-blame. This newfound solidarity was a crucial step in my journey towards healing.

I embraced additional healing practices to help manage the lingering trauma. Yoga became a sanctuary for reconnecting with my body, grounding me and easing physical tension. Meditation brought stillness to my chaotic thoughts, providing glimpses of peace and clarity. Journaling served as a safe haven for my emotions, a private space to freely express myself without fear of judgment.

That following year at Burning Man, I brought this painful experience, alongside my relationship reflections and surfacing traumas, to the temple—a sacred space known for its transformative power. The temple offered a profound way to hold and transmute pain. As I left those burdens there, entrusting them to the fire and the collective energy of the community, I experienced a profound release, feeling lighter and more liberated as the flames consumed the physical symbols of my pain.

At that year's Burn, I was gifted my playa name: C-Love. This new name resonated deeply. It symbolized a new chapter and a new identity that embraced both my creativity and my capacity for love. It later became both my artist and business name. Interestingly, the theme of the Burn that year was Fertility, a theme that unknowingly foreshadowed the significant growth and new beginnings that were soon to unfold in my life.

As our separation period was drawing to a close and we began reconnecting to assess where our relationship stood, I knew I needed to be honest about what had happened during our time apart. I was uncertain about how our connection would feel after so many months and how he would react to the news of my sexual assault. Yet, when we reunited, it felt as though no time had passed. We fell back into our familiar rhythm, and the energy between us was as strong and comforting as it had ever been.

At the annual PSI retreat that we attended, one of our friends shared his experiences of fatherhood with infectious joy and deep love for his baby daughter. His happiness resonated profoundly with me, stirring a heartfelt desire. In a moment of pure openness, I expressed aloud, "I want a love baby too." Little did I know, my words were not just floating into the air, but were potent declarations to the universe, which was listening intently, ready to turn that pure desire into reality.

C-LOVE

Chapter 22
Leap of Faith, I'm Not Coming Back

Not long after declaring my wish at the retreat, I discovered I was pregnant. The news struck me with both a surreal shock and a sense of divine alignment. It felt like all the dreams, healing, and desires for a different life were converging at this moment. Mixed emotions of fear and excitement washed over me as I faced the unknown future, yet I was ready to embrace it wholeheartedly. This pregnancy marked the beginning of a new chapter, a profound opportunity to create the loving family I had always envisioned.

Reunited with my partner, the path ahead seemed filled with promise. Together, we were prepared to navigate this new chapter, drawing on all the lessons and growth we had experienced. This love baby symbolized our enduring connection, resilience, and the deep love that remained the core of our relationship. Embracing this journey, we looked forward to building a future that reflected our shared dreams and values.

Finding out I was pregnant was such a surreal experience, a moment that forced me to face a significant crossroads. Do I keep this blessing or not? I was already working on my ABunnDance class with my business coach and had started conducting some classes. I was also looking into moving down to LA to be closer to him. However, having a baby on the way changed everything. It made everything far more serious and complex. We were required to make quicker decisions than either of us had anticipated.

His family's reaction to our news was disheartening. They judged me harshly based solely on my profession, disregarding the journey I had undertaken and the challenges I had overcome. Their resistance to our relationship added a layer of complexity and stress to an already intense situation, casting a shadow over our joy and complicating our plans for the future.

The disapproval from his family was a persistent burden that strained our relationship. It was tough to navigate their judgments while trying to maintain our focus on building a future together. Despite the challenges, my partner remained steadfast by my side, affirming our bond and commitment to each other and our unborn child. However, the ongoing tension with his family cast a shadow over our happiness and complicated what should have been a joyful time. This situation added a lot of undue stress to our relationship, particularly for him.

Despite the opposition from his family, I was resolute in following my heart and embracing the life growing inside me. I viewed this pregnancy as a divine gift, a tangible manifestation of the love my partner and I shared, and a beacon of hope for a new beginning. However, the road ahead was paved with uncertainty and marred by conflict. I knew that together we would have to confront both external judgments and our own internal fears. Armed with courage and faith, I was determined to forge ahead, believing in the strength of our bond and the future we were destined to build.

Amidst the swirl of doubts and fears, the love and hope within me flourished. I held firm to the conviction that this child was destined to be, that our love could endure the trials before us. The thought of motherhood instilled in me a profound sense of purpose and responsibility, unlike anything I had experienced before. I had long harbored dreams of becoming the kind of mother I never had. I wanted a chance to heal the wounds of the past and break the cycle of mistakes handed down from my mother and hers. This was my chance to nurture a new life with the love and wisdom I had gathered along my journey.

At work, amid the blaring music and glaring lights, a profound unease settled over me like never before. The realization that I was carrying a new life made the club's atmosphere unbearable. Torn between keeping the baby or considering an abortion, I was overwhelmed. The lack of support from his family gnawed at my confidence about our future together, stirring fears of possibly facing motherhood alone—echoes of my own mother's struggles filled my thoughts. Standing at this daunting crossroads, I grappled with the enormity of my decisions: the future of my pregnancy, the sustainability of my job, and the uncertainty of my partner's commitment. The weight of these choices bore down on me, each option heavy with consequence and complexity.

I retreated to the dressing room and called a friend I'd met at a festival in Mexico recently. She listened empathetically as I poured out my fears, then posed a question that cut through my turmoil: "Could you live with the possibility of never having a child? If you terminate this pregnancy and later discover you can't conceive again, could you handle that regret?" Her probing question struck a chord, clarifying my doubts and illuminating the path forward.

Her question resonated deeply, leaving me with a resounding "No." The thought of never becoming a mother, a role I had dreamed of since childhood, was unbearable. This realization hit me hard, making me acutely aware of the long-term impact of my decision. It forced me to look beyond the immediate difficulties and uncertainties and truly consider what I wanted for my future.

Could I live with the regret of not giving this child a chance? Could I forgive myself if I discovered I could never conceive again? These questions swirled in my mind, each one pulling me closer to the answer that was becoming clearer with every passing moment.

I realized that staying at the club was no longer an option. The environment was incompatible with the future I envisioned for myself and my child. Despite the daunting uncertainty about my partner's support and the prospect of potentially raising a child on my own, a strong conviction was taking root within me. I knew it was time to step away from that life, to embrace the challenges ahead, and to commit fully to the path of motherhood and a new beginning.

Tears blurred my vision as I came to my decision. The risk of losing my chance to be a mother was something I couldn't face. The thought of living with such regret was unbearable. I needed to craft a future for my child—one that was safe, loving, and brimming with possibilities.

I called my partner from the locker room, my voice trembling as I laid bare all my fears, doubts, and the resolution I had reached. It was a heart-wrenching conversation, charged with raw emotion and fraught with uncertainty. Despite his uncertainty, I was clear about my decision. I knew what I was choosing and was committed to it, regardless of what he decided for himself. Through the turmoil, I made a choice to step into the unknown, to trust the path unfolding before me, and to take a blind leap of faith towards a new life. This moment marked a profound turning point, where my personal resolve was tested and affirmed, pushing me towards embracing change and the possibilities it held.

I hung up the phone, quickly changed, and left everything behind in my locker, including my work gear and stilettos. With each step towards the exit, my heart pounded with a mix of fear and relief. The fear of an uncertain future mingled with relief from knowing I was making a choice that honored my deepest desires and values. I was ready to face whatever challenges lay ahead. I walked out of the club for the last time, leaving behind the job and industry that had entrapped me for years. I had no plan, but I felt an exhilarating freedom in committing fully to this decision. It was a leap of faith, trusting that I would find a way. I had never felt so alive.

For a decade, I thought I needed to have everything figured out before I could escape the trap I was in. Yet, here I was, finally mustering the courage to leave without any clear plan. Fear had held me back, fear of losing security, fear of the unknown. The real trap was my lack of faith in myself and in the Creator, a disbelief that taking a leap of faith would reveal the next best step. I hadn't been ready to make such a risky, frightening step into the unknown until now.

Over the years, I met many women in the various clubs where I worked. Our backgrounds were as diverse as our reasons for being there—some were involved in prostitution, some in porn, and others were dancers like me - many of whom were single moms. We spent a lot of downtime together in the dressing rooms or waiting on the club floor for customers and during these moments, conversations would naturally unfold. It became clear that many of us shared a common thread: histories marked by abuse. Whether it was childhood sexual abuse, experiences of rape, or ongoing abusive relationships, these stories were heartbreakingly frequent among the women I met and worked with.

Most of the women I worked with in the clubs disliked the job intensely; they simply didn't know how to earn a comparable income elsewhere. Many also harbored a deep-seated resentment towards men and struggled with low self-esteem. It was common for dancers to leave the industry, only to return out of necessity once they became mothers. As I made my own decision to leave for good, I vowed never to return, no matter the challenges ahead. I was determined to find a way to earn a living that was true to who I was and didn't compromise my values.

Moreover, I felt a strong desire to help other women escape this industry. Seeing the struggle and resilience of my peers, I dreamed of one day offering support and resources to those wishing to break free from this cycle and build a better life. This vision of helping others fueled my determination, providing a sense of purpose that propelled me forward on my journey.

Stepping out into the cool night air, I felt the chains of the past begin to loosen. The oppressive atmosphere of the gentlemen's club, with its relentless lights and pounding music, now lay behind me. For a decade I had felt shackled to this job and industry, believing I needed a perfect plan before I could leave, yet here I was, walking away without all the answers. I was FINALLY liberated from the limiting belief that I had to have everything figured out!

Each step I took was a stride toward freedom, shedding the heavy layers of a life that no longer served me. The cool breeze was like a whisper of encouragement, pushing me forward into the unknown. This moment wasn't just about leaving a job; it was about leaving behind an entire way of life that had confined me.

It was a step into a new beginning, a leap of faith into a future I was now free to create.

Walking away without a clear plan was as terrifying as it was exhilarating. I had always been a meticulous planner, someone who needed every detail in place before making any significant decision. Yet, this leap of faith marked a departure from my usual way of navigating life. It demanded trust—trust in myself, trust in my ability to handle whatever challenges might come, and most importantly, trust in my inherent worth. It was a profound shift from planning to simply being, from calculating to experiencing, and from fearing the unknown to embracing it with open arms.

Navigating through the unclear circumstances of my future and my evolving purpose, I resolved to keep my baby and embrace a leap of faith into the unknown. Staying the course in my current lifestyle would only perpetuate the patterns I longed to break free from; I needed a transformative change. This decision marked one of the most significant and daunting leaps I had ever taken. It involved packing up my life in San Francisco, storing a substantial portion of my belongings, and preparing for a new beginning. Initially, we planned to relocate and live with my business coach on the Big Island of Hawaii together. However, this arrangement quickly unraveled, compounding the uncertainty and external pressures of an already complex situation.

When the plan for us to move to Hawaii unraveled, I found myself back at square one, with no clear direction. The intense external pressures forced me to dig deeper within myself, searching for resilience and clarity. It was a time to be resourceful and open to new possibilities, embracing the challenges as opportunities to strengthen my resolve and forge a path that truly aligned with my values and the future I envisioned for myself and my child.

During my pregnancy, the hormonal changes and weight gain brought a flood of old wounds to the surface. Unresolved traumas from my past began to impact our romantic relationship more heavily than before. I found myself unusually sensitive, triggered by things that had not previously affected me so deeply. Frequent flashbacks disrupted my sense of safety, making it difficult to feel secure - even with my partner. The whirlwind of emotions, amplified by pregnancy hormones, created an overwhelming sense of chaos within me. The chaos eventually began to strain our connection and our journey together got more complicated by the day.

Reflecting on that time, I realize I was experiencing the opening of a trauma capsule—a sudden onslaught of repressed memories and emotions that surged to the surface as I entered motherhood. My body was undergoing profound changes, transforming from a shape in which I had finally felt confident in, into something entirely different. As I gained weight, I struggled with the physical discomfort and the loss of familiarity with my own body. The swelling, the difficulty walking, and the fear of not being able to protect my child in a world where I had often felt unsafe all compounded the emotional turmoil. How was I going to protect my child from all the monsters in the world?

Without the tools or a supportive network to guide us through these profound changes, our relationship began to strain and falter. This lack of support deepened my uncertainties about our future together, amplifying my fears as I wrestled with the complexity of it all, often on my own. The weight of the monsters and traps that had marked my past came crashing to the surface, even more intense as I carried a new life within me. The challenges felt relentless, each one highlighting just how much was unresolved, and how much healing was still needed as I prepared to bring my baby into the world.

Chapter 23
Gifts May Not 'Look' The Way We Think They Should

Navigating daily life became a delicate balance, like tiptoeing over eggshells, where even the slightest comment or gesture could trigger intense emotional reactions. During my pregnancy, I found myself trapped in a relentless cycle of fear and anger, desperately searching for some semblance of stability. The intensity of these emotions left me grappling with shame—was this turmoil normal during pregnancy?

As my partner faced his own set of uncertainties, including unsupportive family dynamics and work challenges, his ability to offer the emotional support and understanding I needed diminished. The robust and healing connection we once shared began to fray under the weight of my resurfacing trauma and the looming responsibilities of impending parenthood. This shift in dynamics strained our relationship, rendering it tenuous and fraught with tension. We realized we had to grapple with the altered nature of our bond.

Our efforts to cling to some sense of normalcy became increasingly strained as the cracks in our relationship deepened. Conversations that once flowed effortlessly now stumbled, laden with tension and misunderstanding. I could see the confusion and frustration mirrored in his eyes, a reflection of my own inner turmoil. We were two individuals, each grappling with our personal demons, and we found ourselves increasingly unable to provide the support the other needed. The disconnect widened, pushing us further apart as we each struggled to navigate our individual challenges.

As he began to deliberately antagonize my triggers, the turmoil within our relationship intensified, breeding feelings of distrust and betrayal. I wondered what had happened to my best friend—the one with whom I could laugh, explore, and play. It felt as though we were spiraling out of control, like a shooting star plummeting from the sky. Despite his assurances of support through my pregnancy and the transition from my job, a persistent, nagging doubt clouded his promises. Reflecting on our intermittent relationship over the years, I recognized a lack of consistent commitment, which seemed crucial for navigating such a life-altering journey together. This disparity between his words and actions sowed deep seeds of uncertainty about our future.

Every argument pushed us closer to the brink, and each unresolved issue widened the chasm between us. It felt as though instead of repairing, we were steadily dismantling everything we had built. His actions and words failed to match his promises, exacerbating my feelings of instability. It seemed he was overwhelmed by the depth of my pain and the intensity of my triggers, unable to grasp or manage the complexity of my emotions. Instead of being the pillar of support he had promised to be, he inadvertently became an additional source of stress and anxiety.

The opportunity for a sacred ceremony with a shaman, who my partner had previously assisted, emerged as a beacon of hope amidst our turmoil. Eager for any potential remedy, we embraced this chance, hoping it would restore some equilibrium to our fraying connection. I entered the ceremony with a focused intention to heal the deep-seated wounds of my childhood, particularly the sexual abuse that had become increasingly pronounced with the physical changes of pregnancy.

The ceremony itself was profound, offering clarity and insights that resonated deeply. However, a poignant realization emerged during the process: despite our efforts, it became apparent that the healing was not reaching my partner as I had hoped. As the shaman and the healer focused their energies, it was clear that his heart remained closed. This experience crystallized a painful truth for me—I sensed that he would not remain a constant presence in my life or in our child's life. This foresight was heartbreaking.

When he vanished a week after our sacred ceremony, it confirmed the uneasy realization I had during that healing moment—it sharpened my intuitive 'knowing.' His departure left a gaping void, filled with unfulfilled promises and shattered dreams. It became painfully clear that he was not meant to be a part of my journey toward healing from sexual abuse or to be a co-parent to our child. The ceremony revealed the true nature of his commitment and readiness, starkly highlighting that not everyone is meant to walk our path, especially when their heart remains closed to the journey. Though it was a tough realization, it also showed me that he was just a chapter in my story—one that, despite its pain, brought me the greatest gift of all: my daughter.

The outcome seemed predestined, as if divinely orchestrated. I felt like both a character and an observer in a tragic film, unable to alter the script. This realization struck deeply—I was walking the same path I had always feared, the path my mother had walked. I was now a single mother. The emotions of brokenness, heartbreak, and a sense of failure overwhelmed me. Processing the layers of grief from this breakup took five years, a testament to the deep connection and love I had felt. The depth of bonding that forms when you conceive a child with someone became painfully clear to me; it's a profound tie that deeply roots itself in your very being.

After he left, I faced the profound challenge of raising a child on my own. This reality was daunting, steeped in fear, but at the same time transformative. The clarity I received during our sacred ceremony defined my path—it was a call to reclaim my power and heal deep wounds, regardless of having to walk that path alone. Acknowledging that he was not meant to be a part of our future, I harnessed the strength to focus on the essentials: my healing and the well-being of my unborn child. This realization, though fraught with pain, sparked a profound renewal of purpose, empowering me to put my health and my baby's needs first. My child became the anchor of my decisions, the compelling 'WHY' behind every tough choice. It was this connection that grounded me, steering me towards my true north.

Returning to my mother's house felt like a massive setback, a rewind on my life's progress to the very LAST place I wanted to be. It felt as though the universe was doling out a harsh punishment. This transition was not just humbling, but laden with immense difficulties. Re-entering an environment I had fiercely fought to leave behind, now intertwined with the new challenges of impending single motherhood, weighed heavily on me. It was as if I was undoing all the progress I had made, stepping back into a past I thought I had overcome. It felt like I was returning to a hell I had long since escaped.

Returning to my childhood home—the epicenter of past traumas and the dysfunctional dynamics with my mom—felt like stepping into a time warp. This house, still under seemingly perpetual renovation, was a stark reminder of all the unresolved issues. I found myself sleeping on an air mattress in the living room, surrounded by garbage bags of my scattered belongings - the concrete floor beneath me cold and unforgiving. Every corner of this house echoed with memories of a painful past that I had spent years trying to leave behind. Now, as I faced the daunting reality of single motherhood, I felt broken and defeated. This humbling backdrop was the stage for my new beginning, a stark contrast to the life I had envisioned. It was a harsh reset, forcing me to confront my deepest fears and vulnerabilities head-on.

It seemed that my mom had distanced herself from her previous lifestyle. The woman who had been a negative influence on her had long moved out and, years later, passed away, severing the ties to that tumultuous past. Consequently, the stream of questionable visitors had ceased. Although my mom and stepdad still occupied separate bedrooms, their relationship had evolved into something more functional. They communicated and even spent time together, bringing a new level of stability to the house that hadn't existed in years.

Despite these positive changes, the physical state of the house reflected its history of neglect and constant traffic. The walls and the entire structure bore the marks of wear and tear, making it a less than ideal place to be, let alone a place to raise a baby. It was not the hopeful, nurturing environment one would wish for to raise a baby in.

Walking out of my job without a solid plan while pregnant forced me into a reality I hadn't anticipated—I needed financial support, and fast. So I found myself downtown, applying for government aid. The whole process was deeply embarrassing. Sitting in the waiting room, surrounded by others facing similar struggles, I felt a profound vulnerability I wasn't accustomed to. It contrasted sharply with the independence and resilience I had always prided myself on. Navigating the bureaucratic maze, filling out endless forms, and enduring judgmental glances from staff members made the experience even more challenging.

Reaching out for help as a pregnant, soon-to-be single mom carried a heavy burden of negative judgment and stigma. It was a demeaning experience that made me feel minimized and devalued, as if my single motherhood marked me as unwanted or discarded—like damaged goods. This was a deeply humbling ordeal, sharply illuminating the challenging new journey I was embarking on. The societal judgment only added to the personal and emotional challenges, making each step forward feel even more daunting.

Using food stamps and food coupons from WIC was an ordeal steeped in humiliation. Each time I reached into my purse to pull them out at the grocery store, I felt a surge of anxiety, acutely aware of the scrutinizing glances around me. On one particularly stressful day, as I was about to pay, I realized I had left them at home. The line behind me was long and the impatience of the crowd was palpable as I stood there, sweating under their stares. My mom, who I was buying groceries for, stood helplessly by my side. We were about to leave and face the ordeal of returning, when unexpectedly, kindness shone through. A man in line with his wife stepped forward and paid for our groceries. Overwhelmed with gratitude, tears filled my eyes as I thanked him. This small act of kindness was a beam of light in a moment filled with panic, reminding me that hope and humanity still existed.

This unexpected act of kindness was a profound reminder of the goodness in the world, catching me at a moment when I least expected it, but needed it most. I was deeply uplifted by this stranger's generosity. Though it was a small gesture, it made a significant impact on my spirit. It reinforced my belief that despite hardships, there is always light and support available when we need it most. It also reminded me to stay open to miracles and synchronicity, renewing my hope in possibility.

My mom wasn't working during this time, so the food stamps I received were essentially keeping both of us fed. My stepdad, although living with us, managed his own food separately. Their relationship had not fully recovered; they were together, but lacked real emotional connection and maintaining a somewhat transactional existence. While we managed to coexist, primarily united by the anticipation of my baby's arrival, I was plagued by worries of old patterns resurfacing. My mom had a history of being hypercritical, discouraging, and controlling, often showing little emotional empathy. The potential of returning to these emotionally abusive dynamics once my child was born added a significant layer of stress to an already strained family situation.

The atmosphere at home was tense, as if everything was held together by a fragile thread. My mom and stepdad, though married and sharing the same house for decades, interacted more like roommates than a couple in love. Their relationship had settled into a sort of truce rather than a true reconciliation, marked by a palpable distance between them. They lived separate lives, even sleeping in separate bedrooms. Their interactions were largely transactional, lacking any real intimacy. This disconnect cast a persistent shadow over the household, creating an undercurrent of unease that was hard to ignore. Certainly not the ideal setting to welcome a new baby into the world.

As my pregnancy advanced, I poured my energy into preparing for my baby's arrival. I delved into research and meticulous planning, striving to forge a stable environment amidst uncertainty. I carefully selected and gathered essential baby supplies and gear. Though my mom was supportive in her own way, her personal challenges sometimes hindered her ability to be fully present.

Nevertheless, we found moments of connection and shared anticipation for the new life that was soon to join our family.

Before transitioning to a hospital near my mom's house, I attended one last doctor's appointment in San Francisco. They did my blood work, and it was my first ultrasound to determine the baby's gender. Deep down, I already *knew* I was having a girl—there was an unshakable certainty about it. I felt fine until I laid down on the table, watching the ultrasound screen. When they confirmed I was having a girl, tears streamed down my face like a faucet had just been turned on. I couldn't turn it off!

The news that I was having a daughter, something I had always dreamed of, filled me with overwhelming emotion. At the same time, that joy was tinged with heartache. I was alone, with no partner beside me to share in this life-changing moment. The grief of this reality hit hard. This wasn't how I had ever envisioned this experience to be. It wasn't the dream I had carried for so long, and yet, it was the reality I had to embrace.

As the tears continued to flow, I began to feel a presence holding both my baby and me. It was as if life itself, along with a higher power, was embracing us, offering comfort and assurance. In that moment, I felt held in a way that transcended the physical absence of a partner. There was a profound sense of connection, as though something greater than myself was enveloping me in its care. The warmth of this unseen presence brought a measure of peace to my heart. I felt safe, guided, and cared for by an omnipresent force. I leaned into that energy and allowed it to carry me through the waves of emotion.

The confirmation that I was having a daughter ignited a new layer of motivation and purpose within me. I became even more determined to create a loving, nurturing environment for her—a life filled with the stability and emotional support that I had often longed for. This baby girl symbolized hope, a reminder of my inner strength and my ability to overcome adversity. She represented a chance to break the generational chains that had bound me and my family for so long. I committed every fiber of my being to giving her better than what was given to me, to ensure she would grow up surrounded by love, safety, and endless possibilities.

As I left the doctor's office, ultrasound image of my daughter in hand, I couldn't stop staring at it, even after getting into the car. I had always dreamed of being a mom, of having a daughter, and now she was real. Even though this gift didn't look the way I had envisioned or hoped, I realized I had been so attached to how this gift would appear, I was struggling to accept how it had actually shown up. Still, as I sat there, a renewed sense of resolve settled deep within me. The road ahead would undoubtedly be challenging, but the love I already felt for my daughter was transforming me, igniting a fierce determination to create a better life for us. Whatever it took, I was ready to face it head-on. Her presence had already begun to change me, fueling my strength and commitment to build a future where we could truly thrive together.

From that moment forward, my world centered around the precious life blossoming within me. My daughter and I became an inseparable team, our bond beginning even before her birth. The support was overwhelming; gifts and supplies, both new and cherished, arrived from every corner, a testament to the embrace of the universe. Despite the fractures in my spirit, I felt cradled by an unseen force. My daughter was the miracle I had longed for, my answered prayer—she ignited a profound transformation of my life.

The universe appeared to align in our favor, generously meeting our needs. The outpouring of kindness and generosity from people reminded me that we were far from alone. Each thoughtful gift and message reinforced our connection to a broader community, strengthening my determination to forge a brighter future for us. Remarkably, some of the support came from individuals I had never met—complete strangers who had heard of our journey through friends. It was deeply moving to witness such widespread support emerging from unexpected places.

Sometimes, progress means taking a few steps back. What may seem like regression can actually clear the path for a significant leap forward. This truth crystallized for me amid the complexities of my pregnancy and the process of rebuilding my life from the ground up. It was essential. I realized I had to retreat momentarily and lay down an unbreakable foundation that would support a more profound advancement. I felt at peace and in surrender to this process.

Meeting my ex was divinely orchestrated, a profound encounter that, in retrospect, brought me my greatest gift—not a lifetime partner, but my cherished daughter. This relationship was my first brush with something that felt normal and healthy, a stark contrast to my past experiences. However, it was not built to withstand the intense healing required to confront my deep-seated wounds, especially as I faced pregnancy. We were both too young and unprepared for the challenges stemming from my unhealed trauma. This led him to depart while I decided to embrace the path of single motherhood. My daughter, my answered prayer, remains a steadfast reminder of the power of faith and the profound impact of stepping into the unknown with courage and conviction.

Poem Dedicated to my Daughter ❤ ❤ ❤

I went on an inner journey
Falling into the deepest darkest hole within my being
Where everything including myself lost all meaning
Everything became valueless
Attachments to ideas were shattered
The constructs of my mind began to disintegrate - melt away
I felt like I had died
My heart hurt as if it had been ripped out of my body
In this place where I was surrounded by nothingness
I kept searching for something that meant something
I kept reaching out for answers
Only to be left empty handed
The more I looked outside of myself
The deeper in the hole I fell
The more I looked outside myself the more disempowered and lost I became
In the midst of chaos and people all around, I felt alone
Everything forcing me to turn inward
I began to search my psyche for something of truth
Where its meaning could not be stripped away

Because it stood as evident truth pure and love
And in this moment I reached for my phone and saw you
My little boopity boop boop boop
The light in your angel baby face eyes
Twinkling all so bright- The brightest light I have ever known
Staring at you
Reconnecting with you
The truth of you
My love for you
Brought me back home to myself
Back to the present moment
You are the one thing in my life that stands true that I cannot deny
That cannot be stripped away
Because of you I am beginning to truly know me
Because of you I am learning what love is
Because of you life comes into clear focus
And is beautiful -

July 2015

C-LOVE

Chapter 24
Birthing is Messy

During my pregnancy, the days melded into one another. I found solace in resting, binge-watching favorites like "Merlin," "Once Upon a Time," and "The Flash" on Netflix. It was a time filled with countless hours of crying and grieving, the emotional weight of it all sometimes feeling overwhelming. Simultaneously, I was gathering the essentials for my baby's arrival, preparing to welcome her into the world. With less busyness than in my pre-pregnancy days, I had ample downtime to truly experience and process the myriad of feelings that surfaced.

The upstairs "man-cave" craft room underwent a pivotal transformation, shifting from a cluttered spare room to a cherished sanctuary. We undertook a thorough renovation, discarding the outdated carpet for sleek new panel flooring and infusing the walls with a soft pastel yellow. The furniture was thoughtfully arranged to maximize coziness and warmth. This makeover created a nurturing mommy-daughter den—a peaceful refuge amid life's chaos, inviting us to snuggle up and embrace our new beginning together. This room, once merely an extra space, became a place we yearned to spend time in, wrapped in comfort and love. It was a delightful change from the nights spent on an air mattress on the concrete floor downstairs.

Doctor appointments became a regular rhythm in my life, a blend of excitement and anxiety with each visit. My mom came along, offering some support, and though the medical care was necessary, it often underscored the reality of my situation—the absence of a partner to share these milestones with. Still, each time I heard my baby's heartbeat or saw her image on the ultrasound screen, my connection to her deepened. These moments reinforced my resolve to embrace the journey fully and to nurture the life growing inside me, partner or no partner.

Hearing my daughter's heartbeat and feeling her tiny kicks and movements in my belly were pure magic. Each flutter was a reassuring reminder of the incredible life growing inside me, and these moments brought so much comfort and wonder. Preparing for her arrival became a form of healing—it allowed me to channel my energy into the love and future we were about to share - instead of lingering on past pain. Despite the exhaustion and occasional tears, every day brought me closer to holding my little girl in my arms. The thought of that moment filled me with renewed purpose and determination, making everything else feel worth it.

This time was as much about finding my own inner strength and resilience as it was about preparing for my daughter's arrival. Each small step I took felt like a stride toward healing and transformation. She became my guiding light, inspiring me to move forward with courage and faith. With her as my anchor, I knew our future would be filled with love, joy, and endless possibilities.

Then one day, it hit me—a quiet nudge, like a whisper, urging me to reach out to someone. She was someone who ran night events and I asked if I could set up a booth to face paint guests. Face painting was something I'd started at my first Burn, trying it out on myself and friends, and it quickly became a source of joy and creative expression. I loved seeing people light up as their faces transformed.

Inspired by a fellow artist I admired—someone who had built a thriving business around face painting and creating art on canvas—I realized this could be a temporary solution until something more aligned surfaced. To my delight, the event producer responded with an immediate "Yes," her enthusiasm matching my own. Suddenly, I had a small, but meaningful opportunity to transform my love for face painting into something more, and it offered a way to bring in additional income. This chance reignited my hope, showing me a path forward I hadn't considered before.

I showed up at Supper Club in San Francisco - super pregnant - and set up a small area in a booth near the bar. I handwrote simple signs that read, "1.) Say hi 2.) Sit down 3.) Become art," and taped them above my spot, unsure if anyone would even take a chance on this experience. To my surprise, people came up eagerly. They connected with me, paid the $5-$10 to get painted, and even rubbed my belly for good luck. The act of people rubbing my belly for good luck made me giggle and brought to mind images of Buddha. I thought this would be a short-term gig, something to hold me over while I was still 'figuring out my life.' Yet, this venture kept expanding. This was only the beginning.

This moment marked the genesis of a decade-long business journey. What started as a modest way to make ends meet quickly blossomed into something much bigger, ignited by my heart-driven tagline: "Spreading Love One Brush Stroke at a Time." I realized I wasn't just bringing my daughter into the world; I was birthing my business, C-Love, too. It was a season of ashes and rebirth, a rite of passage into motherhood and full-blown entrepreneurship. Everything I had known was burning down, making way for something new and powerful to rise.

Each night at Supper Club, the joy I brought through face painting rippled outward, reaching more people than I ever imagined. Word spread like wildfire, and soon, my little booth became a beloved fixture at events in San Francisco. People adored the creativity and personal touch I poured into each design, often lingering to watch as I worked my magic, captivated by the transformative power of art.

The connections I formed with each person were profound—a reminder of the importance of human connection and the unique healing that art can bring. Every brushstroke felt meaningful, a way to create beauty and spread joy, and these moments reinforced my belief that joy, beauty, and connection truly give life its richness and depth.

As my belly grew, so did my business and requests poured in for private events, parties, and festivals. The love and support from the community were both overwhelming and deeply affirming. People shared how much they cherished the art and the positive energy I brought to each gathering. It became more than just a 'job' or a means to an end; it was a way to spread love one brush stroke at a time. I felt a sense of fulfillment that was entirely new to me, overflowing with gratitude. This was a dream I hadn't even known I'd had, coming to life before my eyes.

All the business knowledge I'd gathered over the years from workshops and seminars finally found a purpose. I started collecting names and emails from everyone who sat down to be painted, creating an email list that quickly grew. Using Mailchimp, I began sending out newsletters that highlighted the exciting events I'd be part of, along with an inspiring message that reflected whatever I was vibing with at the time. People loved receiving these updates; they became more than just a list of events—they were a source of inspiration and community that connected us all in a shared love for creativity, music and art.

Organizing and compiling my contacts into a cohesive email list was tedious, but so fulfilling. This was more than a list; it was a community of people who had felt the joy and transformation through my art. Each newsletter became a way to nurture those connections, sharing not only details about upcoming events, but also stories, tips, and behind-the-scenes glimpses into the world of C-Love. With every newsletter, I'd send out an intentional flow of love, a blessing woven into each word, hoping it would bring a spark of positivity to their lives. The way people would come up to me, brimming with excitement to tell me they'd received my email, let me know they felt the love I poured into each one. Their enthusiasm was a beautiful affirmation that the connection extended beyond the art—it was personal, a shared energy that reached them in just the way I had hoped.

Realizing that my art was my gift to others and my calling transformed everything. This business was so much more than a way to make money—it was a way to create a positive impact in the world. The more I leaned into this path, the more opportunities seemed to flow my way. I began collaborating with other artists, expanding my skills, and exploring new creative avenues.

Embracing this purpose felt like stepping into alignment with who I was meant to be and who I was all along.

A friend of mine had an old car that technically, the bank should have repossessed, but they never did. So she generously offered it to me, which was a blessing that showed up out of nowhere. Though it needed a good cleaning and some serious elbow grease, it was exactly what I needed to get from home to work and all my doctor's appointments. I hadn't owned a car since that accident years ago when I'd injured someone, so having one again felt surreal. Yet with everything spread out so far, it made life so much easier. I felt incredibly grateful.

Having a car was an absolute game-changer. It allowed me to keep working and make it to all my necessary appointments without the stress of relying on my mom for rides. This gift was a tangible reminder of the support and kindness that surrounded both me and my daughter on this path I had courageously chosen, despite the fear and challenges. It gave me a sense of independence again, helping me navigate this new chapter with more ease, reminding me that even in moments of uncertainty, the universe was providing for us in unexpected ways.

It was a summer morning like any other until a searing wave of pain jolted me awake, filling me with terror. I rushed to my mom, panic thick in my voice. "Something's happening; something is wrong. We need to go to the doctor." She hurried me to the hospital, and just as we arrived, my water broke—it was as if I'd suddenly emptied the biggest pee of my life, soaking me completely within minutes. The pain was all-consuming, a relentless force coursing through my entire body, making it impossible to sit, stand, or find any relief. All I wanted was to hit a pause button, to stop everything for a moment, but there was no escape—it was just too much to bear.

They placed us in a room and gave me pain medication, but it did nothing. The contractions were slow yet relentless, dragging labor out for 42 hours. My daughter was taking her sweet time, progressing just enough that they didn't send me home. The pain felt endless, especially since I've always been hypersensitive about my womb. A sensitivity heightened by past trauma—my abortion and the agonizing aftermath of almost dying while donating eggs.

The only real relief came when the anesthesiologist finally arrived to administer the epidural. For the first time, I could breathe again. As the hours dragged on, I drifted in and out of sleep, the anticipation building with each passing moment. I was eager to finally meet my daughter, the little miracle I had been carrying for so long. My mom, sister, and a couple of close friends stayed by my side. They offered their unwavering support and comfort, which brought a sense of peace amidst the intensity. Despite the pain and exhaustion, a quiet calm washed over me, knowing that soon I would hold my baby girl in my arms—the culmination of all the challenges, hopes, and dreams I had faced throughout this journey.

Finally, it was time. She was on her way out, and the moment I had been waiting for was here. By this point, the pain meds and epidural had worn off, so I felt ***everything.*** My sister had the camera ready to capture this life-changing moment. My mom stood by my head, while my girlfriend—the one who had introduced me to Burning Man—was stationed at one foot, and my mom's friend, who had moved in with us, was at the other. The doctors set up a mirror so I could see everything firsthand. It was raw and surreal, watching my own daughter emerge from my body, witnessing the beginning of her life right before my eyes.

The contractions were enormous and relentless, and I felt like I couldn't do this—like my body couldn't take it anymore—but there was no turning back. I used the word "poop" as our code word for everyone to lift me up for pushing—a choice that came naturally, as I had pooped on the table right away, and the feeling of birthing was like trying to take the biggest poop of my life. Birthing was messy, raw, and completely unfiltered, but at that point, I didn't care about appearances or anything else. I just wanted to get through the pain and finally meet my baby girl. Little by little, with each excruciating contraction and push, my little nugget made her way into this world.

The pain was overwhelming, and I was beyond exhausted, but I pushed with every ounce of strength I had left. The room was filled with encouragement and support, and even though I felt like

I couldn't keep going, the presence of my loved ones gave me the strength I needed to push harder and to not give up.

Then, after what felt like an eternity, she was here. The nurses placed her on my tummy, and of course, she pooped on me—LOL. I couldn't help but laugh, thinking how amazing blessings truly do come with a lot of poop! As we locked eyes, all I could say was, "She's so pretty."

She immediately latched onto my boob, still locking eyes with me, and I cried. I had never felt so much love or connection to anyone on this planet. She was so tiny, so beautiful, and I knew right then that I was going to protect and love her with everything I had. This little soul had instantly changed my life forever.

Once they completed her shots, fed her, and finished all the post-birth procedures, I was finally headed to the shower. After nearly two days of labor, I was desperate to feel fresh. Between my own table pooping mishap, the birthing process, and my daughter's debut poop on me, I felt beyond ready for a reset. The nurses looked surprised at my ability to get up and walk, but they didn't know me yet. I'll move mountains to feel clean.

In the shower, the water washed away the exhaustion, and I felt a renewed sense of energy. As I stood there, I realized that this was the beginning of a new chapter, not just for me, but for my daughter and me together. The strength I had shown in the delivery room was just a glimpse of the resilience and determination I would need as a single mother. As I wrapped myself in a towel and stepped out of the shower, I felt ready to face whatever challenges lay ahead. I was determined to give my daughter the best life possible, filled with love, support, and endless possibilities.

My body felt so strange post-birth, like a balloon deflated but not quite returning to its original form. The pain in my lower region was unreal—like I'd been hit by a semi-truck. It almost felt illegal to be alive and endure this level of pain. Miraculously, I hadn't torn or ripped, which I had definitely manifested after hearing about a friend's experience that left her with an extra flap. We had the most incredible floor nurse, a true angel, who periodically checked in on us. She helped me navigate everything, from those first bathroom trips to breastfeeding, and held emotional space as I tearfully shared my journey to single motherhood. Her kindness and support made all the difference in those early hours.

When the nurses came to press on my belly to expel any remaining blood, the pain was intense, and the sensation felt oddly foreign—like I was a fidget squishy toy rather than a human, let alone a woman. I couldn't help but wonder if my stomach would ever feel the same again, or if my abs would make a comeback. Each touch was a vivid reminder of the incredible journey my body had just undergone, the sheer strength it took to create and bring a human into the world. Despite the discomfort, I felt immense gratitude and awe for what my body had achieved. Creating and birthing a human is no small feat—it's an act of pure power.

I finally got to take my baby girl home, and soon after, I had to take her to her first doctor's visit. I was struggling to get myself ready, wearing what felt like a giant diaper because of the bleeding, peeing myself at every turn, and dealing with milk leaking from my boobs. I felt like a broken mess, but all I could do was laugh and cry at the same time. What a beautiful, chaotic reminder of how raw and miraculous the circle of life truly is!

Amidst the chaos and overwhelm, I found humor in it all. The reality of motherhood hit me in waves—sometimes bringing laughter, other times tears. I realized, in a funny way, that Burning Man had unknowingly prepared me for this. Every moment, whether a small victory or a challenging setback, felt like part of a grand adventure. My daughter was here, healthy and beautiful, and despite the sleepless nights and physical aches, I was filled with a purpose and love that ran deeper than anything I'd ever experienced. This was a journey like no other, and I was all in.

Sitting with my daughter, I'd lose myself in her, tracing the delicate lines of her face with my fingers, memorizing every little detail as if I were preparing to sketch her. Time seemed to pause, creating a quiet cocoon just for us. Feeling her heartbeat as she drifted to sleep on my chest, her tiny hands grasping mine, her gentle breaths against my skin—it was pure magic. Her presence felt like a balm, soothing and mending the fractured parts of my heart that had been broken for so long. She was perfect, and in her warmth, I found a kind of healing I never knew was possible. I loved just being with her.

The sadness crept in quietly, like a shadow slowly overtaking the light. It was confusing, even heartbreaking—I had so much to be grateful for, this beautiful, perfect baby in my arms, yet each day the weight of sadness seemed to grow. I found myself questioning why I felt this way, why I couldn't just revel in the joy and love of motherhood without this undertow pulling me down. It felt like the more I tried to push it away, the heavier it became, making it harder to see the beauty in the little moments that had filled me with happiness.

Looking back, I can see it clearly now: I was experiencing postpartum depression. The exhaustion, the weight of single motherhood, and the resurfacing of old traumas all converged to create a profound emotional toll. The pressure to embody the blissful image of motherhood made the struggle feel even more isolating, as if I was failing at something that was supposed to be purely joyful. I felt trapped in silence, believing I had to bear it alone. But acknowledging it, even just to myself, was the first step toward healing—a quiet admission that allowed me to finally start seeking support.

The extra weight from pregnancy was another struggle layered onto everything else. I'd gained 80 pounds, and unlike some friends or influencers who seemed to snap back effortlessly, my body hadn't bounced back. My midsection was soft and floppy, a constant reminder of the changes I'd gone through. Determined to feel strong again, I started working out, jogging, and practicing yoga. But my efforts had an unintended consequence: my breast milk changed in flavor and stopped flowing entirely. After only two months, I had to switch my daughter to formula. This hit hard, bringing with it a fresh wave of guilt and self-doubt. I felt like I had somehow failed her again, and it was difficult not to feel like a 'bad mom.'

My mom's response only intensified the loneliness I felt. Instead of the compassion I desperately needed, I faced judgment and misunderstanding. Her inability to acknowledge my struggles or extend empathy made me feel even more isolated, like my pain was invisible to those around me. It was heartbreaking, deepening the darkness I was already navigating. I found myself yearning for a lifeline, yet feeling like I was left to face the weight of it all on my own.

The first time I returned to work, tears streamed down my face. I didn't want to go. Every part of me longed to stay with my daughter, but the reality of needing to provide for us pushed me out the door. Leaving her was gut-wrenching, a painful reminder of the sacrifices I had to make as a single mom. Coming back to her, though, felt like a beautiful reunion each time—a rush of joy and relief that made those moments the highlights of my day. I found myself wishing she could somehow go back into my tummy, so I could carry her around with me everywhere, close to my heart again.

As my art business flourished, it brought the blessing of financial stability but also required me to spend more time away from my daughter—a sacrifice that was incredibly difficult for me. My mom stepped in as her full-time *paid* caregiver, which provided her with much-needed income and gave me the peace of mind that my daughter was in familiar hands. This arrangement, though supportive in practical ways, also reopened old family dynamics, adding layers of complexity and emotional tension. Navigating these challenges required constant balancing between gratitude for my mom's help and the need to protect the boundaries I had worked hard to establish.

Amidst the heartache of being away from my daughter, I poured my love and creativity into my art. It became more than just a job; it was a lifeline, a means to provide, a channel for healing, and a way to express who I truly was. The tears and challenges of single motherhood were real, yet so was my fierce determination to create a better life for us. With each event I attended and every brushstroke I painted, I was building a foundation for our future—one filled with hope, resilience, and possibility. Each day brought us closer to the life I envisioned, one where my daughter could thrive in the love and stability I had worked tirelessly to build.

One night after work, as I was heading home, a woman rear-ended me on the Bay Bridge. I felt an overwhelming wave of gratitude that my daughter wasn't in the car. The back window had shattered, spraying glass everywhere—especially into her car seat. She would have been covered in it. Since the car technically belonged to the bank and my friend didn't have the pink slip, the other driver's insurance didn't cover the damage, leaving me with a total loss and, once again, without a way to get to work. It felt like one step forward, two steps back.

Feeling the loss, I vulnerably shared this incident online with my growing community, which had formed around my art. Friends, clients, and even people I'd never met reached out, offering support in ways I never anticipated. Some loaned me money, others donated outright, and many prepaid for future face art sessions. Within just 24 hours, I had enough to buy a car—a newer, more reliable one, and this time, it was in my name. I held the pink slip in my hand, feeling a surge of gratitude and relief. This community had lifted me in my moment of need, reminding me of the power of connection and kindness.

I cried with gratitude, utterly overwhelmed by the outpouring of support from my community. Their generosity and belief in me reaffirmed that this path—with my daughter and my art—was truly aligned with the universe's intentions. This experience was a profound reminder of the strength and beauty of community, and how powerful it is to pursue one's passion, no matter the obstacles. The collective support didn't just give me a reliable means of transportation; it renewed my faith in this path, reinforcing the belief that I was exactly where I was meant to be. Ironically, while this community lifted me up, certain family members saw my asking for help as shameful, while others dismissed my work and urged me to get a "real job." Thankfully, by then, I had learned to tune out the naysayers. This moment cemented my faith that I was exactly where I was meant to be, surrounded by people who saw my heart and believed in what I was creating.

My focus was clear: building a life of purpose, one brushstroke and step at a time.

Instead of letting negativity drag me down, I drew strength from the unwavering support of my community. Their encouragement and generosity were essential, keeping my spirits lifted and my focus clear. Every message, donation, and act of kindness reminded me that my work held real value and that there were people who genuinely wanted to see me succeed.

This journey wasn't just about pursuing my passion—it was about healing and growing with my community. In my younger years, the negative voices were all I heard, and I often found myself shrinking under their weight. Now, I could hear my support so much louder, and the negativity had lost its grip on me. Leaning into my community's belief in me felt empowering and reaffirming, like a long-awaited embrace from the universe itself.

I am forever grateful to each soul who sat with me to become art or supported my journey in one way or another. Every single person added to the foundation of my dream, making it possible for me to keep going, even on the hardest days. Their trust, encouragement, and presence transformed my art into something truly meaningful and gave me the strength to keep pushing forward.

C-LOVE

Chapter 25
Breaking Free

There was this one girl who kept returning to my table at events. She'd eagerly bring more people over to get painted and bedazzled, clearly enjoying the energy and excitement of it all. Eventually, I invited her to be my promo model, which allowed her to attend the events for free, and help me out in a more official way. Later on, she mentioned needing a job and a source of income, and that's when I asked if she'd like to learn the art and become a team member. She agreed, and just like that, my first-ever "C-Love Sparkle Babe" was born. It was amazing to witness this next phase, growing from a solo journey to a shared passion with a teammate.

She picked up the skills quickly, and having her with me at the bigger events was a game-changer—especially with those long lines we'd get! The events were pure joy, immersing us in worlds of art, creativity, music, and a sense of community. The appreciation and celebration from people who kept returning to get "loved up" at our booth filled my heart. Our regulars grew quickly, and it felt like such an honor to be surrounded by a genuine, supportive community.

This warmth and acceptance formed a stark contrast to the lack of encouragement I felt from my family, especially from my mom. Building this community around my art, feeling seen and valued, was deeply healing for my heart and soul. For the first time, my gift wasn't just an outlet—it was a source of connection and affirmation.

Our teamwork was truly transformative. With her by my side, we could finally manage the growing demand, and sharing this journey added a whole new layer of joy and fulfillment to my work. Together, we became a dynamic duo, spreading love and sparkles wherever we went. The authentic connections we built with our clients, along with the genuine smiles and gratitude we received, were priceless. Every interaction reminded me of the magic we were creating, deepening my sense of purpose and passion in ways I hadn't imagined. Her loyalty to C-Love was an invaluable gift to my blossoming dream, fueling it with support and shared enthusiasm.

Each event felt like a celebration of creativity and self-expression. People came to us not just for the face paint, but for a transformative experience that added a spark to their spirit. They left our booth feeling more beautiful, confident, and connected—each brush stroke a reminder of their unique light. It quickly evolved from a job into a calling, a way to touch lives and bring a little more joy and magic into the world.

Through C-Love, I found a way to seamlessly blend my artistic talents with my deep desire to make a difference. It became a platform for self-expression, connection, and healing—not just for those I painted, but for myself and my daughter as well. As the business grew, so did I. I evolved as an artist, a business owner, and a mother, learning to embrace each new challenge with grace and resilience. C-Love wasn't just a business; it was a journey of transformation, purpose, and growth.

As my business blossomed, the old, painful dynamics in my mom's house crept back in. The constant criticism, lack of support, and pervasive feeling of being used pulled me into a space where I felt trapped and unfairly blamed. Any respect for my well-being seemed distant, if present at all. The house itself, caught in the limbo of a remodel and stripped to its bones, became a physical mirror of my own emotional landscape—unfinished, exposed, and haunted by layers of unresolved pain. Each day, I moved through this environment, a stark reminder of the deep healing still needed within myself and within my family.

The constant barrage of negativity and control was stifling. I often felt like I was suffocating under the weight of expectations and criticisms that seemed impossible to meet. It was as if I were a track runner expected to leap through hoops engulfed in flames, with no guidance or support. No matter how much I tried, it felt as though my efforts were never enough.

The dynamic of guilt surrounding me going to work while simultaneously being expected to contribute financially for childcare, was a perplexing and emotionally draining experience. It felt like a constant tug-of-war between being criticized for striving to provide for my daughter, and being coerced into financial obligations. The manipulation and conflicting expectations left me feeling disheartened and frustrated, as if, in my mom's eyes, no path or choice I chose was ever the "right" one.

The weight of these conflicting demands was overwhelming. On one side, I was pouring my energy into building a stable financial future for my daughter and myself through my art business. Yet, on the other, my mom made me feel guilty for not being home with my daughter enough or for relying on her for childcare—despite her being paid. The situation made no sense. My business allowed me to be home during the week, with my busiest hours primarily on weekends, meaning I was around more often than not. Still, she would find ways to make me feel wrong, no matter how I managed my time. The criticism was relentless, a never-ending cycle of being judged for working hard while also being pressured to contribute financially. It was a toxic loop of guilt and resentment that was wearing me down.

My mom's hurtful comments cut deeply, especially when she said things like, *"You don't want to be around your daughter because she looks like her dad,"* and did so in front of her. These words were not just a jab at me, but they planted seeds of pain within my daughter—reminiscent of how she had sown division and hurt between my sister and me when we were younger. It felt as if she was weaponizing my postpartum struggles and throwing them back at me, all while undermining the effort I was pouring into creating a better life.

Here I was, working to support us financially and pave a way out of this unhealthy family dynamic, yet her hand was always out for money in exchange for childcare. It was a constant contradiction—needing my support but shaming me for working to provide it. She'd even interrupt my attempts to parent, taking over and making it hard for me to establish my role as a mother.

I often found myself breaking down in tears, feeling manipulated and abused in my own home as an adult. The familiar weight of guilt, judgment, and constant criticism was stifling, trapping me in a cycle I'd worked so hard to escape. It was like reliving my teenage years all over again, walking on eggshells, trying to anticipate her next comment or accusation. The experience left me heartbroken and weary, yearning for freedom and a truly loving environment to raise my daughter.

The emotional and psychological toll was immense. It felt like no matter how hard I tried, every step forward was met with resistance and manipulation. My mom always told me that she felt it was her job to make my life difficult and she was definitely living up to that belief now. The subtle, yet potent, criticism made me second-guess my choices and doubt my ability to balance work and motherhood. I found myself once again entangled in a situation where I was both dependent on, and deeply hurt by, someone close to me. It was so suffocating.

Despite my best efforts to create a stable, loving environment for my daughter, the constant conflict with my mom made it nearly impossible. This trap was an old, familiar one—a pattern I'd known my whole life. And now, as a single mom with limited options and support, I felt ensnared in that same web, knowing I needed to create a way out but feeling the weight of it all bearing down on me.

It was a perfect storm: navigating the difficulty with my mom, being a single mom, building a business, and dealing with ongoing emotional abuse. This intense combination triggered all my past wounds to resurface in full force. I found myself living in a state of constant fear and suspicion, wary of everyone around me. My ability to feel safe had diminished significantly, pushing my hyper-vigilance into overdrive and making me extremely sensitive to my surroundings.

This heightened state of alert caused me to cocoon myself and my daughter at home much of the time. Venturing out became rare, and when we did, I was the epitome of a helicopter mom, always on edge and unable to relax. I observed other parents at the park, engrossed in their phones or books, seemingly oblivious to their children, and wondered how they could trust so freely. I couldn't fathom it.

To protect myself further, I kept extra weight on my body, hoping to deter unwanted attention from men. The thought of trusting anyone else with my daughter spiked my anxiety to unbearable levels, often forcing us to return home prematurely. My anxiety had become debilitating, coloring every aspect of my daily life and interactions, and significantly impacting my mental and emotional well-being.

Anything I thought I had conquered came roaring back, and I was overwhelmed by it all. I had tried countless avenues of healing—therapy, self-help books, workshops, personal development courses—and while each provided some relief, none truly got to the root of it. It felt as if a part of me remained untouched, a core pain buried so deep that none of these methods could fully reach or heal it. The surface work I had done wasn't enough, and I knew I needed something that would finally allow me to confront and transform the pain at its source.

In my moments of feeling utterly lost, with nowhere else to turn, I found myself reaching toward the one thing I had been avoiding: God. My relationship with God had always been complicated and conflicted. Anger simmered beneath the surface, directed at God for everything I had endured. The abuse, betrayals, heartbreaks—all of it made me question if there was any higher power at all, or if I had simply been left to face these battles alone. Yet, standing at this crossroads with nothing left to lose, I surrendered a quiet plea into the void, willing to reach out, even if part of me doubted whether anything would answer.

As I inched toward the Creator, I felt an equally gentle response. It wasn't some grand revelation, but a quiet, steady opening of my heart. Step by step, I was guided to the Foundation of Spiritual Development in San Rafael, where I learned tools that would change everything—ways to protect, ground, and clear my space, and, most importantly, to connect with God in a deeply personal way. These tools became essential lifelines, helping me shift from reactivity to being responsive. By grounding myself in the present, clearing my energy, and building strong spiritual boundaries, I could finally face the chaos with a newfound inner calm. The peace I found was real, subtle but strong, like an anchor in the storm.

As I grew calmer and more centered, I noticed a surprising and ironic twist: the tension with my mother only seemed to intensify. My newfound peace and refusal to engage in old patterns seemed to unsettle her, almost as if the calm I was cultivating threatened the familiar chaos of our dynamic. Her yelling and criticism ramped up, challenging my serenity at every turn. Maintaining my inner peace required constant effort—resetting my space, reconnecting with Creator multiple times a day. Yet, no matter how hard I tried, it never seemed like enough within the walls of our home. It was as if the higher frequency I was reaching was creating friction within her, stirring up more turbulence and lashing out in response.

To cope, I found myself stepping out of the house as often as possible, seeking refuge in nature's calm. Long walks in the park became my sanctuary, a space to clear my mind and find peace away from the relentless negativity at home. Spending time with friends who truly understood my journey and offered genuine support was a lifeline. These small escapes were essential, helping me avoid the constant tension and giving me the strength to keep moving forward. Each moment outside, each laugh with friends, each mommy-daughter date reminded me of the possibility of a life grounded in peace and positivity.

The man who had quietly supported my diaper drive, a fundraiser organized to provide diapers for my daughter, gradually became a more significant presence in my life. Our conversations extended for hours, delving into topics of healing, dreams, and future possibilities. This connection fostered a deep sense of kinship, despite the physical distance between us.

Living in Wisconsin, he was a father to three children and worked as a "sound magician," utilizing his talents both in healing workshops and as a DJ at various events. Our discussions often revolved around how we could merge our skills to craft transformative healing experiences for others, exploring the potential of combining sound therapy with my own practices.

As our relationship deepened, he shared plans to relocate from Wisconsin, which made the idea of a future together seem more feasible. The distance that once seemed like a barrier began to feel less daunting, opening up new possibilities for collaboration and connection in both our personal and professional lives.

As our connection grew, it became clear we were more than friends. The energy we shared felt like a breath of fresh air, a welcome shift from the struggles at home with my mom. The vision we built together opened new doors in my heart and mind, filling me with excitement for what could be—a much-needed light in a time that had been filled with so many challenges.

After months of intimate conversations, he finally visited me in San Francisco, and we fell into each other effortlessly. Our connection felt so natural, like we had known each other for lifetimes. For the first time in a long while, I felt hopeful about a romantic partnership. But shortly after we posted our first photo together, an intense reaction came from his old "business partner," a woman I hadn't heard much about. When I asked him about her response, he dismissed it casually, assuring me it was nothing to worry about. I decided to trust him, leaning into the connection we had built and the shared dreams we had for our future together.

The warmth and support he provided felt like a soothing balm to my weary soul. In our conversations, we delved into deep topics, shared our dreams, and discovered a shared purpose in helping others heal. The potential for both a personal and professional partnership was exhilarating, a spark of possibility that ignited hope within me. It truly felt as if the universe had aligned to bring us together, opening a doorway to something profoundly beautiful and transformative.

Our time together in San Francisco was nothing short of magical. We wandered through the city, sharing laughter, dreams, and the undeniable resonance of our energies combined. When he DJed a local event and I set up to do my art, it felt as if our worlds intertwined seamlessly, each enhancing the other. The synergy between us created a harmonious blend of creativity and healing, a fusion that felt so fulfilling. This collaboration was not only a beautiful escape from the challenges I faced at home but also a glimpse into a future where our combined strengths and gifts could offer something transformative to others. It was an invitation to something far more profound than I had imagined.

His presence filled a void I hadn't realized had grown so deep. There was a peace and joy in being with him that I had been missing for a long time. His unwavering support and encouragement made me feel genuinely seen and appreciated, and I cherished each moment we spent together.

Despite the initial hiccup with his former business partner, I felt secure in what we were co creating. Our conversations about plans and dreams painted a hopeful picture of a future where distance wouldn't stand in our way. Our shared vision of organizing healing experiences for others was a powerful motivator, lighting a path forward that felt both inspiring and aligned. I was excited to see how this new path would unfold, eager for the day when we could fully unite our talents and dreams into something impactful.

Visiting him in his home state brought some unexpected revelations. The moment I saw he was still wearing his wedding ring from his previous marriage, a wave of unease hit me. I asked him about it, hoping for an explanation that would make sense, and he simply replied that he had "cleared the energy around it." While I understood the idea of clearing energy and detaching from past connections, something about it just didn't sit right with me. Why would anyone choose to keep wearing a ring from a past marriage if they had truly moved on? It felt like a lingering attachment, an unresolved thread, and I couldn't shake the discomfort it stirred within me.

The visit started with a lot of promise, but soon took an unsettling turn. At his workplace, a woman familiar with him approached, focusing her attention solely on him in a manner that felt pointed and exclusionary. Her behavior was not just unwelcoming—it underscored that I was an outsider. It was clear she was there for him and had no interest in me, setting a tone that felt deliberately dismissive.

This encounter led to our first significant argument on the way home, marking the beginning of a disturbing pattern. His responses were defensive, revealing a lack of emotional intelligence that I hadn't perceived before. This shift in his behavior, from the warmth we had shared to a sudden coldness and defensiveness, threw me off balance. It was a jarring contrast to the connection we'd built, and it made me question the depth of his emotional understanding and our compatibility.

The situation escalated further when we were at his house. Unexpectedly, his ex-wife appeared, letting herself in with her own key, as if it were the most natural thing in the world. I was in the kitchen when she walked in, and her presence caught me completely off guard. Her cold stare and the ease with which she entered the home left me confused and uncomfortable, questioning the boundaries and the nature of their current relationship.

Cornered in the kitchen, I felt vulnerable and deeply uneasy. The initial warmth and connection I had felt with him began to dissipate, replaced by a growing sense of confusion and mistrust. I was trapped, with my flight home not until later, struggling to make sense of the tumultuous events and lacking any stable ground in the chaos that had unfolded around me. This experience highlighted the complexities of his personal life that I had not been fully aware of, causing me to reconsider my feelings and the potential future of our rclationship.

These questions echoed in my mind, each one deepening my doubts and turning my initial excitement into worry. *Why was she allowed to walk in whenever she pleased? Why did she still have a key? And why, after everything, was he still wearing his wedding ring?*

It felt like each answer he gave unraveled another layer of complexity, revealing a situation far more entangled than he'd led me to believe. The clarity I'd once felt about us was slipping, replaced by an unease that wouldn't quiet down. It was as if I'd been shown one version of his life, and now the real one was coming to light. I began to seriously question the foundation of our relationship and the sincerity of his intentions, unsure of what was real and what was simply an illusion I wanted to believe in.

I summoned every bit of courage I had and confronted him, hoping for the clarity and reassurance I desperately needed. But his responses were evasive, filled with vague justifications that only heightened my confusion. At the time, I didn't know the term *gaslighting,* but looking back, it was clear he was attempting to blur my sense of reality, making me question my own perceptions.

What had once felt magical and destined was now marred by cracks that seemed impossible to ignore. His lingering attachment to the past, whether intentional or not, undermined the trust I'd tried to build with him. The foundation of our relationship felt shaky, no longer the safe, aligned partnership I'd thought it to be.

This visit, which I had hoped would strengthen our bond, instead highlighted the cracks and inconsistencies in his story. I felt a growing sense of disillusionment and betrayal, as the reality of the situation became more apparent. Despite the strong connection we had initially felt, these red flags were impossible to ignore.

I returned home with a heavy heart, uncertain about the future of our relationship. The magical moments we'd shared now felt overshadowed by doubts and lingering questions. It was a stark reminder that love and connection, as powerful as they are, aren't enough to sustain a relationship—trust and transparency are equally essential. I realized that, despite the spark between us, the cracks in our foundation couldn't be ignored. I had to reevaluate what I truly needed and deserved in a partner, even if it meant facing the possibility of letting go.

As I processed the experience, I realized the importance of listening to my intuition and honoring my feelings. The red flags were there for a reason, and I needed to trust myself enough to heed their warning. This journey of self-discovery and healing was far from over, and I had to stay true to my path, even if it meant letting go of a relationship that no longer felt right.

All the old alarms were going off in my body, making it impossible to feel safe and trust him. Despite the initial promise and the strong connection we had, the inconsistencies and lack of transparency created an insurmountable barrier. Our relationship ultimately fizzled out. We did manage to put together an amazing workshop, helping others transform and hosting an event where his friends experienced the joy of being bedazzled with my C-

Love art. The potential for greatness and co-creation was there, which made it all the more disheartening when it didn't work out. The experience left me feeling bittersweet—grateful for the moments of creativity and connection, yet heavy with the realization that trust is the bedrock of any lasting relationship.

It was so sad to realize that this relationship didn't have the actual legs to go the distance. But I was equally proud of myself for recognizing that and not staying, as I might have in the past. Despite the promising beginnings and shared dreams, the underlying issues and red flags made it impossible to build a solid foundation. In hindsight, I can see that this connection was a dead end from the start—limited by a lack of transparency and integrity. As far as I know, he still hasn't moved from his state, making me feel, in some ways, manipulated and led on. It was a lesson in trusting my instincts and refusing to settle for anything less than genuine honesty and clarity.

Eventually, I uncovered the truth: the woman who had reacted so strongly to our first photo was more than just his "business partner." They had been lovers, and he hadn't even officially ended things with her—she only realized their relationship was over when she saw that photo of us together. I felt a deep compassion for her, understanding the betrayal she must have felt. He seemed to have a pattern—moving from one woman to the next, hoping it would lead to both romance and a business venture. This revelation stung, yet it brought clarity and relief. I was thankful I hadn't stayed involved any longer and that I'd left before things became more entangled. While heartbreak never feels great, this was a healthier ending than others I'd endured in the past. It reminded me that I was making progress—choosing myself, setting boundaries, and recognizing what I deserved in a relationship.

This experience taught me the importance of trusting my intuition and recognizing red flags from the beginning. The pattern of deceit and manipulation was undeniable, but I made a conscious choice to focus on the lessons and positive takeaways. Despite the hurt, this situation became a powerful catalyst for my own self-awareness and growth, showing me how much stronger and wiser I had become. It reinforced my commitment to honor my needs and boundaries, transforming pain into a stepping stone on my journey toward a healthier future.

This ending represented a pivotal moment in my journey. Unlike past relationships, where I often felt ensnared and manipulated, this time I saw the signs early and made the empowered choice to walk away. It was a profound testament to my growth and commitment to self-respect and authenticity. I was learning to trust myself more deeply, honoring my own needs and boundaries with a strength that had taken years to cultivate. This decision reaffirmed that I was finally prioritizing my well-being and embracing a healthier, more fulfilling path forward.

In the aftermath, I poured my energy into my art and my business, using the lessons from this relationship to fuel my determination. I continued to build on the foundation I had created, knowing that every setback was an opportunity for growth. I was on a path of continuous evolution, embracing the highs and lows with an open heart and an unwavering commitment to my own well-being and dreams.

Despite all the healing I had done, the thought of fully stepping into single motherhood outside of my mom's house felt overwhelming. The idea of managing *everything* alone—finances, childcare, and the emotional load—seemed insurmountable. My mother's haunting words echoed relentlessly in my mind: "You're only going to attract a man who'll do the same things to your daughter as what happened to you." These words stirred every fear and self-doubt, making me question whether I was truly capable of building a healthy life for us on my own. Her words felt like a shadow looming over my progress, casting doubt on my newfound confidence and testing my commitment to breaking the cycles of the past.

And yet, I was determined.

Those words, rooted a profound fear within me. I found myself constantly questioning my ability to protect and provide for my daughter, and memories of my own trauma resurfaced, making it hard to imagine a future where she could grow up truly safe and secure. The fear of history repeating itself hovered over me like a dark cloud, shadowing every effort I made to build a better life. I feared that finding a worthy partner who wouldn't harm her might be out of reach, as if past cycles were destined to replay no matter what I did.

Discovering the Shield Maiden program felt like a moment of serendipity. The business page I followed had posted about this upcoming all-women's leadership and entrepreneurship program, and as I watched the inviting video crafted by the facilitator, it resonated deeply with me—as if it were an answered prayer. It spoke directly to my heart, compelling me to join.

Led by Setema Gali, a coach and mentor who is both a husband and father, the program understood the intricate balance between family life and ambition. This was exactly the guidance I needed as an entrepreneurial mom. The program significantly broadened my capabilities as a businesswoman and a mother, instilling a renewed strength and belief in my potential.

We delved into not only entrepreneurial skills and strategies but also acquired resources to craft empowering lives and cultivate leadership skills. My business began to flourish under this newfound knowledge, and for the first time, I saw a future where my dreams were not just dreams but financially viable realities.

Participating in Shield Maiden reinforced my strength in areas where I had felt weak and broken and bolstered my faith in myself, in the power of connecting with other women, and in my spiritual beliefs. It was a transformative experience that reshaped how I viewed myself and my potential in business, as a mom and my personal life.

I wanted to continue with the next round, but the tension at home with my mom had reached a breaking point. The conflicts were consuming, and I knew it was time for my daughter and me to find our own nest—a space where we could settle, thrive, and grow.

The support and camaraderie I found in Shield Maiden were priceless. Surrounded by like-minded women who were also balancing the demands of motherhood and entrepreneurship, I finally felt the sense of community and understanding I had been yearning for. Setema Gali's guidance was invaluable; he helped me recognize my potential and showed me how to harness my strengths effectively. Under his mentorship, my business flourished, and my confidence soared. For the first time, I felt like I was truly stepping into the empowered version of myself that I had always aspired to be.

As my external world blossomed, the internal tension at home became unbearable. My mom and I clashed constantly; the arguments, criticism, and lack of support reached an all-time high. She continually undermined my role as a mother, letting my daughter call her "mom" without correcting her and accusing me of not wanting to be with her, despite the fact that I was working to provide for us. Reaching my breaking point, I realized I could no longer allow this dynamic to continue. The boundaries between her role as a grandparent and mine as a mother were blurred beyond recognition.

It was a confusing push-pull—she guilted me for working yet expected payment for watching her own grandchild. She'd even intervene when I disciplined my daughter, going so far as to spank her despite my clear stance against physical punishment. It was "her house, her rules" all over again—except now it involved my child. I'd finally had enough, my daughter was getting close to starting kindergarten. I knew that to protect both my daughter and myself, I had to make a drastic change.

For my daughter and me to truly thrive, it was essential to create our own space—a sanctuary where we could grow, be nurtured, and heal together. The toxicity at my mom's house served as a constant reminder of the unresolved past I was working diligently to break free from, and it became clear that building a fresh, nurturing environment was no longer just a wish—it was a necessity. This new space would be the foundation for a healthier life, where we could start anew and finally leave behind the patterns that had held us back for so long.

Leaving was one of the hardest decisions I'd ever made. The fear of stepping out on my own as a single mom and taking on such a huge financial responsibility was nearly paralyzing. But the growth I'd experienced through Shield Maiden had instilled a new sense of confidence in me. I knew, despite the doubts and worries, that I had the strength and resilience to create a stable, nurturing home for my daughter. This belief in myself became the foundation I needed to push past the fear and move forward, ready to embrace the unknown for the sake of our future.

Finding our own place was an emotional rollercoaster, filled with excitement and fear in equal measure. Each stage—searching for the right home, filling out applications, and packing up our things—was a mix of liberation and anxiety. There were moments of intense doubt, where I questioned if I could really make it work on my own. But I held tight to the vision of creating a safe, loving home for my daughter and me, knowing that stepping away from the familiar was a necessary step toward thriving.

After five years of relentless dedication, my art business finally reached a level where I felt secure enough to step out of my mom's house. Moving into our own space became a crucial step in breaking free from the unhealthy family dynamics that had held me back. But finding a place was no easy feat. I didn't have credit—not even decent credit—and no regular paycheck to verify my income. All I had were my Venmo transactions and my word to prove my earnings. I was 100% committed to making this happen, no matter the odds. Every setback only strengthened my resolve, fueling my determination to give my daughter and me a place we could truly call our own.

Finding a place that would suit both our needs and our budget was challenging in the Bay Area. I quickly realized that $2,000 a month didn't stretch as far as it used to, leaving us with cramped studios and tiny one-bedrooms. And with my daughter's lively, curious energy, I could feel the owners' hesitation as soon as they saw her. Each rejection felt like another hurdle, but my commitment to building a home for us was unwavering. I was determined to make it happen, no matter how many doors we had to knock on.

Every "no" only strengthened my determination to find a place that truly felt like home. Each rejected application and ill-fitting apartment fueled my resolve to keep searching. The process was exhausting, with doubts slipping in during late nights and long days, but there was no going back. I knew that a stable, nurturing home for us wasn't just a dream—it was a necessity. I was committed to making this happen, no matter how many places we had to look at.

The moment I stepped into the townhome on the border of Concord and Pleasant Hill, I felt a familiar warmth—a positive energy that made me feel at ease. It was more than I could have hoped for: a two-story townhome with two bedrooms, one and a half baths, and partially furnished. The landlady, an older woman with children and grandchildren of her own, was completely unfazed by my daughter's boundless energy. I could feel her understanding and acceptance radiate, a refreshing change from the dismissive reactions we had encountered elsewhere. Standing in that space, I felt a glimmer of hope that this might actually be the home we were meant to find.

I couldn't believe it. My honesty had actually paid off. Despite my unconventional income and lack of formal financial documentation, she chose us because she valued my transparency and sincerity. She shared that other candidates, though seemingly more qualified on paper, had lied to her about something as simple as smoking. Knowing that my openness had set us apart was incredibly validating. For the first time in a long time, I felt truly seen and appreciated for who I was, and it was a reminder that honesty and integrity can pave the way even through the toughest challenges.

Tears streamed down my face as her words sank in—a profound reminder that staying true to myself could indeed open doors, even when the odds felt stacked against me. Moving into our new home felt like a dream finally realized. We began to make the space our own, filling it with little touches of warmth and love. Each day, as we unpacked and settled in, it felt like we were not only creating a home but also building a foundation for a brighter, healthier future.

The townhome quickly became our sanctuary, our own little momma-and-baby-bear fairy den. I decorated it with love and care, filling each room with vibrant colors, art, and photos that breathed life and warmth into the space. My daughter had her very own room—a place she could call hers, where she could play, grow, and feel completely safe. It was a fresh start, a cozy nest filled with love and possibility, ready for us to make new memories together.

In our new home, I felt an overwhelming sense of stability and peace. The constant tension and conflict we'd lived with were finally gone, replaced by freedom and calm. We were able to create our own rhythms and routines, free from judgment and interference. This space allowed me to focus more deeply on my business, which continued to flourish, and—most importantly—to be the mom I wanted to be. Without anyone undermining or intruding on our lives, I could embrace motherhood fully and lead our little family with confidence and love.

This home felt like a divine gift, a door opened by God just when we needed it most. Moving into this spacious two-story townhome after years of being confined to a tiny room was exhilarating yet surreal. It was a new chapter for us—a single mom and her little chick, finally able to spread our wings in our own space. Adjusting to this freedom and space took time; my daughter and I both needed to decompress from the constraints and tension of my mom's house. My nervous system was finally able to begin resetting, free from daily arguments and the weight of constant criticism. This home became not just a shelter, but a place of healing and peace.

It truly felt like a dream—a step closer to the life I had been striving for, with a touch more freedom and room to grow. The shift was profound. The quietness of our new home was a revelation, a stark contrast to the turmoil we'd left behind. For the first time in years, I could breathe deeply, savoring the calm that replaced the toxic dynamics we'd endured. Tears of gratitude flowed often; I was so incredibly thankful for this sanctuary, this fresh start. Each tear felt like a release, a letting go of the past, and a welcome embrace of the peace we were building.

Our mornings were filled with the gentle rhythm of getting ready for the day—our own peaceful routine that set the tone for everything else. In the evenings, a quiet calm would settle over us as we unwound together, sharing stories and cuddles. This newfound stability ignited a sense of confidence and empowerment in both of us. I felt more grounded in my role as a mother, and I could see my daughter blossoming, her spirit thriving in an environment that nurtured and celebrated her. It was as if our new home had given us both the space to grow, to breathe, and to simply be.

It was a sanctuary where arguing, criticism, and disconnection were not the daily experience. Instead, we built a foundation of love, support, and understanding.

In this new space, we found peace and stability that had been missing for so long. The quiet mornings, the laughter echoing through the rooms, and the shared moments of joy and discovery brought us closer together. We no longer had to tiptoe around the unhealthy dynamics of my mother's house. Instead, we had the freedom to create our own flow.

You Can't Break It

What's a heart
I'm not quite sure
Because I don't have all of mine
It's been left here and there
Bits and pieces
Fragments
Spread out through time
Taken away
Or given
And not reciprocated
Either way these parts are gone
Even with glue
I couldn't put it back together
Because the pieces aren't here anymore
Some were stolen
Along with my childhood innocence
And the craziest thing
Is no matter how many get broken off
And subtracted from my heart
It still beats
It still loves
It still gives
Not less
But a whole lot more
No matter how crumbled of a heart

That I have left
It doesn't feel any less
It pumps harder
Cares stronger
Quicker longer
It never fails
You took it
He took it
She took more
Break it
Stomp it
Shoot it
Stab it
But no matter what
It ticks
It tocks
Beats steadily
It won't give up
Not on you, her, him, me
Not on life
People
NOT ON HUMANITY
It will hurt
It WILL bleed
But it WILL get up and keep going
Again and again and
AGAIN...

Cassandra Love Lambert, November 2007

C-LOVE

Chapter 26
Divine Guidance & Trusting Myself

Moving out of my mom's house didn't mean we were entirely free of her influence. It just meant that from Monday to Friday, we finally had our own sanctuary—our own space without her constant control, criticism, and 'rules.' Yet, due to the nature of my work, which primarily took place on weekends, she remained the primary babysitter for my daughter. The fear of making the wrong choice in a sitter and the possibility of abuse haunted me. So, every weekend, I'd drive three hours to drop my daughter off at my mom's house and then another three hours to pick her up after a grueling 20-30 hour work weekend.

While we had moved out and gained some level of freedom, the cost was immense. The long drives, the exhaustion, and the emotional toll of returning to my mom's home each weekend weighed heavily on me. It was like living in two worlds—one where we could breathe and be ourselves, and another where I felt like a puppet being pulled back into old patterns and control. We were no longer under her roof, but her shadow loomed large over our lives.

Despite the strained relationship with my mom and the unresolved issues from our past, I had to acknowledge that in some ways, she was a better grandmother than she had been a mother. Time had taught her hard lessons about protecting children from the dangers of predatory men, lessons she had learned the painful way. With her, I at least knew what to expect; the idea of leaving my precious baby girl with a complete stranger sent my nervous system into a tailspin. The mere thought of it made my body seize up with fear. I couldn't bear the unknowns and potential risks of trusting someone new.

So, we navigated this complicated arrangement together, trying to strike a balance between my need for independence and the practical reality of needing childcare. It wasn't easy, and it was far from ideal, but I made the best choice I could given the circumstances.

I also gained a significant amount of weight during this time—a physical manifestation of the emotional burdens I was carrying. The stress, the constant fear of being fully on my own with a little girl to protect, felt like it anchored itself directly into my body. Each pound felt like another layer of armor, an unconscious attempt to shield myself from the overwhelm and fear. The weight gain wasn't just about the stress of single motherhood; it was a reflection of the complex, tangled emotions I was navigating without the tools to process them fully. It became a visible reminder of the heaviness I felt inside, and the sense that I was carrying the weight of the world on my shoulders. The flood of emotions felt overwhelming and impossible to untangle on my own. I knew deep down that I couldn't navigate this alone—I needed help.

My daughter's fierce tantrums became increasingly difficult to manage as she got older. The intensity of her outbursts would send my nervous system into overdrive. I'd feel a wave of panic wash over me, as though I were in real danger. It was confusing and disorienting to feel this level of fear toward my own child—a small, innocent being who, logically, posed no threat. But the loud screaming, kicking, and uncontrollable fits triggered something deep inside me, making it almost impossible to stay calm. It was as if the trauma stored in my body was suddenly activated, bringing up visceral reactions that felt far beyond my control.

The combination of the weight gain, which felt like a physical embodiment of my unprocessed stress, and the sheer overwhelm of handling her tantrums created the perfect storm. I often found myself crying, turning toward the Creator and asking for help, feeling utterly lost and helpless in those moments. I knew there was something deeper at play, something I couldn't untangle or resolve on my own. It was a call to heal the parts of me that were still wounded and reacting to old, unresolved pain.

Recognizing the need for deeper healing, I sought out a local therapist and returned to EMDR (Eye Movement Desensitization and Reprocessing) therapy—a powerful psychotherapy technique designed to help people heal from traumatic memories and distressing life experiences. My hope was to begin unraveling the intense and overwhelming layers of trauma that had resurfaced, layers deeply intertwined with my own painful childhood and the immense responsibility of now safeguarding my daughter. It's hard to put into words the profound impact that motherhood can have on trauma survivors. It's as if the act of becoming a mother cracks open the sealed vault of old wounds, especially if you grew up without adequate protection.

The challenge of being a nurturing and protective mother, when I had never truly felt protected myself, felt like venturing into uncharted territory without a map. It was daunting, to say the least. Each tantrum from my daughter, every overwhelming moment, seemed to drag the ghosts of my own past into the present, pulling me into a swirling vortex of fear and reactivity. The therapy sessions became a vital lifeline—a sanctuary where I could start to disentangle the complex threads of my history.

This journey was especially grueling as a single mom. I often found myself wondering how different it might have been if I had a solid partner by my side—someone to share the load, offer emotional support, and help me navigate the turbulence. But that wasn't my story. Instead, I faced the weight of it all—both literally and figuratively—alone. The emotional toll was heavy, compounded by the sheer responsibility of managing everything without a partner's steady presence to lean on. The isolation added another layer of complexity, making an already challenging healing process feel even more intense.

Not to mention, the idea of hiring a new sitter was financially impossible—it would have been like paying two rents on top of all the other bills and responsibilities. The relentless financial pressure was suffocating, leaving me no room to slow down, breathe, or relax. If I wasn't physically working, I was thinking about work, spending time with my daughter, or tackling the endless tasks that came with running a household. Downtime became a distant memory.

This constant, unyielding pressure forged a level of independence in me that I hadn't known before. It instilled a "lone ranger" mentality, as I realized everything relied solely on me. The weight of it all was immense, and the responsibility felt crushing at times. Yet, despite the exhaustion, there was a depth of resilience building inside me—a determination to push forward, even when it felt impossible.

The relentless hustle to make ends meet, coupled with the emotional weight of being the sole provider and protector for my daughter, was utterly exhausting. Moments of pure joy and connection with her were often interrupted by waves of deep fatigue and overwhelming anxiety about the future. I had to be strong, resourceful, and resilient, sometimes pushing through at the expense of my own well-being. There was no room for weakness, no time to get sick, no time to fall apart—I felt like I had to be everything, all the time.

While this forged an incredible inner strength, it also left me feeling depleted, like I was pouring from an empty cup. I was constantly in survival mode, treading water just to keep us afloat. It was a lonely, heavy burden to carry, and it made the quiet moments of snuggling with my daughter, or watching her laugh and play, feel like precious glimpses of the life I was fighting so hard to create for us.

I am convinced single moms are superheroes—the kind who navigate the world with resilience and grace, carrying the weight of both the provider and nurturer. We hold the fort down even when we feel like we're falling apart, and we love with a ferocity that defies exhaustion and fear. It's a cape that's invisible but woven from pure grit, determination, and an unbreakable bond of love.

This chapter of my life was a crucible of transformation, shaping me into someone stronger and more self-reliant than I ever thought possible. It pushed me to tap into reserves of resilience and grit I didn't even know I had. Yet, it also revealed the critical need for self-care and the importance of seeking support, even when it felt impossible or out of reach. I learned that while independence is a powerful asset, it's not sustainable without moments of surrender and the willingness to lean on others.

The lessons I absorbed during this time were invaluable. I discovered the delicate balance between fierce independence and the humility required to ask for help. It wasn't about giving up my strength; it was about recognizing that true strength lies in knowing when to rest, when to receive, and when to allow others to hold space for me. This period was as much about becoming the warrior I needed to be, as it was about learning the art of self-compassion and allowing myself the grace to be human. Moms may be superheroes, but they're also allowed to be fully human.

As I continued diving deeper into my healing journey and gaining inner strength, my business, C-Love, blossomed right alongside me. With every layer of myself I uncovered and transformed, C-Love expanded, drawing in a growing community of "C-Love Sparkle Babes." I began attracting other moms who were seeking ways to supplement their income while also craving a creative outlet. These women became part of the C-Love team, bringing joy, sparkle, and connection to every event.

I loved training them, sharing the techniques, tools, and heart behind the art, and watching them light up with newfound confidence. Together, we tackled larger gigs, each event a testament to the power of collaboration and a shared vision. It felt incredible to build something that not only financially supported me and my daughter, but also empowered other moms to shine in their own right. C-Love was becoming a collective—a movement of moms and women spreading love, one brushstroke at a time.

It was incredibly rewarding to help other moms in a meaningful way. Knowing that I was financially contributing to their households while also spreading love, joy, and positivity through our art was deeply fulfilling. We weren't just working together; we were building a community of support. The bonds we formed ran deeper than business. We became a sisterhood, sharing in the ups and downs of motherhood, navigating the challenges of raising children while making people feel beautiful and having fun.

We lifted each other up, whether it was sharing tips on self-care, or celebrating each other's wins. It felt like we were co-creating something much bigger than ourselves—an ecosystem of support, love, and empowerment. This was more than just a job or a business venture. It was a movement, a mission, and a family, all rolled into one beautiful journey of connection and transformation.

As our presence at events in the Bay Area grew, so did our reputation. People loved the energy we brought—the joy, the creativity, and the genuine connections we made with each person we touched. The smiles and laughter we created were contagious, and it became clear that what we were offering was more than just face painting, body art or makeup. Each sparkle, each painted face, was a small act of love, contributing to a larger wave of positivity that rippled through the events we attended.

The business was thriving, and with every new gig, I felt an expanding sense of purpose and pride. It went far beyond just financial stability; it was about the impact we were making. We were creating memorable transformative experiences, bringing a little extra magic into people's lives, and sharing genuine moments of connection. I realized that C-Love was more than just a business—it was a movement fueled by joy, love, and the power of art to transform, uplift, and heal.

While my business was flourishing and I was making a positive impact on others, it often felt like I was fighting an uphill battle behind the scenes. Despite moving out and creating a home for my daughter and me, my mom's control still loomed large. She seemed to find new ways to complicate things, creating unnecessary hoops for me to jump through and adding stress to even the simplest tasks. It felt as though she had unconsciously taken on the role of making my life more difficult, just as she had during my teenage years, almost as if she didn't know any other way to be with me.

It was a painful reminder of the deeply entrenched dynamics we were still caught in—a cycle of control and criticism that persisted, even with the physical distance I had put between us. The emotional toll was immense. While I was working hard to build a life and business that aligned with my true self, the unresolved tension with my mom constantly drained my energy and spirit. It felt like a trap I couldn't escape, especially with the fears I had around trusting anyone else with my daughter's care. As long as my daughter was little, I couldn't see a way out of this entangled arrangement. It was as though I was tethered to the very dynamic I fought so hard to break free from.

The hoops I had to jump through just to get to work and run my business were exhausting. It was as if she couldn't relinquish her need to control and criticize, even though we no longer lived under the same roof. Her influence lingered like a shadow, reminding me that while I was fighting hard to break free and step into my independence, the dynamic between us still needed deep healing. It was a stark reminder that breaking generational patterns is a long, grueling journey, and I often questioned if it was even possible—especially when I felt like I was the only one putting in the work to heal.

Whenever I received job offers, I had to run them by my mom for childcare, and she would rarely give me a clear yes or no. Her vague responses left me in limbo, making it impossible to plan ahead or confirm gigs. I found myself in a constant scramble, trying to coordinate everything at the last minute. Even though I paid her for babysitting, she often refused to help with pickup or drop-off, which meant I had to make the long drive back and forth to Stockton while living in the Walnut Creek area and working events in San Francisco. The constant back-and-forth was exhausting, stretching me thin. And if I showed up to a family event like my niece's birthday party and was visibly tired from the long hours and endless driving, I'd get scolded for dozing off. It was a relentless cycle that made an already demanding schedule even more grueling, leaving me with no room to rest or recharge.

There were countless nights when I found myself drifting off at the wheel, forcing me to pull over at random gas stations just to catnap because I physically couldn't keep my eyes open. The relentless hoops my mom made me jump through, coupled with the long, late-night work hours, took a massive toll on my body and mind. Despite the sheer exhaustion and my nonstop efforts to balance everything, I was met with criticism rather than understanding or support. It added to my growing frustration and deepened my sense of being misunderstood.

I was pushing myself to the absolute limit to provide for my daughter and build a better future for us, yet in my mom's eyes, it never seemed like enough. I couldn't understand why her approval mattered so much to me, especially considering her own parenting track record. By the time she was my age, my siblings and I had already endured significant abuse and trauma. Was she really in a position to pass such harsh judgment when she hadn't protected her own children or been the perfect mother herself? These questions gnawed at me, leaving me to grapple with the complex mix of seeking her validation while knowing deep down that she might never truly give it.

Despite all the challenges, I pushed forward, driven by the fierce love for my daughter and the desire to make my business a success. The hurdles, instead of defeating me, only strengthened my resolve. Each obstacle became fuel for my determination—a reminder of why I had to keep going. I was no longer just trying to survive; I was fighting to break free from the cycle I had inherited, to build a different kind of life for us. The adversity I faced, instead of knocking me down, propelled me to dig deeper and commit even more fully to our future.

I tapped into an unbreakable inner warrior spirit, a part of me I hadn't fully realized before. No matter what came my way, I found a way to alchemize it—to turn every challenge, every setback, into fuel for our journey. It was like discovering a new superpower: the ability to take anything life threw at me and transform it into something that could support and strengthen us. I learned that even the hardest experiences held the potential for growth and could be used for our betterment. This realization became my guiding force, empowering me to move through the obstacles with resilience and grace.

The difficulties I faced were relentless, but I kept hearing my Shield Maiden coach's voice in my head: "Stop wishing for life to get easier; wish for you to get stronger." This mantra became my guiding light, a reminder that strength and resilience were my greatest allies. Each obstacle became a test of my resolve, and rather than shrinking back, I leaned in, fully embracing the opportunity to grow stronger with every challenge. It wasn't about waiting for the storm to pass; it was about becoming the warrior who could weather it. I made a firm commitment to my goal of becoming self-sufficient and breaking free from my mom's control, knowing this was the path to creating a stable, healthy life for my daughter and me.

My first major goal was getting us into our own space, away from the constant chaos of my mom's house. The next goal was even bigger: to reach a point in my business where we were entirely self-sufficient, freeing us from the transactional, unhealthy relationship that still loomed over us. Everything always seemed to come back to money with my mom, and even when I paid her, the way she spoke to me lacked respect. It was manipulative and difficult, making every exchange feel torturous. Although we no longer lived under her roof, the weight of this connection still pressed heavily on my heart.

I decided to use this frustration as fuel. Instead of letting it defeat me, I let it drive me to learn more, take on more business courses, work harder and smarter, pray with more conviction, and surround myself with supportive people who believed in me. Each new piece of knowledge became a stepping stone toward true independence. With every challenge, I reminded myself of the vision I held for our future—one free of manipulation and control, filled instead with respect, love, and stability.

At this point, I felt a strong pull toward a local Christian church and connected with a truly sweet woman there who offered to do one-on-one Bible study with me. I had tried to read the Bible so many times before, but it had always felt like a foreign language—words that went right over my head. Yet, during this season of my life, everything began to click. The teachings resonated deeply, speaking directly to my heart and providing the kind of clarity and comfort I had long been searching for.

It was as if the messages in the Bible were tailor-made for me at this moment, offering insights and guidance I desperately needed. I finally understood why this book had been called a living word—it felt alive, speaking truth into my circumstances in a way that was undeniable.

I also began attending healing retreats through Celebrating Life Ministries, and I brought my daughter with me each time. These retreats became a sanctuary for us—a safe haven where we could find solace, healing, and community. They provided a much-needed reprieve from the challenges of daily life and a space where I could ground myself spiritually. Every time, I would place the relationship with my mom into their prayer bowl, holding onto the hope that we could eventually repair what was broken and transform it into something more peaceful and loving. It was an act of faith and surrender, a way to release the pain I carried and trust that, in time, healing could find its way into our fractured bond.

Despite the ongoing difficulties with my mom, these spiritual spaces gave me the strength to keep hoping for a better relationship. Placing our relationship into the prayer bowl felt like an act of surrender, a symbolic release of control and a gesture of trust that a higher power was at work. It allowed me to let go, if only for a moment, and step back from the heaviness of the day-to-day tension. Opening up to something greater than myself gave me a sense of relief—a chance to believe that healing was possible, even if I couldn't see the results right away. It was a way to stay connected to faith and the mystery of the divine, trusting that the process was unfolding in its own time, even if it didn't match my timeline or expectations.

This deepened my faith in the unseen. With every prayer, every retreat, and each symbolic gesture of release, I was building a foundation of trust in something greater than myself. I began to lean into the belief that there was a divine orchestration at play, even if I couldn't see it yet. It was like planting seeds in the dark soil—I couldn't witness their growth immediately, but I trusted they were taking root. This faith became a guiding force, giving me the resilience to keep moving forward, to keep believing in the possibility of transformation, and to keep nurturing hope, even when the circumstances seemed impossible.

I began to notice a profound shift as my relationship with God deepened. This newfound faith was unlike anything I'd experienced before; it was tangible and transformative. It became a lifeline, one I had no intention of letting go of ever again. For the first time, I felt held and guided by something far greater than myself. I witnessed firsthand the mysterious, yet unmistakable ways God worked through my life, opening doors, orchestrating connections, and constantly supporting us, even when things felt uncertain or impossible. It was as if God was breathing new life into every aspect of our journey, helping us rise above challenges and steadily improving our circumstances. This faith became an anchor, grounding me in a sense of peace and trust I had never known before.

With God on my side, my business flourished, attracting a steady stream of clients and incredible opportunities. It wasn't just about working harder anymore; I was working smarter, implementing the strategies and insights I had gained from the various coaches and mentors who had guided me along the way. We began booking events for major companies like Google, Uber, and Alaska Airlines, as well as collaborating with impactful local nonprofits such as Larkin Street Youth, Hack Cancer, and The Guardsmen.

Seeing these doors open and the momentum build was like watching the seeds I had planted over the years finally blossom. Each new gig was a confirmation that the path I had chosen was aligned with something greater, and the vision I held of a self-sufficient life was becoming tangible. The success wasn't just about financial stability—it was a testament to the power of perseverance, faith, and trusting the process.

Being asked to set up a face-painting and bedazzling station at Gia Coppola's wine booth at BottleRock was a thrilling opportunity. I was over the moon with excitement, knowing this was a big moment for C-Love. They asked me to incorporate their logo into my art, blending it into my bedazzling designs to help draw people to their booth. And it worked like magic! As soon as a few people started walking around with my art on them, word spread, and a long line quickly formed. I was busy non-stop, painting and connecting with people from morning until night each day.

The energy of the festival was electric, and being part of such a high-profile event sparked something new inside me. I realized I didn't just want to collaborate with others' booths—I wanted a C-Love booth of my own at BottleRock and other major festivals. I envisioned a vibrant, colorful space where festival-goers could come to be transformed, showered with joy, love, and sparkle. It would be a place where creativity and connection could thrive, leaving everyone who stopped by feeling seen and uplifted. This experience planted a powerful seed of possibility, expanding my vision for what C-Love could grow into and igniting a new level of passion and ambition for my business.

The energy of BottleRock was electrifying! The music, the food, the art, the wine—all of it came together to create an unforgettable atmosphere. Working with Gia Coppola's team was a highlight; they were enthusiastic about my work and made me feel like a valued part of their activation. The crowd's response was amazing; I loved watching people's faces light up as they saw their reflections adorned with my bedazzling art. It was deeply gratifying to witness that moment of joy and surprise, knowing that each brushstroke brought a little extra magic to their festival experience. This was a true celebration of creativity and connection, and it left me feeling inspired and ready to dream even bigger.

Each interaction reminded me why I embarked on this journey in the first place. The smiles, the laughter, and the sheer delight on people's faces made every ounce of effort worth it. I loved witnessing how my art could transform someone's day, even if just for a moment. It was this impact—the joy, the connection, the spark—that fueled me to keep pushing forward and to dream even bigger. As I stood there amidst the music and the energy of BottleRock, I knew I had to have my own C-Love booth at this event in the future. I didn't know *how* I would make it happen or what it would take, but I was certain of one thing: this vision was worth chasing down, no matter the obstacles.

I had no clue who to talk to or even where to begin in securing a booth at BottleRock. I started by reaching out to other vendors, exploring potential collaborations, but none of them panned out. It felt discouraging, but I was far from ready to give up on this dream. Determined to make it happen one way or another, I decided to pivot. The following year, I would set up my station down the road in a parking lot, catching people on their way into the festival. If I couldn't be inside just yet, I'd create my own opportunity right outside.

As always, the universe and God had their own plans, orchestrating a series of connections I couldn't have anticipated. One day, while I was painting faces, I met a woman who happened to be connected to someone with her own parking lot, right next to the event grounds. She generously offered me a place to stay at her house during the festival for the next year—an incredible blessing I hadn't expected.

A year flew by, and there I was, setting up at the corner of the parking lot, determined to make the most of the opportunity. As I laid out my paints and brushes on the first day, I could hear the unmistakable sound of Stevie Wonder playing live inside the festival. It transported me back to the few safe moments of my childhood—familiar, comforting, and filled with a sense of nostalgia. As fate would have it, one of the first faces I painted belonged to a young woman who was working the event. She was ecstatic with her face art and, without hesitation, took me to meet someone who played a pivotal role at BottleRock every year. The introduction left me buzzing with a mix of excitement and nervous hope.

I followed up later by connecting with him on Facebook, trusting that this could finally be the key to making my dream of having a C-Love booth inside of BottleRock a reality. It felt like yet another sign that when you take bold steps toward your dreams, the universe takes steps toward you, too. It was a powerful reminder that perseverance, committing to an intention and a little faith can open doors you never imagined.

After returning home from the festival, riding the high of all the incredible moments, I came across a Steve Jobs quote that hit me hard. It inspired me to write a raw, vulnerable post about my own life and the harsh things I'd overcome to get to where I was. I poured my heart into that post, not expecting much, but to my surprise, it went viral.

The person I had met at BottleRock saw it and was moved enough to share it with someone higher up at the BottleRock corporation. That person read it and reached out to me directly, telling me about exciting plans they had for the next year. They were going to create an actual spa experience at the event, and she wanted to connect me with the woman in charge of running it.

It felt like a divine orchestration—proof that when you show up authentically, even the harshest parts of your story can pave the way for incredible opportunities.

WOW, it's incredible how God orchestrates things through people, and how powerful it is when you follow those intuitive nudges and act with authenticity. When I look back, I realize how misguided the advice was from those who told me not to share my story. They thought I was playing the *'victim,'* but the reality was the opposite: by sharing my truth, I was stepping into my power by 'owning' my story, not shying away from it.

The more I shared openly, the more connections I made and the more support I received. I had so many people thanking me for my transparency and vulnerability—it made them feel seen, less alone, and more connected. It taught me that showing up as my whole self, scars and all, was the key to unlocking not only my own potential but also creating space for others to feel empowered in their own stories.

I learned that sometimes, the very thing people criticize is exactly what makes you unstoppable.

Sharing my journey—the raw struggles and the hard-won triumphs—was something I felt deeply called to do. It resonated with people on a profound level, offering them a sense of hope and connection. The messages of gratitude and encouragement I received from those who found strength in my vulnerability far outweighed the criticism from the naysayers. It was a powerful reminder that being unapologetically real and honest is what truly creates impact.

I made a conscious choice to tune out the naysayers completely. It never felt right to have people trying to silence me when I felt a deep, authentic calling to share my experiences. Their attempts to diminish my voice only strengthened my resolve to be open and genuine. I realized that by sharing my story, I was not just healing parts of myself but also offering a beacon of light to others who were navigating similar paths. My vulnerability became a bridge, connecting me to those who needed to know they weren't alone in their struggles.

Being true to myself and my journey allowed me to connect with people on a deeper, soul-level. It created a community rooted in support, shared experiences, and genuine understanding. I found that authenticity attracts authenticity—the more open and raw I was, the more I drew in the right people. Those who resonated with my story were the ones who mattered most. They were the ones who saw the real me, celebrated my growth, and became part of the incredible community we built together. It reinforced my belief that when you show up as your true self, you naturally attract the people who are meant to walk this path with you.

The experience at BottleRock, combined with the outpouring of support from the community, affirmed the incredible power of vulnerability and authenticity. It was a living testament that when we are brave enough to share our true selves, we open the door for divine orchestration. God's work often manifests through the people we meet and the connections we make, and it all starts with having the courage to show up fully and unapologetically. It was a powerful reminder that when we trust the process, step into our truth, and follow those inspired nudges, miracles unfold in ways we could never have planned.

The call came in from the woman managing the spa, and she laid out the details. This was going to be the most expensive booth I'd ever taken on—by a long shot. Not only was there a hefty vending fee, but we also had to pay additional fees per sale. On top of the financial weight, it was clear she wasn't entirely sold on the idea of our art being there. She expressed doubts, suggesting that our edgy, artsy style might not align with the more elegant, chic vibe of the BottleRock clientele and spa atmosphere.

But deep down, I knew we would be a hit. I had a strong feeling that our art, our vibe, and the energy we brought would stand out in a memorable way. So despite the doubts, I took a leap of faith, put my money on the line, and said, "Yes." It felt like another defining moment—one where I chose to trust my instincts, bet on myself, and believe in the magic we were capable of creating.

Being a part of the Live Love Spa at BottleRock was a crash course in growth, both as a businesswoman and as a leader for my Sparkle Babe team. The level of preparation required was intense—filled with a whirlwind of logistical challenges and financial hurdles. One of the biggest, most unexpected issues came at the last minute: we learned that all our booth fabrics needed to be treated with flame retardant spray. This wasn't something I had planned for at all, and the stakes were high. Without the treatment, we would have been forced to strip down all the decor—a decor that we had meticulously set up, piece by piece, for hours. It was an integral part of our booth's vibe and I was determined not to lose it.

It turned into a mad scramble, but with the help of many angels who showed up in the nick of time, we managed to find a business that sold the spray. We got it applied and secured the signed paperwork just as the festival doors were opening. In that moment, I learned a valuable lesson: when you're on the right path, even the most impossible situations can work out—sometimes by the skin of your teeth.

Despite the initial doubts and uncertainty, we became an incredible success at BottleRock. Our art resonated with the festival attendees far beyond what anyone had expected. Lines formed at our booth, and the joy we brought to each person who came to get sparkled was palpable. To our surprise and delight, we even ended up on the front page of the Napa Newspaper that year. This recognition was a powerful affirmation—validating all the hard work, late nights, and risks we took. It felt like a beautiful full-circle moment, proving that when you trust your vision and take bold leaps of faith, the universe rises up to meet you.

Being part of BottleRock and proving the skeptics wrong was a pivotal moment for my business. It reinforced my belief in the power of staying true to my vision and taking bold steps, even in the face of uncertainty. This experience didn't just boost our reputation; it solidified our place in the festival scene and deepened the bond within our team. We felt like we had overcome a huge milestone together. The success we achieved, despite the challenges, was a testament to our collective passion, creativity, and resilience. It was more than just a win—it was a validation of everything we'd built and a launchpad for even bigger dreams.

Our booth quickly became a beloved staple at BottleRock, a consistent space where festival-goers could come year after year to get bedazzled and experience the magic of C-Love. It was more than just a booth—it became a family. The connections we made with returning clients, the smiles, the laughter, and the shared moments of joy created a sense of community that made each year feel like a reunion. We weren't just adding sparkle to their day; we were adding a touch of love and connection, making our little corner of the festival a place people sought out, remembered, and cherished.

This experience taught me a few invaluable lessons: the importance of staying open to the magic of connections, trusting my intuition, and following it, no matter how unexpected the path might seem. It also reminded me of my worth—that I am deserving of amazing things and opportunities. We became a fixture at BottleRock every year after that, and I continued to refine and elevate C-Love, enhancing our offerings and expanding our reach. Each year was an opportunity to grow, to learn, and to serve our community with even more love and creativity. The journey was filled with challenges, but the rewards were far greater, proving to me time and again the power of resilience, authenticity, and faith.

Year after year, our presence at BottleRock became stronger and more impactful. Each event brought fresh opportunities, deeper connections, and an ever-expanding network of clients and supporters. We evolved from being a new face in the crowd to a beloved fixture, recognized for our vibrant, artistic energy and the joy we brought to festival-goers. Our booth wasn't just a place to get bedazzled; it became a destination, a space where people came to feel uplifted, express themselves, and share in the magic we created. It was a beautiful testament to the power of showing up authentically and building something rooted in love and connection.

C-LOVE

Chapter 27
Sometimes 'Chosen' Family Shows Up More Than Blood

Reconnecting with my 'chosen aunt' was a divine gift. She had been a steady presence throughout my life, popping in and out of my world like a guardian angel since my birth. She lived closer to us than my mom, in Hayward, and offered to watch my daughter for free. I was blown away by this gesture—it felt like such an incredible act of love, especially when compared to my mom's transactional approach from day one. It made me question the authenticity of my mom's role as a grandma, especially when I thought about all the times she made things so difficult for me, giving me vague or unclear answers about childcare and hindering my ability to accept gigs.

Anyone in the events industry knows how quickly you need to respond to job offers—if you can't say yes immediately, clients will move on and find someone else. So when my mom played these control games, it was not just frustrating; it directly affected my livelihood and our financial stability. Having someone I could genuinely trust with my daughter was a huge relief. It felt like a massive weight had been lifted off my shoulders. This chosen aunt's willingness to step up and help was a true Godsend. It gave me the space and freedom to focus on growing my business without the constant stress of navigating my mom's manipulative tactics.

Having her in my life felt like a breath of fresh air. Not only did she help with my daughter, but she also provided a safe, non-judgmental space where I could vent and share my true feelings without fear of criticism or scolding. I could talk openly about my business ideas and plans, and she'd listen with genuine interest, offering thoughtful feedback and encouragement. It felt like I finally had the mom figure I had always longed for—supportive, nurturing, and truly present.

Her and her husband's kindness and willingness to step up lightened the burden that often felt unbearable. It was the kind of support I didn't even realize I had been missing, and it made me feel a little less alone in this journey. I am forever grateful for their presence in our lives, for being the family I needed, especially in a time when everything felt overwhelming. Their love was a reminder that I didn't have to carry the load all by myself.

Every gesture of support from them was deeply meaningful, particularly because they were significantly older than my mom and had their own health challenges to manage. They couldn't always be available, but the moments they were able to offer support meant the world to me. These instances provided a precious glimpse of independence from my mom's involvement, allowing me to experience a sense of freedom that was both rare and invaluable. This brief relief from my usual responsibilities offered not just practical help but also an emotional reprieve, giving me a taste of what it might be like to have a support system that allowed me more autonomy and less reliance on my mom.

I poured my heart and soul into C-Love, continuously refining and expanding our services, always striving to create unforgettable experiences. It was more than just a business; it was a living, breathing manifestation of my passion and purpose. However, life has a way of surprising us, bringing unexpected challenges that we can't always anticipate or control. Despite the success and the incredible journey of growth, I never imagined this beautiful, divine creation would come to an end—or even a temporary halt.

Yet, I've come to understand that life's twists and turns, as unpredictable as they may be, often hold deeper meanings. Although C-Love may not look the same as it once did, the lessons, memories, and connections from this chapter are woven into the fabric of who I am. The experiences and the love shared through this venture will forever be a part of me, fueling whatever comes next on this wild, ever-evolving journey.

The constant driving back and forth to my mom's house was wearing me down, physically and emotionally. It became clear that I needed to find a way to create income from home—a shift that would allow me to be more present for my daughter and bring some much-needed stability to our lives. But beyond the logistical need, this realization awakened a deeper calling within me. I wanted to make a more profound impact on women's lives, moving beyond the surface-level beauty that C-Love had offered.

I yearned to help women feel beautiful on the inside too, to heal the wounds and traumas that had dimmed their light. I wanted to be a part of their deeper transformation, guiding them through their own healing journeys. I envisioned creating a space where women could feel seen, heard, and held as they worked through their inner struggles. This desire for a more meaningful, lasting impact was becoming undeniable—a calling I knew I had to answer.

Indeed, the adage "When the student is ready, the teacher will appear" has profoundly resonated with my experiences. At a pivotal moment when I was deeply contemplating my path and seeking greater depth in my endeavors, the Passion to Profit program came to my attention. Enrolling in this program was transformative and inspired me on multiple levels. It equipped me with the essential foundational skills necessary to elevate my visions to the next level.

The program taught us practical skills such as how to create a website and utilize design tools like Canva. For the first time, I could visually manifest my ideas, providing a clear and tangible glimpse into what my business could become. This ability to see my concepts take shape was not only affirming but also empowering. Having these tools at my fingertips allowed me to pivot toward creating a more impactful, heart-centered business, making my dreams seem even more attainable. This shift was a significant step in my journey, enhancing my confidence and capability to build something truly meaningful.

Not long after, a friend reached out and asked if I would be willing to be one of her practice clients as she was completing her training in a new healing modality. She offered me three free sessions. I jumped at the chance, curious about what new layers of healing and transformation might be available. Little did I know, this would be a pivotal moment that set the stage for my next chapter, deepening my own healing journey and expanding my vision of how I could help others heal.

When she came over for our first session, I wasn't sure what to expect, but I was open and curious. The modality she introduced me to was Clinical EFT Tapping (Emotional Freedom Techniques), an evidence-based therapeutic treatment that merges Neuroscience with Intuitive Practice.

EFT is a powerful method for safely releasing unwanted emotions, thoughts, and feelings like sadness, fear, anxiety, anger, guilt, shame, hurt, and grief. It works by reducing the emotional intensity associated with traumatic memories, phobias, and deep-seated fears. As we tapped through that initial session together, I felt an immediate resonance, like a switch being flipped on inside me. It brought back the familiar feeling I used to get in the acting classes at Seydways Theatre in San Francisco—a deep, intuitive "this is it" sensation.

At that moment, I realized that EFT was the thing I had been searching for, the next evolution in my journey. It was the tool I could use to help people go beyond surface-level transformations and truly heal on a deeper level.

The very next day, I felt a surge of excitement and clarity. Without hesitation, I signed up for my first training class toward becoming certified in EFT Tapping. The course was that summer in San Diego through EFT Universe, a well-respected organization in the field. I was eager to dive headfirst into this new modality, knowing how profoundly it had impacted me in just a few sessions.

I had experienced firsthand the incredible lightness that followed each session my friend had gifted me. Unlike other healing modalities I had tried, EFT Tapping seemed to get right to the core, uncovering and releasing deep-seated emotional pain. The results felt lasting and genuine, not like the temporary relief of a band-aid. It was clear to me that this was more than just another tool—it was a pathway to true, lasting transformation. I was ready to learn everything I could about it, so I could bring this powerful healing to others.

The more I learned about EFT Tapping, the more everything clicked into place. It was the perfect blend of psychology, energy work, somatics, and personal development. It addressed issues at their core, going beyond surface-level healing. I realized I had found a crucial missing piece in my own journey of transformation—one that I could also use to help others on a deeper level.

Integrating EFT (Emotional Freedom Techniques) Tapping into my work was a transformative experience. It opened up a new avenue to deeply connect with and support the women who sought me out. These women often came with profound emotional burdens: mother wounds, father wounds, struggles with attachment styles varying from anxious to avoidant, experiences of abuse, challenges with C-PTSD, and a desire to feel safe in their bodies again after periods of dissociation or living disconnected from their physical selves.

EFT Tapping provided a gentle yet powerful means to address these issues. This modality has a unique capacity to delve into the core of emotional pain and facilitate a release in a way that is both gentle and profound, leaving a sense of peace and tangible relief. It felt like discovering a key to unlocking profound healing, not only for myself but for the individuals I supported.

The ability to offer such a significant tool was not just a professional enhancement but a personal gift. I felt a deep sense of responsibility and eagerness to share this effective technique with a broader audience. EFT Tapping wasn't just another method; it was a transformative approach that could change lives by restoring emotional balance and fostering deep, lasting healing. I was ready and enthusiastic to bring this powerful tool to the world, eager to see the positive changes it could engender in others' lives just as it had in mine.

Incorporating EFT Tapping into my work felt like the most natural evolution of my journey. It seamlessly aligned with my vision of creating a space where women could come to heal, not just on the surface, but from the depths within. It was a powerful way to address the wounds left by facing life's monsters and breaking free from the traps so many of us find ourselves caught in. This wasn't about enhancing outer beauty anymore—it was about igniting true empowerment, cultivating self-love, and facilitating profound, lasting transformation.

I wanted every woman who came to me to feel seen, heard, and held with deep compassion on her path to wholeness. This was about getting to the root of the pain and helping women reclaim their inherent power, guiding them gently back home to themselves. It was a chance to heal beyond the surface, to mend the invisible scars, and to help them step fully into their authentic, vibrant selves.

C-LOVE

Chapter 28
Emotional Availability Can Be Deceiving

Dating as a single mom—or better yet, *attempting* to date as a single mom—could honestly fill an entire book. The characters I encountered, the ridiculous situations I found myself in, and the kind of nonsense this "modern dating" scene delivered were nothing short of legendary. At this point, I thought I had finally mastered the art of holding my boundaries and confidently say ing "next" when things weren't right.

Or so I thought.

I met this guy through Bumble who, at first glance, seemed genuinely nice and refreshingly simple. I appreciated how easy it felt to stay within my window of capacity with him—no emotional roller coasters, no overthinking. He was a dad with a son just a year older than my daughter, and he presented himself as divorced, framing the mom as the "bad guy" in their story.

We went on a few dates, and I couldn't help but notice how thoughtful and helpful he was. It was such a contrast to the "Peter Pan" types I had encountered in the Bay Area—men who were nowhere near dad material, let alone potential husband material. This guy felt different, like a breath of fresh air. For the first time in a long while, I allowed myself to think, *Maybe this could actually work.*

He went above and beyond in ways that felt so thoughtful and intentional. If he knew I'd be outside working all day, he'd get me an external charger to ensure my phone wouldn't die. After I returned from Burning Man, he unpacked my entire U-Haul and even helped me clean it. When he knew I hadn't eaten, he'd bring me food without hesitation.

What stood out most was his emotional availability—he would talk to me about anything and everything, holding space for my feelings with such ease and patience. On nights when I was driving home late, he'd stay on the phone until he knew I was safely inside. He never complained about helping; in fact, he seemed to genuinely enjoy doing things for me, planning dates, and being of service.

For the first time in a long time, I felt truly cared for. It was such a beautiful feeling, a reminder of how good it could feel to be with someone who showed up in the little and big ways without making me feel like a burden.

And yet, beneath the surface of all this care and thoughtfulness, a flicker of fear began to take hold. My system couldn't help but whisper, *"What's the catch? There's no way someone is this perfect."* It felt almost too good to be true, and that old, familiar anxiety crept in, casting shadows over the sincerity of his actions. I found myself second-guessing, wondering if this was real or if I was bracing for the other shoe to drop. It was like my nervous system, trained by past experiences, couldn't fully relax into the possibility of someone genuinely showing up for me.

Despite the fear, I chose to lean into the moments of kindness and support. His thoughtfulness and attentiveness were unlike anything I had experienced in a long time, and I wanted to believe in the sincerity of his actions. I made an effort to stay present, to appreciate the care he showed me without letting my fears overshadow the experience. It was a delicate balance—a dance between hope and caution, trusting enough to let myself enjoy the connection while remaining vigilant for any red flags. Each gesture felt like a small test, not of him, but of my ability to trust and receive without expecting the worst.

Heading to San Diego for my first EFT certification workshop marked a significant milestone, and the timing couldn't have been more perfect as it coincided with a Greatness Gathering networking event. I had been following this organization on social media for years, captivated by their mission to build houses for families in Mexico who lacked livable homes. The idea of participating in one of their builds had long been a dream of mine, something I held as a bucket list experience.

Witnessing the transformative impact of the organization's work through social media was inspiring, but I knew that experiencing the group's energy in person was crucial before committing to travel abroad with them for a house build. The synchronicity of both events happening concurrently felt like a nudge from the universe, affirming that I was on the right path. This alignment seemed to confirm that I was exactly where I needed to be, offering a chance to combine my personal development through the EFT workshop with exploring a meaningful volunteer opportunity that could extend the reach of my newfound skills and compassion.

During the gathering, the founder led us through an exercise, and I found myself paired with a girl who, as it turned out, was also in my EFT certification class that weekend. The connection felt significant, as if we were meant to cross paths and support each other on this shared journey. It was a beautiful reminder of how aligned opportunities can bring people together in the most unexpected and meaningful ways.

We clicked immediately, bonding over our aligned goals, similar experiences, and the excitement for what lay ahead. It was serendipitous how well we connected, and she quickly became not just a friend but an invaluable guide to Encinitas, California, where we were staying. She was a treasure trove of local knowledge, taking me to the most amazing spots in the city and introducing me to an incredible network of people.

Encinitas itself had a vibe that was impossible to ignore—it felt vibrant with possibilities. The laid-back atmosphere, stunning beaches, and the palpable sense of community engagement made the city feel like a hidden gem, perfectly suited for healing, personal growth, and nurturing entrepreneurial spirits. This environment, coupled with the new friendships I was forming, enriched my experience, making every moment in Encinitas a significant part of my journey.

Everywhere we went, I encountered vibrant, like-minded individuals who were just as committed to their paths as I was. It was like the town had its own magnetic pull, drawing in people who wanted to live intentionally and connect authentically. Being in that space was rejuvenating and inspiring, sparking ideas and dreams of what life could look like surrounded by such a community. It left a lasting impression on me, one that I knew would influence the next steps in my journey.

Encinitas felt like a haven, a place where I could truly see myself thriving. We explored cozy cafes with the hum of meaningful conversations, holistic health shops brimming with intention and care, and serene oceanfront spots where we could meditate and reflect on our journeys. Each location added a layer to the sense of belonging and connection I felt in this vibrant community.

The people we encountered were warm and welcoming, embodying the very spirit of the town. They radiated kindness and authenticity, sharing a passion for personal development and healing that mirrored my own. It was refreshing, even invigorating, to be surrounded by individuals who not only understood the journey I was on, but were walking their own parallel paths. Encinitas wasn't just a beautiful place—it felt like a glimpse into the life I was striving to create for myself and my daughter, filled with connection, growth, and peace.

The time I spent in Encinitas wasn't just a break from routine; it was a profound glimpse into the lifestyle I longed to cultivate. The effortless balance of work, play, and spiritual growth I witnessed there resonated deeply with my soul. It was as though the town itself exuded a sense of purpose and harmony, with people who seemed to live with intention, joy, and a connection to something greater.

Being there ignited a yearning within me—not only to embrace this energy, but also to infuse it into my own life and business. I wanted to create a space where this kind of balance and fulfillment could flourish, both for myself and for the women I worked with. Encinitas felt like more than just a place; it felt like a vision of what was possible, a template for the life I was ready to create.

Learning EFT was absolutely fascinating. At first, I'll admit, it felt a bit awkward to sit there tapping on myself while repeating setup statements and phrases. I couldn't help but feel a little self-conscious, wondering if I looked silly. But as the sessions went on, the awkwardness faded into the background as I started to feel better and better. And honestly, when something makes you feel *that* good, looking a little silly stops mattering entirely.

The class was filled with incredible people from all over, each one bringing their unique experiences, energy, and perspective. It was inspiring to be in a room with so many individuals, all committed to growth and healing—not just for themselves but for the people they hoped to help and serve.

Our instructor, Naomi, was everything you could want in a teacher: smart, savvy, and deeply compassionate. She had this remarkable ability to hold space for everyone in the room, creating an environment that felt safe, supportive, and encouraging. Under her guidance, I not only gained skills but also a deep sense of community and connection, which made the learning experience all the more meaningful.

Throughout the class, I released so much—especially the fear and uncertainty surrounding this new relationship and the person involved. Each session chipped away at the anxieties that had been clouding my judgment and holding me back, replacing them with a growing sense of clarity and peace. The repetitive tapping and processing allowed me to let go of the "what-ifs" and the worst-case scenarios my mind had been looping through.

By the end of the class, I felt noticeably lighter, as though a weight I hadn't fully realized I was carrying had been lifted. There was a sense of hope blooming within me—not just about the relationship, but about everything that was beginning to blossom in my life. It felt like I was shedding old fears and stepping into a version of myself that was more open, grounded, and ready for what lay ahead.

After a few months of dating, we finally decided the time was right for our children to meet. To make it convenient, we arranged to meet halfway between Pleasant Hill and Roseville, in Vallejo.

Dinner went surprisingly well—the kids got along beautifully, and everything seemed to flow naturally. It felt like a milestone, one that indicated our relationship was moving in a positive direction.

But as the evening came to a close, something shifted. When it was time to leave, he walked us to our car, but instead of heading to his own vehicle, he lingered, acting oddly. His behavior didn't match the ease of the rest of the night. That small, out-of-place moment set off an alarm in my body. I couldn't help but wonder what was behind his hesitation. It was subtle, but enough to plant a seed of doubt, adding a layer of uncertainty to what had otherwise been a pleasant evening.

The next playdate we arranged was at an ice skating rink, and it turned out to be a lot of fun. The kids were laughing, skating (or attempting to), and the day felt lighthearted and enjoyable. However, as we were walking out to the parking lot afterward, things took an unexpected turn. He casually mentioned not having his usual car and needing to use another one temporarily.

When he got into the car, it was a super old beater, completely at odds with the story he had told me about his life. My nervous system immediately went on high alert. To make matters worse, his story about the car kept changing each time he brought it up, adding layers of inconsistency that were impossible to ignore. His lack of transparency left me feeling uneasy, casting a shadow over what had otherwise been a fun outing.

Despite these red flags, I tried to be understanding. I reminded myself that life can get complicated, and I wanted to give him the benefit of the doubt. To manage my growing anxiety and confusion, I kept tapping with my EFT classmates, working through the discomfort and trying to make sense of his behavior.

One pattern that stood out was how he consistently came down to where I lived instead of inviting me to visit him. Eventually, he revealed that he had moved in with his dad, explaining it as a way to support his father, who was also going through a divorce. While I wanted to believe his story and admired his intention to help his dad, something about the situation didn't sit right. It felt like there was still more he wasn't sharing, and the inconsistencies in his behavior kept my guard up, despite my efforts to stay open and understanding.

When I finally went up to meet his dad and see his home, I felt a bit more at ease. It was nice to put a real place to the story he had shared, and meeting his dad was a positive experience. However, the lingering unease didn't entirely disappear. The fact that I had spent months not knowing where he had been living still felt strange, like a shadow over our connection.

The inconsistencies in his stories and the way he withheld details continued to gnaw at me. It created an undercurrent of doubt that was hard to ignore, even though there were plenty of positive aspects to our relationship. I wanted so badly to trust him fully, to let go of the questions swirling in my mind, but the lack of clarity made it impossible to feel completely safe. It was a tug-of-war between the hope and potential I saw in us and the red flags I couldn't deny.

I kept tapping on all the feelings that kept bubbling up around these unsettling pieces, trying to process them and move forward. I reminded myself that no one is perfect, and everyone has their own baggage to carry. Divorce can be messy and painful, and I told myself that maybe he was just embarrassed about rebuilding his life from the ground up.

He often painted his ex-wife as the bad guy, which tugged at my empathy, making me want to give him the benefit of the doubt. Tapping became my lifeline in moments of doubt, helping me feel more at ease and reconnect with the hope I had for this relationship. Each session soothed my nerves, allowing me to hold space for the possibility that he was doing his best under difficult circumstances.

Then Thanksgiving came, and with it, the truth. He wasn't actually divorced. He wasn't simply in a custody battle with his ex—he was still in the process of divorcing her, with no timeline for when it would be finalized. This revelation hit like a ton of bricks. Suddenly, all the stories, the secrecy, and the ever-changing explanations about his living situation and the car snapped into focus. It all made sense now, and the deceit was undeniable.

I felt deeply betrayed. The trust I had been carefully trying to build, despite the red flags, was shattered. All the compassion I'd extended, the understanding I'd tried to hold, now felt misplaced.

The foundation of our relationship, which I had hoped was solidifying, crumbled beneath me. It wasn't just the lie—it was the erosion of trust and the realization that he hadn't been honest about something so fundamental was utterly devastating.

I had poured so much energy into understanding and supporting him, even when my instincts had screamed that something was off. I had worked through my doubts and fears, tapping away at the unease, trying to trust and move forward. Yet here I was, facing the harsh truth that the foundation of our relationship had been built on a lie. It felt like all the effort I had invested—the emotional labor, the compassion, the vulnerability—had been for nothing.

When the truth came out, I completely lost it. The anger and betrayal hit me like a tidal wave. I wasn't just upset about the lies themselves, but about the fact that my choice had been stolen from me. Had I known he was still married, I wouldn't have gotten involved—or at the very least, I might have kept things platonic until his marriage was fully finalized. Instead, I had been led into a relationship under false pretenses, and now all the inconsistencies, the shifting stories, and the secrecy made sense. The weight of all the lies stacked on top of each other was unbearable. I felt like my trust had been manipulated, and the realization was infuriating.

Each red flag I had overlooked now blazed vividly in my mind—the constantly shifting stories about his car, the evasive explanations about his living situation, and the misleading comments about his relationship status. It was like watching a puzzle come together, and the final picture revealed betrayal. I realized I had been deceived from the very beginning, and the weight of that truth hit me hard. To be misled about something so fundamental wasn't just disappointing; it was a direct blow to my ability to trust.

He often shared stories about his years as a soccer coach, speaking warmly of the young girls he mentored and describing them as "little sisters" to him. I found it touching and admirable, a reflection of his character—or so I thought. Then I discovered something that completely contradicted his words: he had been liking nude images and sexually suggestive images of a few of them, now in their early twenties. It left me feeling deeply unsettled. How could this behavior possibly align with the familial bond he claimed to have with them? It didn't. When I confronted him about it, he had no explanation. Instead of addressing it, he shut down, leaving me questioning everything about him and his integrity.

With all the trauma I had endured with men and my fierce protectiveness as a mom to a little girl, discovering this sent me into a spiral of anger and hurt. I felt an overwhelming surge of protectiveness and betrayal, unable to reconcile his actions with the trust I had placed in him. My immediate instinct was to leave, to grab my things and walk out the door. I actually did walk to the front door, expecting him to care, to stop me, to show any remorse or concern—but he didn't. Instead of leaving like I should have, I hesitated. I wish I had just walked away at that moment. It would have saved me from what came next.

Instead, I paused, lingering at the door, clinging to a sliver of hope that he might say something—anything—that would make sense of his actions, that would show remorse or offer an explanation to ease the sting of betrayal. But there was nothing. Just silence. Indifference. The gravity of the moment settled heavily around me, the weight of my past traumas pressing down, amplifying the distress swirling in my chest.

I stood there, frozen, torn between my instinct to leave and the desperate hope that he might acknowledge the hurt he had caused and make things right. I wanted so badly to believe in the goodness I thought I had seen in him, in the potential for redemption and change. He seemed just as paralyzed, like a sad puppy with its tail between its legs, unsure of how to proceed. I stood by the open door, debating whether to walk out and never return.

He had always been so sweet to me, going above and beyond to be helpful and of service—a gentleman in many ways. Could this be something I could forgive, something from which we could grow stronger? I wasn't sure. Ultimately, I closed the door and sat next to him in silence, processing the weight of the moment, before we left to go to dinner and pick up his son. The decision to stay, at least for now, weighed heavily on me as I tried to reconcile my feelings with the reality of our situation.

I longed for things to return to the way they were before this incident, for the ease and comfort we once shared. Yet, deep down, I knew something fundamental had shifted—the seeds of doubt had firmly taken root. Trust, once shattered, proves incredibly difficult to rebuild. No amount of silence or denial could undo the revelation of his actions or the impact they had on our relationship. This realization hung heavily over me, a stark reminder that some things, once changed, cannot simply be mended back to their original state.

As the trust between us eroded, I found myself questioning him more, feeling increasingly unsafe when we were apart. Our communication started to deteriorate; we argued more frequently, yet often he would shut down and cut off communication entirely, leaving issues unresolved and tensions high. The damage that had been done seemed to continually ripple outward, tainting what had once felt like a blessing in my life. The broken trust cast a shadow over everything, turning what had once been a source of joy and comfort into a constant source of stress and uncertainty.

A month or so later, still grappling with the confusion and emotional weight of my relationship, I needed a shift in perspective. To cope, I decided to focus outward and joined a trip with the Greatness Collective to San Diego, an experience aimed at making a tangible difference. We were scheduled to cross into Mexico to build two homes for families living in dire conditions—under tarps and made of scrap wood, without any real protection from the elements.

These families lacked stability and a proper place to call home. The opportunity to provide them with sturdy roofs, solid walls, and floors raised off the dirt filled me with a renewed sense of purpose and hope. This project was not just about building homes; it was about restoring dignity and creating a safe, secure environment for these families. Engaging in this meaningful work allowed me to channel my energy into something positive, offering relief from my personal troubles and a chance to contribute to something larger than myself.

The experience was transformative. Seeing their current living conditions firsthand was a stark reminder of how much we often take for granted. Working side by side with others to build these homes, brick by brick, was both humbling and empowering. Visiting orphanages and spending time with children with special needs deepened my perspective even further.

This journey was exactly what my heart needed—to step out of my personal struggles and immerse myself in service. It brought a much-needed shift, a reminder of the resilience of the human spirit, and the profound impact of community and giving. These families would now have a safe place to call home, and being part of that change was nothing short of life-changing for me as well.

Being surrounded by a community of truly caring and compassionate individuals was pure medicine for my soul. The collective effort to build homes and bring joy to these families wasn't just about construction—it was about restoring hope, creating stability, and making a tangible difference in their lives. It filled my heart in ways I didn't realize I needed, reigniting my sense of purpose and connection.

Witnessing the harsh conditions these families had been living in was a humbling experience. Seeing children laugh and play in the dirt, despite their hardships, reminded me of the resilience of the human spirit. Watching their faces light up as their new homes took shape was profoundly moving. This experience wasn't just about giving—it was about receiving, too. I received perspective, gratitude, and the healing power of being part of something so much bigger than myself.

Witnessing the harsh conditions these families had been enduring was a deeply humbling experience. They had no running water, no toilets, no showers, no floors—and yet, they radiated joy and gratitude, their eyes sparkling with hope and resilience.

It made me pause and reflect on my own life, realizing how much I often took for granted—the comforts, the conveniences and the opportunities I had access to. This experience was a powerful reminder of the blessings in my life and the immense privilege of being able to give back in a meaningful way.

Spending time with the children at the orphanages was equally heartwarming and humbling. Their resilience and pure joy, despite their challenging circumstances, left me in awe. Each smile, each laugh, and each small moment of connection felt incredibly profound.

I found myself deeply moved as we played games, exchanged stories, and shared moments of simple human connection. The way their eyes lit up, even with the smallest gestures of care and attention, reminded me of the transformative power of love and presence. It was a beautiful reminder that, even in the face of adversity, the human spirit can shine brightly when nurtured by compassion and kindness.

The entire experience starkly contrasted with the turmoil I had been facing in my personal life. It offered a much-needed shift in perspective, helping me step outside of my own struggles and see the bigger picture. Witnessing the joy and resilience of those with so little reminded me of what truly mattered—connection, gratitude, and the ability to bring light into others' lives. I felt a renewed sense of clarity and purpose, eager to return home with a fresh outlook and a commitment to making changes.

When I got back, I was determined to apply the lessons I had learned. It was time to reassess my relationships and focus on the ones that fostered positivity, growth, and mutual respect. The trip to Mexico had not only filled my heart with gratitude but also equipped me with the strength to make the tough, yet necessary decisions for my daughter's well-being and mine. It became clear that creating a life aligned with love, peace, and purpose would require letting go of anything that no longer served us. The journey had given me the courage to start that process with unwavering resolve.

The relationship had morphed into something unrecognizable, its initial sparkle dulled by deceit and inconsistency. Despite all the EFT Tapping I did to calm my nerves and release my emotions, the uneasy feelings wouldn't go away. I was furious—at him for not being honest from the beginning, and at myself for allowing the situation to drag on. I was stuck between frustration over not being able to walk away and the attachment I had developed after investing so much time and energy.

The cycles of love-bombing followed by emotional withdrawal were draining. He would shower me with affection and grand gestures, only to pull away and ignore me shortly after. The emotional rollercoaster left me dizzy and unsure of what was real. His gaslighting made it even harder to find clarity, as my mind became tangled with doubt and confusion. My nervous system was constantly on high alert, making it nearly impossible to focus on work or other areas of my life. I was caught in a loop of frustration, trying to reconcile the reality of the relationship with the idealized version I had once believed in.

The emotional rollercoaster left me completely drained, caught in a relentless cycle of second-guessing myself and my feelings. Every time I contemplated leaving, the fear of losing the fleeting good moments or breaking the attachment I had formed held me hostage. I was stuck in a perpetual state of anxiety, walking on eggshells, never knowing which version of him I'd encounter next.

At work, my mind would drift to the latest argument or his baffling behavior, making it nearly impossible to stay present or give my best effort. The love-bombing phases were intoxicating, offering just enough of an emotional high to keep me tethered to the relationship. But the withdrawals and gaslighting were devastating, eroding any sense of stability or self-worth I had painstakingly tried to rebuild. It felt like I was losing pieces of myself with each passing day, trapped in a web of confusion and emotional chaos.

I felt stuck in a relentless loop, trapped between the truth I knew deep down and the hope that clung stubbornly to the surface. This relationship was unhealthy—that much was clear—but breaking free felt like an insurmountable challenge. The cycles of manipulation and the rollercoaster of emotional highs and lows had woven a toxic thread through my life, quietly unraveling my sense of self. It wasn't just the relationship; it was the way the unease and confusion seeped into every corner of my world, clouding my ability to find clarity or peace.

I knew something had to change, but the weight of my attachment and the persistent hope that things might somehow improve kept me tethered. I had walked straight into another trap—one I thought I'd learned to avoid, but somehow hadn't. This one was more tangled, more difficult to escape than I cared to admit.

Yet, amidst the chaos, a small, steady voice inside me whispered louder each day: *This isn't sustainable. You deserve more.*

Unhealthy Relating

He asks me what's wrong
I debate on whether to share
This always starts a fight for no reason
I decide to be honest
... "I have anxiety because I'm leaving and we are not and have not been connected"
He goes into frustration
... "I don't know how to help you"
I say
... "I didn't ask for help"
He says he wants to help
I say
... "it's not just one moment that led to this... it's been all summer"
He says
"it's not just you"
I say
"I didn't say it was"
He huffs...
I shut down
I shouldn't have said anything
Cuz now he's frustrated
He was frustrated before the huff
He erupts
"we aren't going to make it, it's you, it all your fault...I'm allowed to breathe"
I didn't say he wasn't
It's these tiny moments that get messed up
He erupts
Raises his voice
Positioned 'he's right and has power over'
The chain reaction starts with me telling the truth about how I feel
That's when his frustration begins

He would rather act as if everything is fine all the time
Fine is death
Fine means not fine
Fine means barely a pulse and just getting by
Fine never means fine
I feel dead in this relationship
And now I am in my anxious fight or flight response
He blames me and in a way I do too
I need to stop saying how I feel or the truth
Prevent the entire spiral
Just say "I'm fine"
At least that doesn't cause this chain of events
Where I then feel worse than I did
His frustration didn't start with the huff
It started with his comment ... "I can't do anything for you"
The more I try to explain the chain of events
The more he yells at me and over me
Him yelling doesn't change what's happening or make him right
I cover my ears
My nervous system is shaking
I hate sharing my feelings with this human being
He has zero patience and erupts with so much anger
So fast over the smallest words or things
I feel like I have to be so careful about anything I say
I feel like I'm walking on eggshells
And all he does is point at me and say it's me
Versus looking at how quick and easily he erupts into anger
He feels justified because I said he was frustrated and he wasn't
He doesn't care about my reality or experience
What he says goes
He only cares about his reality
His way or no way
He is my mom
I have been dating my mom
I hate it
I don't feel happy here in this relationship

This is not dreamy
This is not magical
This is not true love
This is a nightmare
He makes me feel dull, small and dim
I don't feel seen
I don't feel heard
I don't feel appreciated
I don't feel loved
I don't feel cherished
I don't feel cared for
I feel tolerated
And in turn I tolerate him
But this is not love
It's tolerance
And it's death

Cassandra Love Lambert

C-LOVE

Chapter 29
Miracles Can Be Birthed Out of Chaos

I found myself setting up my C-Love bedazzle station at 1015 Folsom in San Francisco for yet another Burning Man fundraiser for Airpusher, completely unaware that life as I knew it was about to change. As I meticulously arranged my glittery tools and decorations, adding the finishing touches to my C-Love art station, one of my Airpusher buddies approached me with an unusually serious expression.

He started talking about something called COVID. I wasn't much of a news watcher, so I had no idea what he was referring to. He explained that it was spreading rapidly in China and expressed his growing concern about its potential global impact. His tone was heavy as he warned me to stay safe and mentioned that events like these might have to stop entirely. Before walking away, he wished me and my daughter well, leaving me slightly puzzled but unconcerned.

As I returned to my station, I brushed off his warnings, focusing on the fun and creativity of the night ahead. *China is so far away,* I thought. *There's no way this will affect me.* Little did I know that those words would echo in my mind as the world began to shift in ways I could never have imagined.

As the weekend unfolded, the whispers about COVID turned into a steady stream of conversations. More and more people began talking about it, and the news was suddenly saturated with reports of the virus spreading to other countries. The gravity of the situation started to sink in. What had initially seemed like a distant issue now felt uncomfortably close.

A growing sense of unease crept in as I wondered: What would this mean for my business, my daughter, and the life we had worked so hard to build? The uncertainty was unnerving, and while I tried to ignore it and focus on the present, it was impossible to ignore the unsettling feeling that change was looming.

"Don't count on being able to work next weekend," my dad warned as I arrived to pick up my daughter from my parents' house after a busy weekend of work. I paused, looking at him with a mixture of confusion and skepticism, not fully grasping the weight of his words. To me, it felt like one of those moments when the world braces for something catastrophic—like the Y2K frenzy or one of the countless apocalyptic predictions I'd heard growing up.

Each time, the panic had passed, leaving little more than a collective sigh of relief. This felt no different, just another passing storm of exaggerated headlines. I shrugged it off, hoping it was just another hoax. I wasn't about to spiral into fear over what seemed like nothing. The thought of taking it seriously felt absurd; after all, the world had cried wolf too many times before.

Then, the very next day, reality hit hard. One by one, like dominoes falling, every event and gig on my calendar was canceled. The shock was palpable, and the feeling was surreal, as if I were trapped in a nightmare I couldn't wake up from. In my quest for clarity and understanding—something I rarely ever felt compelled to do—I turned on the TV to watch the news.

There I was, glued to the screen, absorbing every update with a mix of horror and disbelief. I reached out to my boyfriend, who seemed just as bewildered by the unfolding events. Yet, in his usual supportive manner, he was ready to stand by and help with whatever was needed. It was a small comfort in the midst of an increasingly uncertain world.

The images and reports flooding in from around the world were harrowing. Every news cycle brought more updates of rising infection rates, hospitals pushed to their limits, and cities going into lockdown. It was like watching a disaster movie unfold in real life. The magnitude of the pandemic became starkly evident, painting a picture of a world grappling with an unprecedented crisis. The weight of the situation hit me hard—life as we knew it was changing dramatically, and the future was shrouded in uncertainty. This stark new reality brought a sense of helplessness that was hard to shake off, as the global scale of the crisis sank in.

As the news unfolded, a whirlwind of questions overwhelmed me: How long would this pandemic last? How would we survive without a steady income? How could I ensure my daughter's safety and well-being amidst such chaos? I harbored deep reservations about the hastily developed vaccine—what if it compromised my health? And how was my daughter supposed to continue her education? The weight of these pressing concerns bore down on me. Yet, despite the swirling storm of fear and uncertainty, I knew I needed to summon the strength to be the stable foundation my daughter relied on.

As the reality of ongoing closures and cancellations settled in, a thought struck me with overwhelming force—I needed to find a way to keep providing for my daughter amid this chaos. The steady stream of event cancellations meant I had to pivot, and fast. I had previously toyed with the idea of creating Bedazzle kits, but the thought of actually bringing this idea to life was daunting. I felt lost, unsure of where to start or how to transition this concept into a tangible product that could sustain us financially.

My boyfriend and I hunkered down together, dedicating hours to scour the internet for the best materials for the Bedazzle kits. We compared prices, read through countless reviews, and discussed various options. He was incredibly supportive, helping me brainstorm names for the kits—names that were creative, catchy, and would resonate with my target audience.

As the supplies began to arrive, my kitchen transformed into a makeshift assembly line. Together, we meticulously assembled each kit, piece by piece. It was a labor of love and partnership, turning a challenging situation into an opportunity to adapt and grow. This collaborative effort not only brought us closer, but also laid the groundwork for a new chapter in my business.

As we prepared each Bedazzle kit, we paid close attention to detail, making sure they were packed with everything needed to create a fun and engaging experience. Each kit included a variety of gems and jewels, adhesive, detailed instructions, and some unique touches that made them stand out. My boyfriend's meticulous approach and his unwavering support lightened the workload, turning the process into an enjoyable activity. His presence made the task not just easier but also infused it with joy and creativity, reinforcing the bond between us as we worked together towards a common goal.

I launched C-Love DIY Bedazzle Kits along with virtual sparkle parties, creating a vibrant way to stay engaged with my community during the shutdown. These virtual gatherings were more than just tutorials; they were lively, interactive sessions where participants could learn how to use their kits to bedazzle themselves from the comfort of their homes. This connection was vital during a time when many felt isolated and disconnected.

To further support this new venture, I reached out to my community through a heartfelt post and email. I outlined various ways they could help sustain the business amidst the pandemic. Options included pre-paying for future makeup sessions and Burning Man Braids, purchasing a Bedazzle Kit, booking one-on-one EFT Tapping sessions, or simply making a donation. The response was incredible—so many stepped forward to show their support, reminding me of the strength and generosity of the community I had built over the years. This wave of support was not just a financial lifeline; it was a powerful affirmation of the bonds created with art.

The response to the C-Love DIY Bedazzle Kits and pre-sold services was overwhelmingly positive—I sold over 300 kits in just two months! Additionally, the pre-sales of my art services and Burning Man braids for future festivals provided a crucial financial buffer, allowing me more time to navigate these uncertain times. The outpouring of love and support from my community was incredibly heartwarming. Every message, purchase, and donation reinforced the strong connections we'd established and reminded me that I wasn't alone in facing these challenges. The solidarity shown by everyone was not only uplifting but also a powerful testament to the community's strength and generosity.

The virtual sparkle parties turned into a real hit. People embraced the interactive element, which offered a lively and engaging way to connect during the pandemic's isolation. Watching everyone light up with their creations filled me with immense joy and fulfillment. It felt like we had conjured our own little festival in the virtual space, brimming with laughter, creativity, and a warm sense of community. These sessions not only brought sparkle to their days but also deepened our connections, making each virtual gathering a celebration of resilience and collective joy.

The overwhelming support from so many during this challenging time truly left me in awe. These were the same souls to whom I had brought sparkle over the past decade with my art. There was a bittersweet sadness in realizing that while I could no longer physically adorn them, their support had become a shining beacon of solidarity for both me and my daughter. Their contributions, whether through purchases, donations, or emotional support, reminded me of the deep connections we'd forged through the simple act of sharing beauty and joy. This solidarity not only helped us navigate those uncertain times, but also deepened the gratitude and love I felt for my C-Love community.

I was grateful that my boyfriend was willing to handle the shopping during the pandemic. He was meticulous about safety—he wore a mask every time and even wiped down all our groceries in the backyard with disinfectant before bringing them inside, then he'd change clothes and shower immediately afterward. His respect for the precautions we needed to take brought me some peace of mind. As a single mom, the uncertainty of COVID-19 made me extremely cautious. The health of my daughter and myself was not something I could gamble with. However, even with his helpfulness, our relationship began to strain as more issues arose that didn't align with my values.

One evening, while we were relaxing on the couch, he received a text from a porn site. This was a complete violation of my boundaries. He tried to brush it off, claiming he had no idea why he would receive such a message. The trust issues that were already simmering beneath the surface suddenly intensified. I felt deeply betrayed and disappointed. Despite all the good moments and support he had provided, incidents like this made it incredibly hard to fully trust him.

I found myself in a tough spot. While his help during the pandemic was invaluable, and I genuinely appreciated his support and presence, these misaligned actions and breaches of trust were becoming too significant to overlook. It was becoming increasingly clear that our relationship harbored deeper issues that needed to be addressed.

After a particularly heated argument about something now forgotten, he abruptly stopped all communication. Overwhelmed by the lies, half-truths, and confusion, I felt compelled to reach out to his ex-wife, despite my fears. I needed clarity, and I hoped she could provide it. When we spoke, she revealed a side of him I hadn't seen. She told me he had slandered her name and ruined her business due to tax fraud, among other things. He also owed her a significant amount of money—details he had conveniently left out of our conversations. This new information was eye-opening and deeply troubling.

Reaching out to his ex-wife was a difficult but pivotal decision for me. It brought clarity and validated the unsettling feelings I had been wrestling with. The truths she revealed painted a clearer picture of the patterns I had sensed, but hadn't fully understood. This conversation underscored the critical importance of transparency and integrity in relationships. The lies and manipulation I had encountered weren't just sporadic issues; they were part of a consistent pattern that deeply affected, not only our relationship, but others before mine. This realization was crucial for my healing journey and reinforced my commitment to seeking and fostering honesty in my future relationships.

There was no going back from the truth I uncovered as I finally began to process everything. I grieved for what could have been and eventually healed from the deception. This profound experience fueled my passion to speak up and share my story. It inspired me to create "The Gaslighting Series," aimed at helping other women recognize the signs of manipulation and covert narcissism early on.

This drive to empower others led me back to a business coach I had met a few years ago while doing makeup for her and her friends on New Year's. She specialized in helping people create businesses online—a path I knew I needed to pursue, especially with the world in lockdown. The timing of this reconnection felt divinely guided, and I was eager to adapt my business to thrive under these new circumstances. I had a call with her to discuss the possibilities, but the investment was significant. It required some serious thought and consideration on my part.

As I laid on my bed, tears streaming down my face, I mourned the loss of my beautiful business—something I had birthed while pregnant and deeply cherished—and the recent relationship that had ended. It felt as though I was cursed with the worst luck in love and relationships. Each heartbreak seemed harder than the last, compounding my sense of loss and loneliness. The dream of finding a love like the one my godfather had, a love that felt safe and true, seemed to drift further out of reach with each disappointment. This growing despair made it feel increasingly impossible to find what I so desperately yearned for.

Amid the grief of my halted art business and the recent end of my relationship, I found myself recalling the recent conversation I had had with the business coach whose expertise in online business creation now seemed incredibly relevant. Her advice echoed in my mind with a new sense of urgency. With a blend of desperation and renewed hope, I decided to invest in her program. This felt like grabbing a lifeline, providing a new direction for my career as a Somatic Practitioner during a time when the world was shifting drastically toward virtual interactions. It was a crucial step toward adapting and learning how to sustain my practice and make a living from home.

The transition was challenging, but deeply transformative. The pandemic had stripped away the familiar, forcing me to confront my deepest fears and insecurities. However, it also pushed me to discover new strengths and possibilities within myself. The training and guidance I received from my business coach proved invaluable. She equipped me with the tools and confidence needed to turn my pain into purpose, allowing me to channel my experiences into something that could help others heal. This period reshaped my career and expanded my capacity to impact lives positively through my work as a Somatic Practitioner.

C-LOVE

Chapter 30
The Responsibility of Helping Others in Their Healing

Working with my business coach was a crucial step in navigating the challenges brought by the pandemic. She guided me in pivoting my skills and offerings to the online space, which was essential since in-person events were still being affected. With her help, I successfully built an online presence that could sustain my business. This allowed me to continue providing for my daughter and serving as a Somatic Practitioner and healer, helping others navigate their paths to healing even amidst global uncertainty. This shift not only maintained my professional life, but also expanded my ability to reach and impact more people than ever before.

Embarking on this journey with my business coach was the start of an incredible transformation. As I delved deeper into the program, I uncovered innovative ways to channel my experiences and skills into something profoundly impactful. The pain and challenges that had once seemed overwhelming became the foundation of my new venture— and my Pain into Power Process was born. This process has equipped me to guide others in their healing, using my experiences as a beacon of inspiration and strength. Every step forward not only deepened my understanding of my own path, but also expanded my capacity to positively influence and guide others on their healing journeys.

Today, the **Pain into Power Process** is more than just a program—it's a lifeline for those wrestling with their traumas and challenges. By weaving together Somatic practices and EFT Tapping, I've crafted a holistic approach that nurtures the physical body, mind, spirit, and nervous system. This method allows clients to release deep-seated pain and reclaim their power, catalyzing profound and lasting transformations in their lives.

Launching my new venture at the time was exhilarating yet daunting. I felt a profound responsibility to those entrusting me with their healing journeys. The weight of ensuring I didn't negatively impact others was immense, as I took the ethics of this work very seriously. Despite the pressure, the positive feedback and transformative results from my clients reinforced my belief in the effectiveness of the Pain into Power Process. Each success story not only validated the method, but also fueled my passion and commitment to continue this important and sacred work.

Balancing my role as a solopreneur and Somatic Practitioner alongside my duties as a single mother during the pandemic was both challenging and incredibly rewarding. Helping others heal opened new pathways for my own healing, creating a deeply reciprocal process. This journey not only fostered my professional growth but also infused my life with a profound sense of purpose and fulfillment. The more I engaged in this work, the more I found myself enriched and committed to this path, underscoring the transformative power of giving and receiving healing.

Reflecting on this journey, I realized that the pause in my art business was a profound turning point. It nudged me into exploring new avenues and led me to a deeper calling. My Pain into Power Process transcended just a career shift; it became a mission deeply aligned with my life's purpose, making sense of all the monsters and traps I had encountered along the way.

At the same time, my daughter's school closure introduced another layer of complexity. The initial homeschooling efforts didn't mesh with my need to rebuild our financial stability and my business. Inspired by another mom who had navigated homeschooling her child solo, I decided to create our "Mommy-and-Me School." I became the headmaster in our home classroom, allowing me to weave my daughter's education into our daily lives around my working schedule.

The adventure of tackling homeschooling brought a profound new appreciation for teachers into my life. Managing the pivot in my business while ensuring my daughter's well-being added immense pressure. Some days, it would take us two hours just to get through a single worksheet due to her resistance. These moments were energetically and emotionally taxing, leaving me drained and overwhelmed. However, these challenges also brought invaluable lessons and deepened my understanding of my daughter's needs and our dynamic. This understanding strengthened our bond and reinforced my resolve to make it work. On days when the worksheets became too much, I realized what she truly needed was time and undivided attention. We would set aside the schoolwork to go for walks, immerse ourselves in nature, enjoy ice cream, and watch her favorite shows or movies while snuggling. These moments were just as educational and crucial for her development and our relationship.

Our days became a delicate balancing act between homeschooling, my work commitments, and maintaining a semblance of normalcy during our isolation. Being both a teacher and a business owner required creativity and flexibility, as I strived to keep my daughter engaged and motivated while also pushing my business forward. The tug-of-war between work and quality time with her was constant and often overwhelming. There were moments when the weight of this dual responsibility felt unbearable, and I would battle feelings of inadequacy. I often felt like a failure or a bad mom, especially on days when traditional education took a backseat to what she really needed—quality time, play, and her mommy's undivided attention. In a world where no one else could step in, these moments of connection became our lifeline.

Navigating my daughter's learning difficulties, especially with reading and writing, was a deeply challenging experience. Each day felt like an uphill battle, her resistance and frustration stirring the waters around us relentlessly. The tantrums and meltdowns during our learning sessions triggered my nervous system severely, leaving my brain overwhelmed and foggy, impacting my ability to focus on work or anything else.

Realizing that teaching her these essential skills was beyond my current abilities, I reached out for help. I contacted a friend who was a teacher, hoping she could tutor my daughter. Thankfully, she agreed. This decision was a lifeline for both of us. Without her support, I feared we might sink under the weight of homeschooling and the pressures of running my business. Her involvement not only alleviated the educational challenges but also gave me the space to breathe, refocus, and strike a healthier balance between my professional duties and my role as a mother. This support was crucial, allowing me to be more present with my daughter and less overwhelmed by our daily challenges.

Slowly but surely, my daughter started to show progress in her reading and writing skills. The tutor's patience and expertise truly made a difference, and with each session, I could see small but significant improvements. It was a gradual process, but each little victory brought a wave of hope and joy. Watching her gain confidence and seeing the light in her eyes when she correctly read a word or wrote a sentence on her own was deeply rewarding. Witnessing these moments of triumph not only filled me with pride, but also reinforced the value of reaching out for help when needed.

With the help of the tutor, I could finally focus more on my business, knowing that my daughter was in good hands and receiving the support she needed. This significantly alleviated the immense pressure I had been feeling. Our days gained more structure and became more manageable, which allowed me to breathe a little easier. The weight of trying to manage everything on my own began to lift, bringing a newfound sense of balance and relief to our daily routine.

The certification in Clinical EFT Tapping that I had pursued a year earlier turned out to be another pivotal element in navigating the challenges brought by the pandemic. As our trainer finally gave us the green light to begin accepting payments for our work, I couldn't help but see the divine timing and orchestration in it all. The global pause caused by the pandemic, while full of uncertainty, pushed me to start charging for my services with this powerful healing modality. It felt as though God was guiding me towards a deeper purpose, rooted in my own journey of healing, so that I could effectively support others in theirs. It was a clear sign that it was time to step out of my comfort zone as a lifelong student and embrace my role as a practitioner and guide, propelled by a loving nudge from the divine.

This shift in my life felt profound. The call to embrace a deeper purpose, anchored in my own experiences and growth, became undeniable. My art business, which had been a lifeline and a source of joy, transformed into a catalyst for a more significant transition. It nudged me towards fully embracing my role as a healer—a responsibility I had grappled with accepting for a long time. Now, it felt not only right, but necessary. Integrating my journey with the transformative power of EFT Tapping, I could see the profound impact it had on others. This alignment with my personal mission resonated deeply, confirming that I was on the right path.

With the world effectively on pause, my parents really stepped up in significant ways. My dad would come over to watch my daughter, allowing me to run essential errands like grocery shopping—I was too worried about exposing her to COVID to bring her along. He even helped with rent during those initial tumultuous months of transition. As social distancing limited our interactions outside, we found new ways to strengthen our family ties. We made holidays larger-than-life to create special memories for my daughter. For Halloween, we all dressed up, loaded up on candy, and played games at my mom's house, making it a magical night for her. That Christmas, my parents showed up dressed as Santa Claus and Mrs. Claus, igniting my daughter's face with joy and excitement. Their presence and support during this time meant the world to me. It was heartening to see a global crisis bring out the best in my family, not the worst.

The pandemic brought an unexpected resolution to the transactional dynamic I had with my mom regarding babysitting. With no need for a sitter due to lockdowns and my ability to work from home, she began to spend time with my daughter simply as a grandmother, without any financial exchange. It felt as though all the prayers I had placed into that prayer bowl about my relationship with my mother were finally being answered. This shift was a profound relief, freeing me from a complex web I had been entangled in since I embarked on the path of single motherhood. I felt deeply grateful for this unexpected silver lining. This trap had indeed come full circle, and I felt liberated from it. This newfound freedom was not just a huge relief but a significant turning point in my journey as a single mom and entrepreneur. Tears of gratitude filled my eyes, realizing I had made it through that seemingly never-ending season. Feeling so light, it seemed I could do anything.

This period of time was transformative in many ways. The unexpected closeness with my family brought a sense of healing and connection that I hadn't felt in a long time, probably since they got married decades ago. Despite the challenges and uncertainties of the pandemic, these moments of bonding and support were precious. They helped me navigate through the difficulties with a sense of gratitude and hope, providing a stark contrast to the isolation and anxiety of the outside world. This newfound unity was a silver lining, a reminder of the enduring strength of family ties through even the toughest times.

Navigating the ups and downs of life with my family, especially with the complexities that trauma introduces to dynamics and seasons, has truly been a rollercoaster. Each twist and turn has brought its own challenges and revelations, shaping how we interact and support one another. It's a journey that tests resilience and teaches profound lessons about healing and growing together, despite the shadows the past might cast. Through it all, the experience underscores the importance of understanding and patience in the face of deep-seated issues that affect familial relationships.

During this time, my relationship with my parents, particularly my mom, began to transform in unexpected ways. The removal of our previous transactional babysitting arrangement allowed us to reconnect on a much deeper and more genuine level. I began to see her in a new light, and to my surprise, she revealed a side of herself that was nurturing and kind—a side I hadn't witnessed in a long time. This shift was a profound reminder of the power of prayer and the importance of being open to the unexpected ways in which our needs might be met. It felt as though all the prayers I had placed into that prayer bowl over the years were now weaving their way into our interactions, mending old wounds and easing long-held resentments.

In this new environment, my daughter flourished. The love and attention she received from her grandparents brought a sense of stability and joy that was palpable. Watching her happy and well-cared-for reinforced my belief that, despite the chaos swirling around us, we were on the right path. The pandemic indeed came with its fair share of obstacles and challenges, but for us, it also brought numerous blessings. I am profoundly grateful for this season of life and remain in awe of how mysteriously and wonderfully God works to turn our prayers for healing into visible miracles.

C-LOVE

Chapter 31
A Real Relationship Will Also Take Work

Responding to comments and reactions on social media had become an essential part of my new online business approach. Engaging with my audience in real-time allowed me to foster deeper connections and provide immediate support and encouragement. One day, a response to one of my stories caught my attention. It came from someone I had been virtually introduced to through a friend I met at the Greatness Collective and had done EFT training with. He was going through a tough breakup, and his emotions were all over the place.

As we exchanged messages, I shared some tools and resources that could help him navigate his emotions. I offered him a meditation I typically give my clients and suggested a withhold list exercise to help him process his feelings more effectively. Our interactions grew from brief exchanges to longer, more meaningful conversations. He appreciated the support and guidance I provided, and I felt a deep sense of fulfillment from being able to help someone navigate such a challenging time in their life. This connection not only helped him but also reinforced the value and impact of the work I do.

Our conversations deepened as we shared more about our lives. He opened up about his past relationship and the struggles he was facing, while I shared insights from my own experiences and the strategies that helped me navigate my challenges. This exchange of stories and advice fostered a genuine connection, enriching our dialogue. It was incredibly fulfilling to engage with someone who seemed to value emotional intelligence and focused on personal growth. Discussing and exploring these topics was a passion of mine, so finding someone equally enthusiastic about these discussions was inspiring.

Over time, our exchanges evolved from supportive guidance to sharing more personal aspects of our lives. We found that we shared many common interests and values, and a genuine friendship began to blossom. Despite the physical distance—he was in San Diego and I was in the Bay Area—we discovered inventive ways to stay connected and continue supporting each other. This unfolding relationship underscored the incredible power of social media and the internet to bring people together. It was fascinating to see how these platforms could forge meaningful connections between individuals who might never have met in person otherwise.

The pandemic really changed the dynamics of relationships; physical location became irrelevant as in-person interactions were off-limits for everyone. He would spend hours playing Minc craft with my daughter over Zoom, turning what were essentially virtual meetups into family dates. Our connections flourished in a purely digital space, transcending physical distance and proving that genuine relationships can thrive under any circumstances.

His connection to people who were connected with the Greatness Collective—a community known for its commitment to personal growth and positive change—added an extra layer of comfort. Knowing he was surrounded by good people enriched the trust and bond we were developing. It was so seamless that one day, my daughter asked if he was my new boyfriend, a moment that made me realize how naturally he had blended into our lives before it even fully dawned on me that there was a romantic possibility brewing between us.

Our friendship had blossomed over time, and we finally decided it was time to meet in person. After taking the necessary health precautions—masking up and observing isolation periods—he flew up to visit us. Once we were all together, our connection deepened quickly; it felt as if everything fell into place effortlessly. Our first outing as a family—my daughter included—was a trip to the San Francisco California Academy of Sciences. Although we all had to wear masks, we had a wonderful time. It was the first time my daughter and I had gone to a public place for fun since the pandemic began, so having him there to help break us out of the isolation we had been in for a year was incredibly refreshing.

During his visit, we went on numerous hikes, ate out, and had many deep conversations; the time flew by. My daughter especially loved the moments when he gave her undivided attention and played Minecraft with her. After a delightful couple of weeks, he had to return to San Diego to spend time with his family, who were visiting, while we headed to Florida to reconnect with my sister and nieces.

We were both excited about his return after my trip, looking forward to picking up right where we left off and continuing to explore the promising connection we had started. The initial meeting had confirmed our compatibility and deepened our bond, making the anticipation of our next reunion even more thrilling.

My sister was now living in Miami, with two beautiful daughter and her husband. About six years prior, my sister and her then boyfriend decided to make their relationship official by getting married at the courthouse shortly after my daughter and their first daughter were born. This marriage marked a significant turning point in their lives. Motivated by their growing spiritual commitment, they started attending church regularly and felt a strong conviction to align their daily lives more closely with their biblical beliefs.

To support this new chapter back then, I moved to Walnut Creek, CA, after leaving my mother's house. This move was strategically planned to ensure that we were close enough for our daughters to easily spend time and play together. The proximity allowed us to support each other as young families, sharing the joys and challenges of parenting while fostering a strong bond between our children. Living close to my sister and niece provided cherished moments that were both heartwarming and invaluable.

Being able to have my niece over for sleepovers, dinners, and play dates was particularly special. We spent hours engaging in arts and crafts on the back patio, coloring, and playing games. These activities not only brought joy but also strengthened our bond, creating beautiful memories and moments of deep bonding. Living closer allowed us to share everyday experiences and support each other in ways that distance simply wouldn't permit.

However, not long after we moved and settled in, they made a drastic change. My brother-in-law secured a job as a border patrol agent at Miami Airport, prompting their move to Florida. Over the years, I visited them a few times in Florida, including when my second niece was born. Despite my desire to be close to my sister and my nieces, Florida never felt like the right place for me, so I never considered moving there permanently. This geographical distance was disheartening because I had hoped for our children, the cousins, to grow up together and for us to see each other regularly

Becoming a mom brings its own set of challenges and responsibilities, such as caring for the kids, managing the household, and working, which made it increasingly difficult to maintain a close relationship. Consequently, my sister and I found ourselves drifting apart over the years, not seeing or talking to each other as much as we would have liked. This reality was tough to accept, as ideally, I had envisioned a life where we could be more integrated into each other's daily lives, supporting each other through motherhood.

It had been quite some time, perhaps since my niece was born four years ago, when we decided to visit my sister during the middle of the pandemic. That first visit since the outbreak began was incredibly precious. The pandemic really highlighted the importance of close connections with loved ones, making every moment feel sacred. The change of scenery and the warmth of family time provided deep comfort. We laughed, shared stories, and created new memories, including a delightful trip to Legoland. My daughter absolutely loves rollercoasters, so this trip—especially after being isolated for so long—made her beam with so much joy and happiness. Seeing her so happy truly lights me up; there's nothing quite like seeing her light up with excitement.

During my visit, I noticed a shift in the frequency and quality of communication with my new boyfriend, who seemed increasingly preoccupied with his own family back in San Diego. While I understood and respected his need to focus on his family, it left me feeling somewhat unsettled. His reduced outreach caused me anxiety and made me wonder if I was still on his mind. This contrast in his usual attentiveness triggered a reaction in my body, a sort of mini alarm that something wasn't right. For him to transition from being very attentive to scarcely available was jarring and didn't sit well with my nervous system.

Realizing how deeply attached I had become to him in such a short time was more challenging than I had anticipated. This early and intense attachment brought back fears from past relationships, making me question my vulnerability. Opening up so quickly and so deeply stirred a complex mix of emotions, highlighting the tension between my desire for closeness and the fear of being hurt again. This experience served as a reminder of the delicate balance required in new relationships, especially when past traumas linger in the background.

As our relationship continued, a growing unease took root within me, fueled by his continued engagement with his recent ex on social media. Early on, before our relationship became serious, he had suggested I follow her for business advice. However, as we grew closer, I couldn't help but notice that he remained actively engaged with her posts, some of which were quite revealing, featuring her in attire that highlighted her cleavage. This persistent interaction hinted at possibly unresolved feelings or, at the very least, a desire on his part to maintain a connection and seek her attention. This behavior struck me as unsettling and raised questions about the depth and exclusivity of our connection.

Moreover, he casually mentioned that they were messaging each other during a work Zoom call—since she was a client at the company he worked for—and he seemed amused by this. This lack of boundaries in their communication and relationship amplified my discomfort, triggering feelings of insecurity and prompting me to address the issue directly with him.

I expressed my need for clearer boundaries regarding his interactions with her, explaining how his current level of engagement did not make me feel safe or secure in our relationship. It was crucial for me to communicate these feelings to see if we could align our expectations and reassure the trust needed to continue building a healthy relationship.

He responded to my concerns by promising to cease all personal interactions with her, emphasizing that he didn't want to jeopardize the good thing we had started creating together. His response appeared sincere and initially soothed my anxiety, providing a momentary relief. However, the situation had already planted seeds of doubt about the security and stability of our connection. Despite his assurances, I found myself questioning whether I could genuinely trust his choices and his word moving forward. This internal conflict made me ponder the true depth of our relationship and whether such trust issues could be resolved or if they would remain a recurring concern.

Initially, I felt heard and respected regarding my need for safety. However, not long after, on a phone call, he mentioned the possibility of moving to another country for several months with a coworker. This idea set off more alarms for me, reigniting my insecurities. As a mother, the thought of getting involved with someone who might abruptly leave the country for a long period of time seemed unstable, inconsistent, and unsafe. It made me question the reliability of building a future with someone so ready to make a dramatic life change without considering its impact on us. This uncertainty wasn't the stable foundation I sought in a lifelong partnership, nor did it seem conducive to building a family life with my daughter.

As time passed, I began to question whether this person, to whom I had grown so attached so quickly, possessed the maturity necessary for a relationship that already involved a family. It seemed he didn't fully grasp the differences between being in a relationship with a young, single woman and being with a mom who has a seven-year-old daughter. Some of his ideas were unexpected and disorienting, lacking the stability and security needed to lay a solid foundation for our relationship. This created a shaky and unpredictable environment, leading me to doubt whether our relationship could sustain itself long-term. The uncertainty made it difficult to envision a stable future together, casting shadows on the longevity of our connection.

I found myself wrestling with whether my heightened sensitivity was a byproduct of the pandemic and the isolation it enforced or if it truly stemmed from legitimate concerns about him. His uncertain future plans and the looming possibility of physical distance between us only compounded my fears. Despite these mixed signals and growing doubts, I chose to continue exploring the relationship, influenced partly by his affiliation with The Greatness Gathering—a community I deeply respected for its integrity. His association to this community made me hesitant to quickly dismiss him, urging me to give the relationship more time to unfold and develop, hoping that further engagement might clarify my feelings and the potential for a lasting bond.

Navigating trauma within intimate relationships presents a profound challenge. It often becomes difficult to trust your instincts and intuition, as trauma can blur the lines between past experiences and current realities. Self-doubt frequently overshadows decision-making, and a desire to be forgiving or to offer the benefit of the doubt can cloud judgment. This dynamic raises critical questions: Am I interpreting this situation and this person accurately, or are my reactions influenced by past traumas? Is this moment genuinely reflective of current issues, or is it a trigger from the past masquerading as the present?

These questions underscore the complexity of dealing with trauma in relationships. The intensity of feelings in the moment can make it seem unquestionably relevant to the present, reinforcing the perception that the reaction is directly tied to what's happening now. However, distinguishing whether these strong emotions are truly about the current situation or are echoes of the past is incredibly challenging. This confusion is a common struggle for those navigating post-traumatic reactions, making it essential to approach such situations with self-awareness and, often, professional guidance to help discern and heal the underlying issues.

After returning home from Florida, I was determined to finally address my lingering concerns about his interactions with his ex. The thought of confronting him was daunting and filled me with intense anxiety; the prospect of facing the truth was so unsettling that it made me feel physically ill, my body shaking—a clear trauma response. Despite my resolve, I continuously found myself creating reasons to delay the conversation. The apprehension was overwhelming, and every moment felt like a battle between my need for clarity and the fear of what that clarity might reveal.

Days after his return, when we took my daughter to the park, the right moment finally arrived. We sat on a bench watching her play, and the anxiety I'd been holding onto was clearly visible on my face—I've never been able to mask my emotions well. Seeing my discomfort, he gently probed, asking what was troubling me. His direct inquiry felt like a doorway opening, providing a space to voice my concerns and fears openly and to gauge his reaction. This was a pivotal moment, offering a choice between retreating into silence or embracing the vulnerability required for honest communication. I knew that how I chose to proceed could significantly impact the future of our relationship.

When I finally gathered the courage to discuss his ongoing engagement with his ex on social media, I was seeking clarity and reassurance. His initial silence in response was disconcerting; it felt as though the ground was falling away beneath me. After a tense moment, he handed me his phone. As I scrolled through, the reality hit me hard—I discovered they had been texting and messaging on Instagram. Although the messages themselves weren't overtly inappropriate, my heart sank as I felt a wave of dizziness and began to shake, overwhelmed by the sense of betrayal.

The core issue wasn't the nature of their exchanges but the fact that he had explicitly promised to cease communication with her to foster a sense of security in our relationship and to respect a boundary we had set together. By breaking that promise, he not only continued communication but also significantly undermined the trust and safety we were trying to build. This breach of trust was deeply hurtful and made me question the foundation of our relationship and his commitment to our future together.

The realization that he had lied to me triggered a profound sense of insecurity and mistrust. At that moment, in my eyes, he transformed from someone I was growing to trust to a 'liar' whose words I could no longer rely on. This shift was not just disappointing—it cut deep, awakening old fears and amplifying my doubts about whether I could truly rely on anyone. His actions contradicted his promises, and that breach of trust felt like a significant betrayal, reshaping how I saw him and our potential future together.

Feeling deeply betrayed, my pain was only intensified by his reaction. Instead of acknowledging his actions and taking responsibility, he became defensive. He accused me of attacking his character and dismissed my feelings as an overreaction. He attempted to rationalize his behavior, minimizing the significance of what had happened and its impact on me. This dismissal of my valid emotions—particularly when I was most in need of empathy—deeply hurt and frustrated me.

His inability to offer compassion or understanding was palpable. When I cried, he just stared blankly, showing no sign of empathy or connection. This response only widened the rift between us, making the breach of trust feel almost irreparable. It undermined the foundation of our relationship and shook my confidence in his sincerity, casting a long shadow over our future together.

In the weeks that followed, the atmosphere between us grew increasingly tense, filled with unspoken grievances and a palpable strain. I was wrestling with deep disappointment and anger, while he seemed more concerned with defending his actions and his character and minimizing their impact rather than genuinely understanding how deeply they had hurt me. The trust we had been carefully building felt irreparably shattered, leaving our once-promising connection feeling precarious and fraught with instability. The early days of our relationship, which should have been filled with discovering each other and joyful exploration, quickly gave way to a harsh reality where both our wounds were laid bare, clashing and intertwining in ways that were too complex to navigate smoothly. This rapid shift from a very short-lived honeymoon phase to confronting raw and unresolved issues was jarring, making it clear that our path forward would be anything but easy.

Despite my efforts to manage my emotions through EFT and other healing practices, the core issues in our relationship remained unresolved. I found myself questioning whether the emotional toll was worth it, especially considering my past traumas and my need for a stable, trustworthy partner. The weight of these doubts and the constant conflict underscored the need for change. This wasn't the kind of relationship I envisioned or desired for myself and my daughter.

This experience highlighted his difficulties with managing his emotions, holding emotional space, expressing empathy, and fully owning his mistakes. Despite these significant issues, we continued to date and eventually became a couple. When he moved up from Encinitas, he quickly began to take charge and make changes around the house, often without considering my preferences. It felt like a bull in a china shop, as he bulldozed through everything, from rearranging the pillows on my bed to adjusting the temperature in the house. It soon became clear that he needed more space than our two-bedroom, two-story townhouse could provide.

In many ways, I was scared of him and his anger. His outbursts were unpredictable and intense, making me feel like I was walking on eggshells. The fear of triggering his anger made me question my decisions and second-guess my actions constantly. Yet, despite this, I also loved him. There were moments when his inner child side would come out—playful, caring, and sweet. These moments created a confusing juxtaposition between love and fear, making it hard to clearly see the relationship's true nature.

This relationship cracked open a trauma capsule, bringing up deep-seated issues that I hadn't fully reckoned with since my daughter's birth. It surfaced all my attachment wounds at once, intensifying my emotional turmoil. The strain of these unresolved issues pushed our relationship to its breaking point, mirroring past experiences, especially with my daughter's father. Just like then, it became evident that this relationship might not have the resilience to withstand the firestorm of unresolved traumas and the intense pressures we were facing.

Desperate for solutions, I reached out to Derek Hart, someone whose expertise I had known and trusted for years. We had first connected through mutual friends, and I had followed his work on attachment styles and relationships, resonating deeply with his teachings on how he supported couples in connecting and healing. Previously, Derek had also supported me in creating a 20-video series on gaslighting for women, which allowed me to work closely with him and build a sense of safety in his guidance.

We underwent several sessions with Derek, which illuminated our conflicts and offered strategies to manage them. While these sessions weren't a magical cure, they provided valuable insights and tools that helped us address some of our issues. Alongside our sessions with Derek, I continued my personal journey of healing, engaging with various practitioners and healers. My aim was to delve into and begin healing the deep-seated wounds that had resurfaced, striving to mitigate the overwhelming internal activation that often pushed me beyond my capacity to cope. This dual approach—couple's therapy with Derek and personal healing work—was crucial in managing the immediate challenges in our relationship while also addressing the underlying issues within myself.

The couple's therapy sessions with Derek provided some clarity and a temporary sense of hope. We explored our patterns, communication styles, and the deep-seated fears that fueled our behaviors. Yet, these sessions also underscored the profound emotional gap between us. Although we made some progress, it frequently seemed like we were merely applying band-aids to much deeper wounds, rather than achieving the substantial healing we needed.

For my own healing, I continued to explore and engage with new therapeutic modalities that could benefit, not only myself, but also my clients. I pursued certifications in Somatic Attachment Therapy and Brainspotting, delving deeper into these practices. As I experienced healing from these techniques and learned to apply them more effectively, I noticed a significant change in myself—I became less reactive and started to practice pausing more in the relationship, which helped me manage my responses and interactions more thoughtfully.

Somatic Attachment Therapy opened new pathways for me to deeply connect with my body, teaching me how my physical sensations relate directly to my emotions and the parts of myself that needed love. This awareness helped me effectively identify and soothe my triggers, lessening their impact on my daily life. It also taught me to recognize the parts of myself seeking validation from my partner, guiding me to validate myself instead.

Brainspotting was transformative in a different way. It enabled me to process and release trauma stored, not only in my brain, but also in my nervous system and body tissues. This approach accessed deeper layers of healing, helping me uncover and address buried emotional pain.

These practices profoundly influenced my personal growth, gradually allowing me to gain more control over my reactions and emotions. I had emerged from the overwhelming flood of trauma-induced responses. These tools didn't just help me manage my present; they began reshaping my future and steering me toward a healthier, more grounded existence.

The transformative effect of these healing modalities on my conflict management was profound. As I integrated the practices into my daily life, I found myself able to remain calmer during disagreements, which significantly improved my communication skills. Instead of succumbing to impulsive reactions, I learned to pause—take a moment to breathe, regulate my system, and assess the situation thoughtfully before responding. This newfound ability to soothe myself and take a step back created a buffer that reduced the intensity of our arguments, paving the way for more constructive discussions. While this shift greatly enhanced the dynamics of my relationships, it didn't make the process effortless, especially when dealing with deeply ingrained triggers or particularly sensitive topics.

As I evolved through my healing practices, the dynamics of our relationship began to shift. My partner noticed the changes in how I managed conflict and responded to stress, and this influenced his behavior too. Though our relationship remained challenging, the emotional rollercoaster we were on started to stabilize somewhat. The peaks and valleys of our interactions became less extreme. We experienced moments of genuine connection and understanding amidst the ongoing challenges, offering glimpses of what a healthier, more balanced dynamic could look like between us. These changes didn't resolve all our issues, but they opened up new possibilities for growth and understanding within our relationship.

This personal journey of healing and growth within my own relationship significantly enhanced my ability to support my clients facing similar intimate relationship challenges. Relating to their struggles on a deeper level, I could offer them tools and techniques that had proven effective in my own life. The modalities I incorporated into my practice, such as Somatic Attachment Therapy and Brainspotting, became powerful aids, helping others navigate their healing journeys and improve their relationships.

Life seemed to continuously present me with difficult scenarios, as if preparing me to help others facing similar hardships. I often joked about wanting to emulate Buddha in my life's work—careful what you wish for, right? But this path, while challenging, has been profoundly rewarding, allowing me to transform personal trials into professional triumphs, aiding others in their own quests for healing and fulfillment.

Deciding to move out of state was a pivotal moment for us. We were outgrowing our two-bedroom home, particularly with both of us working from home and evolving into a small family unit. Texas emerged as an attractive destination. The relentless inflation in California, along with my reservations about the educational system and certain progressive educational policies that seemed to infringe upon parental rights, fueled our decision. Relocating to Texas was not just a practical move for more affordable living—it was also a step towards an environment that better aligned with our values and promised a brighter future for my daughter.

During a work trip, we took the opportunity to scout out a few locations within Texas. The first two towns didn't feel right at all, and even Austin, where the work event was held, was a definite no for me. But when we arrived in a suburb of Houston, I was immediately struck by an expansive, energetic feeling of affirmation. The first house we viewed was nearly perfect—it was brand new, having been previously inhabited by only one older man. Despite my initial hesitation, convinced that it was the house we surely wouldn't secure, it turned out to be the only one that approved us—and that happened within the same day. We hadn't even made our way back to California when we were already signing the lease.

Everything happened swiftly after we decided to move forward with the house. It was a beautiful four-bedroom home, offering ample space for my partner and me, an office for each of us, a vast backyard for my daughter, and a garage. We were more than doubling our living space compared to the cramped two-bedroom townhome we had been squeezing ourselves into. I could hardly believe that this was going to be our new home.

The move to Texas was fraught with a whirlwind of challenges from the start. As we were preparing to head back to California, we contracted COVID for the first time. We attempted to isolate from my daughter to prevent her from catching it but she hated this because she just wanted to be close to us. Ironically, she ended up contracting it but handled it surprisingly well, and was just happy not to be isolated from us anymore. I, on the other hand, developed a severe cough that made breathing difficult, requiring an inhaler for the first time in my life—despite being vaccinated, which made me question the vaccine's effectiveness.

Juggling, packing, planning, and caring for my daughter and partner while feeling miserable was overwhelming. To add to the stress, we encountered issues with a moving company that seemed dubious, prompting a hurried trip to the bank—masked up and cautious—to prevent unauthorized withdrawals. I felt so guilty for potentially exposing others to COVID and having to physically be there in order to change my account to avoid being scammed.

Miraculously, we tested negative on the morning of the move, allowing my parents to help without risk. As if in answer to my weary question, "What else could go wrong?" the universe seemed determined to show us exactly that. Our journey continued to unravel in ways we hadn't anticipated. Not long after resolving the banking issues, another challenge arose, the moving company double-booked our truck, giving us one that was too small and arriving hours later than my booking. This left us scrambling with a vehicle that was too small for all our belongings. We found ourselves making tough decisions on what to keep and what to discard, as we tried to squeeze a life's worth of possessions into the undersized truck.

The complications didn't stop there. During a quick run to the hardware store, a car collided with my back bumper as I was reversing out of my parking spot. The driver, clearly under the influence of hard drugs, accused me of hitting him, though it was clear he was at fault. Sensing a scam, I exchanged information and documented the damage. I took a moment to center myself and connect with my higher power, and as suspected, he never filed a claim.

Finally, with the house spotless and our belongings packed, we set out on the road, hopeful that the worst was behind us. Yet, fate had one more test in store. As we merged onto the freeway, the bikes and bike rack unexpectedly detached from the back of my car, clattering across the asphalt and vanishing from sight. It was a heart-stopping moment, instantly escalating our stress to new heights. We pulled off at the nearest parking lot to call the police and gather ourselves.

This last incident pushed us all to our emotional limits. My partner, who had remained strong throughout the ordeal, broke down for the first time since we'd been together, overwhelmed by the chaos of the day. I, too, was a complete mess, barely holding it together. Thankfully, the bikes and rack didn't cause an accident on the freeway—somehow, they seemed to have been quickly picked up by someone passing by. Still, the mere thought that we could have caused serious harm to others was devastating. After navigating so many hurdles, this final scare felt like too much to bear.

In the midst of this turmoil, I felt compelled to reach out to my spiritual mom and mentor from the Foundation of Spiritual Development. I needed to ground and re-center my energy and to draw on my faith more deeply. Her response was a beacon of serenity in the storm. She guided me through the process, helping me to reconnect with my spiritual practices and reminding me of the strength and peace that come from maintaining that connection. Her support was invaluable, providing me with the spiritual sustenance needed to navigate the chaos and re-anchor myself in stability and hope.

The remainder of our journey turned a corner toward the lighter side, becoming smooth, fun, and filled with adventure. We made our way through various cute Airbnb stops, each offering a unique place to rest and recharge. Along the route, we indulged in meals at quaint little diners, enjoying the local flavors and the charm of small-town hospitality. These stops became delightful interludes that punctuated our trip with moments of joy and relaxation, allowing us to collect memories that would last a lifetime. It was a wonderful way to transition into our new life, gradually leaving behind the chaos of the move and embracing the exciting possibilities ahead.

Despite the series of curveballs and challenges we faced, we finally arrived in Houston, ready to start settling into our new home and life. The spacious environment felt like a breath of fresh air, a true fresh start marking the beginning of a new chapter for us all. I set up my home office, turning it into a sanctuary for both my work and personal growth. My daughter was immediately taken with the backyard, finding joy in the ample space to play and explore. Together, we began discovering the local community, each outing bringing us closer to making this new place feel like home.

The extra space in our new home brought a profound sense of relief and significantly eased the anxiety that had been weighing heavily on us. As we settled in, the calmness of our surroundings began to permeate our relationship, fostering healing and stability. It became increasingly clear that this relationship had the depth and resilience to endure, providing a level of stability that had been absent in previous relationships. My partner was committed for the long haul, and my daughter now had a home in a family-oriented neighborhood—a nurturing environment where she could truly thrive. This move wasn't just a change of location;

it was a transformative step towards building a stable and flourishing family life.

As we settled into Houston, my nervous system began to truly calm down and heal. The significance of one's environment in the healing process cannot be overstated, and our new surroundings provided the peaceful and supportive atmosphere essential for my continued journey of self-discovery and transformation. Although Texas was the last place I ever imagined I would call home, it was precisely where my intuition led me. This unexpected destination has proven to be a place of profound transformation and growth for all of us, confirming that sometimes, the most unexpected paths lead to the most rewarding destinations.

Our new home in Houston quickly transformed into a sanctuary, offering us a space where we could all breathe a little easier. The additional room allowed for personal retreats, providing each of us the necessary space to grow both individually and as a family. My daughter thrived in this new environment, making new friends and exploring the local parks and activities. This sense of belonging and the newfound stability we experienced were healing in themselves, reinforcing the importance of setting roots in a nurturing community. Our move to Texas, though filled with initial hurdles, unfolded into a period of significant personal and collective growth, affirming our decision to embrace this new chapter.

I've come to understand that the fairy tale ideal of love and relationships is often just that—an ideal rather than reality. A partner doesn't arrive in our lives fully formed and flawless. Relationships require ongoing effort, mutual commitment, and a capacity for repair when imperfections and challenges emerge. The relationship I find myself in may not match the storybook vision I once held, but it is grounded in reality. It is a partnership characterized by genuine growth and learning. This has taught me that real love isn't about perfection but about navigating life's ups and downs together, building resilience, and evolving side by side. This real, imperfect relationship has been a profound teacher of what it means to love and be loved.

Perfection isn't the goal in relationships; instead, growth, understanding, and mutual support take precedence. Every challenge we've faced has not only tested our bond but has also strengthened it, drawing us closer together. The moments of tension and conflict, while certainly difficult, have offered invaluable opportunities for learning—about each other and ourselves.

Navigating a relationship where both partners have endured childhood trauma presents a unique dynamic. We find ourselves in a delicate balance, where our interactions can either trigger old wounds or foster profound healing. The outcome hinges on our continual choice to engage in the work necessary for growth. It's a path that could potentially lead us into unhealthy patterns, or alternatively, bring about the deepest healing for both of us. Recognizing this, we remain committed to couples therapy as a vital tool in our journey. Therapy helps us learn and practice the behaviors and skills that weren't modeled for us in our formative years. This commitment to actively working on our relationship is essential in transforming our past adversities into a source of strength and mutual healing.

What truly matters in our relationship is our willingness to address issues head-on, to listen attentively, and to support each other through all the ups and downs. It's about committing to the work, especially during those times when it feels challenging or uncomfortable. In this new chapter of my life, I've embraced the reality that love and relationships are fundamentally about partnership, consistent effort, and ongoing growth. They require showing up every day, being fully present, and making the conscious choice to choose each other, particularly in tough times. This approach to love, while far from perfect, is deeply fulfilling and genuinely real—it's about building something lasting and meaningful together, based on mutual respect and shared growth.

In relationships, making an empowered commitment is crucial, rather than being swayed by fleeting emotions. It's important to recognize that relationships aren't always going to feel 'good', nor are they designed to make you happy all the time. They involve a balance, with ebbs and flows, where the emphasis isn't on avoiding mistakes but on rising from them—together. It's about dusting each other off, moving forward, and learning from those mistakes.

In today's world, where noncommittal flings and a plethora of options can make it difficult to settle on one person, finding someone who is willing to do the hard work is vital. Look for someone who doesn't shy away from challenges or adversity—someone who is willing to go to therapy with you and who is committed to building a life together. These are significant green flags. Such a partnership, built on mutual effort and a readiness to face life's challenges, becomes a powerful and enriching journey that far transcends the superficial connections that often characterize our modern dating landscape.

Our move to Texas, despite its initial series of challenges, has become a pivotal part of our relationship journey. It has provided the necessary physical space and environment to nurture not only our relationship, but also our individual growth. Texas has transformed into a sacred place of healing and personal transformation for us as a family, enabling us to cultivate a life that truly reflects our values and aspirations. Here, my daughter has thrived, experiencing the kind of childhood I always hoped for her—a childhood filled with joy, growth, and the freedom to explore her interests in a supportive and loving environment, neighborhood and community.

My Pain into Power Process has flourished here, allowing me to assist more women globally in transforming their emotional traumas and challenges into their superpowers. Living in the outskirts of Houston, I've embraced new roles that amplify my voice and extend my reach. I've become a writer, contributing articles to various publications, and I am now stepping into the roles of author and keynote speaker, which further expands my impact.

Working through the layers of fear that once kept me hidden, I've overcome the silence imposed by past abuse. Speaking up and out more than ever, I've released the silence I felt compelled to maintain since being threatened by Bobby. This journey of vocal empowerment is not just about personal healing but also about inspiring others to find their voice and reclaim their power, illustrating the transformative potential of turning pain into a source of strength and empowerment.

Helping women navigate their pain and transform it into strength has been an incredibly rewarding aspect of my work.

Witnessing the profound transformations and growth of my clients and supporting them through this alchemical process of turning their deepest struggles into their greatest strengths, truly reinforces the value and importance of what I do. Each story of empowerment and every breakthrough I witness not only fuels my passion but also deepens my dedication to this path. It's a privilege to be part of such powerful journeys, and it continually inspires me to keep moving forward, expanding my reach, and enhancing my methods to better serve those who seek healing.

Stepping into the role of a writer has truly opened new avenues for me to share my experiences and insights. By contributing articles to various international publications, I've been able to reach a broader audience, offering guidance and support to those who may be navigating similar challenges. The feedback from readers has been incredibly heartwarming and affirming. Knowing that my words can make a difference in someone's life, even if it's just one person, is deeply fulfilling. If my writing can touch a soul, offer a new perspective, lighten someone's burden, or plant a seed of hope, then it's wholly worth it. This positive impact motivates me to continue contributing in this way.

Becoming an author and a keynote speaker marks an exhilarating new chapter in my life. It offers a unique opportunity to compile my experiences, lessons learned, and tools into a cohesive narrative that can inspire and guide others on their paths to healing and empowerment. Speaking allows me to connect with audiences on a deeper level, sharing my story and the "Pain into Power Process" in ways that resonate and motivate. It's a privilege to stand before others, not only as a guide but as a testament to the transformative power of facing and reframing our deepest challenges.

In embracing these new roles, my goal is to cultivate a larger community focused on support and transformation, creating a space where women feel truly seen, heard, and empowered to reclaim their lives. The journey from pain to power represents one of the most profound transformations, and I am deeply honored to both guide and witness this incredible process in others.

As I continue to grow and evolve, I remain steadfast in my commitment to authenticity, vulnerability, and the relentless pursuit of healing and empowerment. The challenges and experiences that have shaped my journey illuminate a life filled with purpose and passion—a life dedicated to helping others discover and harness their strength and power. This mission drives me every day, fueling my dedication to make a meaningful impact and inspire change in the lives of those I have the privilege to reach.

I've discovered the immense power that lies in following my passion and the magic that unfolds when I truly step into my purpose. This journey hasn't been easy—each challenge has tested my resolve, but these obstacles have only made me stronger and more determined. Through these experiences, I've learned to trust the process and believe in my own capabilities, embracing the understanding that I have the power to create something both beautiful and meaningful. This belief in myself and my mission has been fundamental in shaping a path that not only fulfills me but also allows me to contribute positively to the lives of others, turning adversity into opportunity and despair into hope.

Reflecting on my two-decade commitment to healing, I see it as a testament to the power of love, creativity, and perseverance. This journey reminds me that, even amid uncertainty, it's possible to create a life aligned with my true self. It all began when I chose to surrender to the calls of my soul, following them unreservedly—a decision that has profoundly shaped my life and my daughter's life. This path hasn't just been about self-improvement; it's been a profound transformation that has allowed me to live authentically and vibrantly. If I can embark on this journey of self-discovery and healing, so can you. It starts with listening to your inner voice and daring to follow where it leads, trusting that this is the path to a fulfilling and meaningful life.

The Ultimate Prescription

For every mistake I've made
I've made someone bleed
If not another
Then it was me
So much blood has been shed
So many scabbed-up scars
Gotten me connected

To the pain of the world
To tap into this river
Is to tap into what it means to be human
Had to surrender
End the struggle of fighting against the current
Accept what is
And sit in it
Let go of all deflective maneuvers
Remove all masks- layers- barriers
Stand still and open
Transparent
Naked
Transcendent
Grieving the losses
Without any judgment
Opening the gates of forgiveness
Clearing the way for space
Where love can enter
Pour over the hurt- the pain
Heal the wounds where blood was shed
To combine
Reunite
Become whole
Treat the infection of separation that disconnects all of life's creation's
Build bridges of understanding
Compassion
To Arrive
At a Higher State of Consciousness
The Ultimate Prescription
For the tangible physical reality of unnecessary suffering
The disease that's been killing us
Since Adam and Eve in the Garden of Eden
Since the beginning of the beginning
The cure is in motion
It's trickling through the masses
The Ego's downfall is now on the horizon
It cannot thrive where awareness is prevalent

Gives meaning to all the blood that's been shed
Purpose
Where darkness used to reside
We now have the light of reason
Open your arms and embrace it
Life as you've known it has now ended

Cassandra Love Lambert, June 2008

C-LOVE

Chapter 32
Becoming My Own Hero, If I Can You Can Too

What a life, am I right?! Searching for healing, I encountered a significant challenge in finding the right support to transcend my trauma. I was seeking someone who not only understood the depths of my pain but could also guide me effectively through the darkness. However, I often encountered coaches, practitioners, therapists, and mentors who, despite their claims of being able to help, hadn't experienced anything remotely similar to what I had gone through. This lack of shared experience led to a disconnect; I didn't feel fully understood or seen, which seeded doubt in their ability to genuinely support me.

After two decades dedicated to my healing journey, I've reached a profound realization: the healer I was desperately searching for was always within me, waiting to be realized and embodied. The hero I had been hoping and praying for was me all along. Much like Dorothy from *The Wizard of Oz*, I had the power within me all along. Through years of relentless dedication, growth, and self-discovery, I have transformed into the very person I once needed—someone capable of transforming trauma into triumph. This journey of becoming has shown me that the most significant changes happen from within and that our greatest challenges can lead to our most extraordinary transformations.

Walking through the fires of my own experiences, I've learned the art of alchemy—turning darkness into light. This journey has not only healed me, but has also empowered me to guide others through similar paths of transformation. I've become a testament to the power of self-healing, embodying the resilience and strength that I aim to foster in those I help. This transformation reinforces the idea that sometimes, the most profound guidance comes, not from external sources, but from within ourselves—through our own trials and triumphs.

Now, I have the privilege of helping other women navigate their own paths to healing. I guide them through their pain, support them in transforming their trauma, and empower them to find the light within themselves. I help them to find the power within and rise to becoming their own hero's too. My story is a testament to the resilience of the human spirit and the power of self-transformation. It is a reminder that even in our darkest moments, we have the strength to heal and the potential to become a beacon of hope for others. This role allows me to share not just my techniques but also my personal journey, providing both a roadmap and a source of inspiration for those embarking on their own healing journeys.

By sharing my story—the good, the bad, the ugly in its rawest form—I hope to inspire you to find your own path to healing and to embrace the power within you to transform your life. No matter how daunting the journey may seem, remember that you are not alone, and there is always a way to turn your pain into power. Each step you take on this path, no matter how small, is a step toward reclaiming your life and discovering your strength.

In sharing my vulnerabilities and triumphs, I aim to show that healing is not a linear journey but a complex, deeply personal process that can lead to profound self-discovery and empowerment. Let my journey be a reminder that every challenge holds the potential for growth and transformation. You possess all the tools needed to navigate this path, and by embracing your journey with courage and openness, you can not only heal but also become a source of inspiration and strength to others. We are walking each other home.

Healing, I've learned, is far different from what I initially envisioned. It's not about reaching a point where all challenges or obstacles vanish, nor is it about becoming impervious to the things that once triggered deep emotional responses.

Healing is more of a lifestyle—a continuous process of cultivating your day-to-day life to nurture and support your well-being. It involves building the capacity to fully experience all your emotions, including the difficult ones, without overwhelming suppression or denial. Healing means developing resilience to handle life's challenges and obstacles more effectively and learning to resource yourself in moments of distress.

This approach to healing emphasizes adaptability and growth rather than achieving a static state of being "cured." It's about making intentional choices each day that contribute to your long-term health and happiness, recognizing that while the journey may involve setbacks, each step forward enriches your ability to live fully and authentically. This ongoing process is integral to a fulfilling life, allowing you to continuously evolve and strengthen in the face of life's complexities.

Healing is a dynamic and deeply personal process that involves crafting an environment where you feel safe and supported. It's about setting boundaries that honor your individual needs and capacity, allowing you to navigate life on your terms rather than forcing yourself to accommodate situations or behaviors that don't resonate with your well-being. This kind of boundary-setting creates a 'safe playpen' where you can explore and grow without the fear of being overwhelmed or invalidated.

Owning all aspects of your identity and showing up authentically is a crucial part of this process. Healing encourages you to embrace every facet of who you are, including the parts that you may have once wished to hide or change. This authenticity means being true to yourself in your interactions and choices, fostering deeper connections and a more fulfilling life.

Additionally, healing involves establishing a routine of self-care that caters to your physical, mental, and spiritual needs. Whether it's through meditation, physical activity, journaling, or simply spending time in nature, these practices are about more than just maintenance; they're about actively nourishing and rejuvenating yourself. Such routines not only improve your overall well-being but also help you to maintain your equilibrium in the face of life's inevitable stresses.

Recognizing and honoring your emotions is another fundamental aspect. It's important to allow yourself to feel and process your emotions freely and without judgment. This acceptance is crucial for healing, as it helps you understand that all your feelings are valid and form a significant part of your human experience.

Through these practices, healing fosters a deepening trust in yourself and your instincts. You develop a clearer understanding of your own needs and desires and become more attuned to what truly matters to you. Ultimately, healing empowers you to live a life that is not only aligned with your values but also true to your authentic self, enhancing your sense of fulfillment and purpose.

I've come to realize that when a memory ceases to ignite our bodies with activation and its vibrancy fades, it has been fully processed into the memory banks of our brain. However, if a memory still sends shockwaves of emotion through us, it's a clear indication that part of us is still trapped in that moment, reliving the pain of that traumatic event repeatedly in our subconscious, day after day.

In my healing practice, I've learned the profound importance of processing these memories. Each step forward in my journey of inner healing has allowed me to rescue parts of myself that have been ensnared in those nightmares, aiding me in becoming more whole and liberated. There is truly nothing more freeing than releasing these fragments of my being from the torment they've endured. This process of liberation not only heals me but also empowers me, reinforcing my belief in the transformative power of facing and embracing our deepest fears and pains.

In my **Pain into Power Process**, I guide my clients through this very journey, helping them transform their deepest wounds into their greatest strengths. The essence of our work together involves delving into those dark memories and liberating parts of themselves that have been trapped in nightmares. By addressing and healing these parts, we not only relieve the pain of the past, but also unlock a newfound strength and resilience within them. This process is not just about recovery; it's about reclaiming power and identity, enabling each person to emerge stronger and more whole from the trials they've endured.

I discovered that traditional talk therapy felt quite redundant for me. I grew tired of discussing the same issues repeatedly without any noticeable change in the sensations my body experienced in connection to those memories. Despite my commitment and regular attendance in therapy, my life seemed stagnant.

In response, I developed a process for my clients that focuses on releasing these bodily sensations tied to memories, without the need to delve into extensive detail about each experience repeatedly. This approach allows the sensations to be processed and released, paving the way for new possibilities and changes in their lives. This method has not only been transformative for my clients but also a vital part of my own healing journey.

The journey of inner healing is about breaking this cycle. As we engage in our healing work, we gradually rescue these trapped parts of ourselves, liberating them from their confines. This process not only helps us become more whole, but also restores our inner peace and strength. Each step towards healing is a step towards reclaiming our power and transforming our pain into a profound source of resilience and power.

Healing involves integrating the fragmented parts of ourselves, bringing them back into the present moment where they can be seen and acknowledged. This visibility allows for their release, integration, and embodiment. It's about gently tending to our wounds, giving them the care they need to heal. By doing so, these once painful memories and experiences lose their grip on our emotions and reactions.

This process enables us to move beyond being defined or controlled by our past hurts. Instead, we gain the freedom to respond to life's challenges with a greater sense of calm and resilience, not out of past reflexes but from a place of healed strength and wholeness. This transformation not only enhances our personal well-being, it also improves our interactions with others and allows us to engage more fully and authentically in our relationships and everyday life.

Through powerful modalities like EFT Tapping, Somatic Attachment Therapy, and Brainspotting, we gain the tools to access and gently release stuck memories from our nervous system, body, and brain, little by little. These approaches enable us to tap into our body's deep wisdom, helping us pinpoint where these memories are stored and understand their current impact on our lives. This process isn't just about dealing with past trauma; it's about reconnecting with ourselves on a profound level, allowing for true healing and transformation as we begin to understand and harmonize our body's responses to past events. These therapies offer a path to recovery that is both holistic and deeply respectful of the individual's pace and emotional landscape.

As we work through and unpack the painful events and memories, we actively create space for new experiences and ways of being to emerge. This process allows us to respond to life from a place of presence and authenticity, moving away from old wounds that keep us stuck in repetitive cycles of reaction and recreating the same narratives and patterns. Each memory we heal brings us a step closer to reclaiming our power and reconnecting with our true selves. This transformation is not just about moving past pain, but about embracing a new identity shaped by resilience, understanding, and self-compassion. Every step in this journey is a step toward a more authentic and empowered version of ourselves.

Healing is indeed not a linear journey; it's a continuous process of peeling back layers—like those of an onion or the spirals of a staircase—and uncovering deeper truths about ourselves. This path demands patience, consistency, compassion, and a readiness to confront the uncomfortable parts of our psyche. Each step moves us closer to a state of wholeness. As we transform our pain into power and our wounds into wisdom, we not only heal ourselves but also gain invaluable insights that enrich our understanding of life and our role within it. With every layer we shed, we emerge stronger and more integrated, capable of facing life with renewed clarity and resilience.

By engaging in this deep, transformative work, we heal not only ourselves, but also extend a ripple effect to those around us. We become a source of healing, a balm to our families, and a bridge of resolution to the wounds of our ancestors, as well as a foundation of strength for our children and those alongside us. We transform into beacons of light and love, inspiring others to embark on their healing journeys. Together, we can cultivate a world where authenticity, compassion, and connection are the norms—a world where everyone has the chance to move beyond merely surviving day to day, into a life of healing and thriving. This shift doesn't just change individual lives; it reshapes communities and generations, forging a legacy of health and wholeness that impacts the world at large. This is sacred work and a sacred path.

Being the first in my family to actively seek healing and support marked a significant turning point not just for me, but also for my loved ones. My dedication to finding a way through the challenges we faced inspired my sister to embark on her own journey of healing by starting therapy. This ripple effect of healing within our family was profound.

I also integrated these efforts into my parenting by involving my daughter in a few of my therapy sessions. My therapist remarked that she was the most confident 5-year-old he had ever met, a testament to the positive environment I strived to create for her amid our healing processes.

Recently, we reached another milestone. During a holiday gathering with my mom and stepdad, we managed to spend the entire week together without a single argument or fight—a first for us. At the end of their stay, we celebrated this achievement with high fives, acknowledging our collective progress. This peaceful interaction was a heartening sign of how far we had all come in understanding and supporting one another, highlighting the transformative power of continued healing and effort in improving our family dynamics.

I'm currently in my longest relationship with a man, and while it's not 'perfect,' its strength lies in our mutual commitment to making it work. He willingly engages in the necessary efforts, including attending therapy with me and dedicating himself to our relationship's growth. Unlike the 'Prince Charming' archetype that characterized my past relationships, he entered my life as someone real, flawed, and utterly human. This shift from seeking an idealized partner to embracing a genuine, flawed individual has transformed my approach to relationships tenfold, breaking old patterns and fostering a more profound, realistic connection.

Also, it has been deeply meaningful to reconnect with my long-lost younger sister on social media, whom I haven't seen or spoken to verbally since I was two years old. She found me years ago and began following me, and I followed her back. Since then, we've exchanged messages sporadically, offering support and encouragement for each other's lives and accomplishments. Observing her life unfold from afar, seeing her married and happy, brings me immense joy. Her support in the journey of writing this book, especially her active participation in the pre-sale by purchasing a copy, has been incredibly heartwarming and affirming. This connection, though primarily digital, has enriched my life and provided a sense of familial bond that was missing for so long.

I am deeply grateful for this connection. It offers a window into her life and allows for a form of relationship that we've not been able to have in person. I cherish this bond and hold onto the hope that one day our connection can grow stronger and perhaps lead to a more direct relationship. This possibility of eventually deepening our ties keeps me optimistic about the future.

Witnessing my daughter's innocence and experiencing how a childhood can unfold without the shadow of abuse is profoundly heartening. The efforts I've made to provide her with a safe, loving environment have been both healing and rewarding. It's a gift to see her grow up free from the burdens I carried, and it reassures me that the past patterns of abuse are not repeating in our family.

She is a beautiful soul, brimming with life and vitality, and seeing her thrive in this way fills me with immense joy and pride. Her happiness and well-being are constant reminders of the importance of breaking the cycle of abuse and the transformative power of providing a nurturing upbringing. It's a testament to the possibility of change and the positive impact we can have on the next generation.

Last year marked a profound moment in my life when I reunited with my God family after many years apart. The separation had been due to the shame I felt for returning to a dysfunctional environment, a decision that weighed heavily on me for almost two decades. Coming back to them, I was enveloped in the warmth of their unconditional love, which was incredibly healing.

Introducing my daughter to this nurturing atmosphere was especially meaningful. It was as if no time had passed, and we seamlessly fit back into the place where we've always belonged. This reunion not only mended old wounds but also reinforced the strong bonds of family and acceptance. It was a powerful reminder of the enduring nature of love and the potential for healing, regardless of past choices.

At last, I have reached a place in my life where I can wholeheartedly embrace every moment—the joyous, the painful, and the downright challenging. I recall the times when people spoke of this profound acceptance, and I struggled to believe such a state was attainable. It seemed like a myth, a kind narrative spun to offer comfort. Yet, here I am, standing at this juncture, feeling this truth in every fiber of my being. I now understand that each piece of my journey has been essential. Any variation in my path might have changed the essence of who I am. And who I am now is someone I deeply respect and truly cherish. I love who I have become!

Reaching this place of acceptance and appreciation didn't happen overnight. It has been a long journey filled with years of deep inner work, confronting my shadows, and celebrating my light. Each challenge, heartbreak, and triumph has sculpted me into the person I am today. Every experience has served as a teacher, leading me towards a greater self-awareness, enhanced compassion, and fortified resilience.

My journey of self-love and acceptance is far from over; it is a continuous path of growth and transformation that I embrace with all my heart. By sharing my story so openly, I hope to inspire you to embrace your own journey, find the courage to heal, and uncover the beauty and power that resides within you.

We all have the capacity to transform our pain into power, to turn our struggles into masterpieces, and to build lives that not only make us proud, but also fill us with purpose and passion. It starts by embracing our stories, owning our truths, and loving ourselves unconditionally. After reading these pages, my hope for you is to discover your own path to healing, to navigate your journey with compassion and courage, and to step into the light of your true self. Together, we rise.

C-LOVE

Keys I Want You to Take Away from My Life

Listen to your intuition and follow through on the messages it shares with you: Even if you don't see proof, celebrate the wins that manifest each time you do. Your intuition is a powerful guide, and trusting it can lead you to amazing places and protect you from things that may be harmful.

Be honest and show up as yourself: Many doors opened for me just by humbly showing up as myself and being honest. Authenticity attracts opportunities and genuine connections.

Ask for help and allow the support: Sometimes, the help we need comes from outside our immediate family. Be open to receiving support from unexpected sources, and recognize that we don't have to do everything alone.

Nurture and establish a relationship with a higher power: Whether you call this God, the Universe, Nature, Creator, or Source, there is a divine energy here to help us. Establishing that connection can provide guidance, strength, and comfort in difficult times.

Make your inner healing work a priority: Healing that occurs on the inside will transform your reality on the outside. I highly recommend somatic work to speed up the process and collapse time. Invest in your healing journey—it's the foundation for everything else in your life.

Treat everyone with kindness: You never know who you are meeting and who they may become tomorrow. Leave positive impacts and spread love wherever you go. Kindness creates ripples that can change the world.

Take inspired, imperfect action: As you take action, you can pivot and adjust along the way. Imperfect action is better than no action. Don't wait for everything to be perfect before you start moving toward your dreams.

No one is coming to save you: You are the one you have been waiting for. You have the power to heal and become your own hero. It's time to own that and step into your power.

By integrating these keys into your life, you can navigate challenges with resilience, create meaningful connections, and manifest a life that aligns with your true self. Trust in your journey, embrace your unique path, and know that you have the strength within you to overcome any obstacle.

C-LOVE

Next Steps on My Journey

Currently, I am working on becoming a professional keynote speaker. I recently got accepted to speak on the 2025 Women Thrive Summit Stage, where I will deliver a signature talk and step into this new dream. Next up will be a TED Talk. I'm excited to embrace these bigger roles of responsibility, so I can spread more light and have a greater impact by helping more people transform their pain into power.

If you have a stage where you'd love to have my story and message, please feel free to reach out to me. If you know organizations that could benefit from my message of inspiration and hope, please share my book and profile with them. If you know someone who is in the middle of their struggle, gift them a copy of this book. Let's keep paying it forward and spreading seeds of hope.

Are you curious about the **Pain into Power Process**? Do you feel called to work together more intimately? Feel free to visit my website and book a consultation call to see if we are a fit to work together in transforming your pain into your power. Let's embark on this journey of healing and empowerment together.

Scan this QR code to get all the gifts I have set aside for you, and to see behind the scenes memorabilia from different stages of my life.

Claim your Gifts HERE:
https://intothelightwithc-love.com/gift

C-LOVE

Victim Impact Statement

Before you read my Victim Impact Statement, here's a brief explanation: This statement details the profound effects of the sexual abuse I endured. It's an exercise my therapist encouraged since I never had the chance to speak up during the trial with Bobby. Writing this allowed me to voice the duration and depth of the abuse and its lasting impacts on my life. Creating such a statement can be profoundly healing, offering survivors a way to articulate their experiences and process trauma. I highly recommend that any abuse survivor writes their own impact statement and shares it with trusted individuals as a vital step in their healing journey.

Cassandra Love Lambert, Victim Impact Statement

When I was five and in kindergarten, we moved to this small apartment on San Bruno Avenue. My mom went to work and Bobby would stay home with me, he was my baby sitter. One day he called me into the bathroom and had his pants down and private out. It was the first time I had seen a naked grown man. He had magazines with naked women out on the counter and he told me to lick jelly off of his private part. I felt trapped. Like I could not say "No!" or walk away because he was in charge of me. I did what he told me to do even though I was scared and didn't want to. After the jelly was licked off he then had me touch his private part with my hand and rub up and down until white stuff went into the toilet. I did not know what that was at five years old. It was gross and reminded me of snot coming out of your nose when you're sick. He also was staring at the girls in the magazines the entire time he had me performing these tasks. He told me I better not tell my mom or else... After having seen him kick her in her tummy when she was pregnant, I took that to mean he would hurt her even more than I had already witnessed.

I felt gross, confused, alone. This became part of his routine with me when my mom was at work and not at home. Sometimes he would have me touching him in different ways. Sometimes he would lay me down and touch me, either with his hands or with his mouth and tongue. I hated how it felt when he touched me because it would burn in my private area between my legs. Sometimes after he had me touch him or he touched me, he would make me shower. He would wash me meticulously and stare at me. I couldn't hide or run away. I didn't like this either, but I didn't get a choice; I was at the mercy of what he wanted, when he wanted it. My voice and choice was taken away.

There was a time one of my friend's came over and I thought I would be safe from his activities. I was not. He came into my room with us and he was naked. We couldn't run away or leave. We were trapped. He directed us to also get naked, to touch each other, and to hump my big teddy bear. This was the only time he did something with me and someone else at the same time.

These sessions with him doing things with me and to me happened a lot from the time I was five years old until I was eight. It wasn't until I was eight that my mom finally left him. I'm not sure what prompted her to finally make that decision, but what I do know is that she was completely unaware of what he was doing to me when she wasn't around.

After we moved out, he would still take me and my sister out to do things and we would come to his new place in the city. That's when he started to take my sister to the bathroom instead of me. I felt horrible because I couldn't protect her and she was only three years old. She was so little I couldn't believe he would do that to her. This incident catapulted me to talk to my best friend at school, whom Bobby had also touched with me at my house. She told me I had to tell my mom in order to help my sister. I had so much fear and shame around telling my mom.

We walked out to my mom's car together, but I was too terrified to speak, so my friend spoke up for me. My mom was in shock. Without hesitation, she drove me to one of her friend's houses where we called the police and filed a report. I couldn't bear to talk about what happened, so I wrote it down instead. It turned into a long essay, detailing everything he had done, every incident, with as much detail as I could muster. It was one of the hardest things I've ever had to write.

After telling my mom and writing out everything in a report Bobby was still able to see and take my sister for visits. Only now I wasn't able to come with her, so she was alone and on her own. I was so scared for her especially with the information now out in the open. It took months, maybe even a year or more for the legal system to stop allowing him to take my sister on his own. He came to Latchkey one day while we were there, and he took her right off of the playground and no one stopped him.

It took months before he had to see my sister via supervised visits, and it took even longer for him not to be able to see her at all. This made me feel so helpless and powerless. Like I had made things worse by telling, versus better. It didn't feel like the 'system' really protected kids, it felt like it protected the 'monsters.'

These four years of my life with Bobby and his behaviors, choices and actions have negatively impacted my life in countless ways, even to this day, 35 years later. I have spent over $200,000 on two decades of healing work with different healers and practitioners, yet I still have triggers that prevent me from living a 'regular' life. I still navigate life with Complex Post Traumatic Stress Disorder (C-PTSD).

Throughout my teens and twenties, I struggled deeply with thoughts of suicide and a persistent desire not to be alive. I often found myself engaging in risky behaviors, like driving under the influence, secretly hoping for something drastic to happen. Miraculously, I always made it home unscathed, even surviving five car accidents in a single month during an especially turbulent period in my early twenties, while in an extremely abusive relationship.

When emotions overwhelmed me and I stepped outside my window of tolerance, I turned to self-harm—slapping, punching, or clawing at my arms. The physical pain was a grim relief, momentarily easier to handle than the profound emotional anguish that seemed to permeate my existence from within.

To this day, I have to skip or fast-forward certain scenes in movies and shows, or I use the Vid Angel App—an app that filters specific content out of shows and movies for me. This helps me manage my triggers and ensures that my viewing experience remains comfortable and enjoyable without unexpected content that could be distressing. It's a valuable tool that allows me to engage with media while still protecting my emotional well-being. I have to skip or filter scenes in movies and shows that show nudity, semi-nudity, or sex scenes.

I still have difficulty feeling safe in my body or feeling okay about my body. I struggle with having sex and tend to check out even when I am in a loving relationship. Challenges with my partner persist, and sometimes I still check out, and struggle to be present. I don't understand what love is or isn't, or what a loving touch is or isn't—it all feels the same. Dissociation occurs even when touched by someone I love.

Navigating relationships with deep-rooted attachment wounds is incredibly challenging. My past experiences have left me feeling insecurely attached, often on edge and in a state of hyper-vigilance, always bracing for the next disruption. This underlying anxiety makes it difficult to feel secure with a partner, especially regarding fidelity. The fear of being betrayed, whether through actions like watching porn, lusting with the eyes or emotional cheating, looms large and perpetuates a cycle of distrust that makes it hard to feel truly safe in a relationship. This deeply embedded distrust colors my interactions and can make intimate connections feel perilous, even when I deeply desire to connect and build a trusting bond.

Navigating social spaces and the digital world can be incredibly challenging for me, especially in environments where there's a lot of exposed skin, like beaches or pools. These settings trigger activations in my body, a response tied deeply to my past traumas. The pervasive oversexualization in our society, often reflected in marketing strategies involving nudity or partial nudity, complicates my interactions with social media and the internet. It's a constant effort to protect my mental and emotional well-being while trying to engage with the world around me in a healthy way.

Navigating the world with triggers from sexualized and semi-sexualized visuals is especially challenging while in a relationship. It intensifies the activations in my body whenever I notice my partner seeing certain images on social media, or even just someone passing by in revealing clothing. This aspect of my life has been incredibly difficult to manage. It's crucial for me to find a partner who understands the depth of my experiences and is willing to be extraordinarily sensitive and protective concerning these triggers. While I diligently work on healing internally and reducing these triggers, it requires continuous effort to face these fears and try to function in a world where I often feel unsafe and uncomfortable. The journey demands not only constant work on myself, but also a profound level of understanding and support from my partner. It requires someone who can truly grasp the depth of my experiences and offer the kind of sensitivity and support that helps me feel secure. This level of empathy and patience isn't common, making it difficult to establish and maintain relationships that feel safe and nurturing.

It's crucial for me to find a partner who not only respects my journey but is also committed to actively participating in it. I need someone who understands the depth of my experiences and is willing to help create a healing environment, rather than inadvertently reinforcing the wounds and traumas I've worked so hard to overcome. Finding someone with this level of understanding and commitment has felt close to impossible, but it remains a vital part of what I need in a relationship.

Throughout my life, I've found myself in and out of numerous abusive relationships, a pattern I now recognize as being rooted in early grooming and the silencing of my voice. This cycle severely impacted my self-esteem and self-worth, leaving me struggling with my identity as a woman. I've even resented my own body, wishing I could rid myself of the curves that seemed only to attract unwanted attention and abuse.

In a bid for control and perhaps a sense of empowerment, I turned to exotic dancing. I thought it would transform my circumstances—make me like one of those unattainable women in the magazines Bobby had, rather than the little girl forced to lick his penis. Unfortunately, this environment only deepened my trauma, echoing the abuses of my past rather than providing the escape I had hoped for and it became a trap that was hard to get out of due to building my life around the finances it provided.

The trauma I endured has significantly impacted my relationships within my family, especially with my mom and sister. The divide between my mom and me has deepened, largely because of how she's handled the situation—often using my trauma as leverage in arguments or exacerbating my triggers without regard for my feelings. This has only intensified my sense of isolation and distrust toward her. My relationship with my sister has also been a rollercoaster of closeness and distance, complicated by our shared traumatic past. Seeing my sister, who reminded me of Bobby during our childhood, would trigger distressing memories, making it difficult for me to be around her comfortably. Rather than cultivating understanding and compassion, my mom's tactics have only driven a deeper wedge between us, obstructing any chance for healing or genuine connection in our family. This trauma, inflicted by Bobby, has profoundly affected our family dynamics.

I've felt alienated, because I didn't get to develop my sexuality in a healthy or normal way. Sex and sexuality was taken and forced onto me. I don't even know what that is or how that would feel. My innocence was taken away and can never be returned. My first sexual experiences were with a grown man, while I was five years old. You cannot change or erase that.

Love in a relationship feels so foreign to me. Once sex is introduced, the confusion in my body ramps up—it's as if love and sex can't coexist because of the abuse I experienced. I've struggled with my weight, battled anxiety, and grappled with feeling unsafe in this world. The damage inflicted by the abuse seems endless, and there's no way to completely erase its impact. Over time, I've just become better at navigating life with the cards I've been dealt, learning to manage the aftereffects so they don't control or rule my life any longer.

I never had the chance to see Bobby brought to justice in court, to confront him legally for what he did to me, my sister and mom. He eventually died from a rare disease that liquifies the internal organs—a fate I attribute to karma and divine intervention. Yet, I never had the opportunity to face him, to tell him about the deep scars he left on my life. Writing this book is my way of speaking up, of reclaiming my power and my voice that were taken from me. It's a declaration of my resilience and a step toward healing, a testimony that while I may not have had my day in court, I will not be silenced.

Bobby might be gone, but the legacy of the damage he inflicted lives on within me and my family, decades after he's stopped breathing. This is the stark reality of childhood and sexual abuse; it's an enduring battle, not just against the memories, but against the deep-seated impacts they embed within a person's life and body. It's a constant effort to heal and reclaim parts of myself that were unjustly taken. While Bobby's death may have brought some sense of karmic justice, the work I need to do to mend the scars he left is ongoing—a testament to the profound and unfair impact of such abuse.

Sexual abuse isn't just something that impacts someone in the moment; it impacts them for their entire life. What Bobby did continues to impact my ability to have a normal healthy life.

And this happens every day to other children all around the world, right in our neighborhoods, often unnoticed. It's crucial that we bring these issues into the light and provide a voice for those too vulnerable or scared to speak up. We need to advocate for justice against the 'monsters' of this world and ensure that no child has to endure what I went through. It's time to stand up, speak out, and fight for the innocence that deserves to be protected.

Children are precious and represent our future; they deserve to be protected and nurtured at all costs. If you observe or witness anything that seems 'off,' it's crucial to report it and advocate for them. Be an angel and an ally to a child who may be silenced and trapped. We must all be vigilant and proactive in

safeguarding the innocence and wellbeing of every child, ensuring they have the safe and supportive environment they need to thrive.

C-LOVE

Thank Yous and Acknowledgements

First and foremost, I am so grateful for my daughter. She is my why for everything I do. I love her more than words can ever say. She has been my answered prayer, divine intervention and greatest teacher. I am grateful for my partner/boyfriend, Jared, for stepping into our lives and being my partner for the past three years. His family has been so loving and supportive, welcoming my daughter and me with open arms. Thank you to my sister for being supportive and being there when I have needed her.

A huge thank you to my Into the Light Angels, Kaya Stanely, Penelope Jane Smith, Christine Innes, Don Ratliff, Michele Comeau Correa, Kelley Beveridge, Claudia Noriega-Bernstein, Matt Baumann, and Therese Marie Clinton for supporting and cheerleading this project. Thank you for Ramonda Jankunaite and Women Thrive Media for supporting me in really propelling this book forward and launch it and supporting me in stepping into being the empowered thought leader and woman I was always meant to be. Heather and She Rises Studios for granting me this opportunity to begin writing my book and help my dreams come true and to fruition. Thank you to PSI Seminars and their Intention Program for being right on time and helping me embark on this journey in actualizing my book. I am eternally grateful for all you have taught me and the PSI community. Thank you to everyone in my small group from Intention for all your love and support, as I have been on this journey and working on this goal.

Thank you to my current therapist, Jennyfer, for helping me delve deeper within via Brainspotting and parts work. Thank you to Jess Johnson for being my EFT Tapping buddy for the past year and a half. It's been an honor to be a part of each other's ongoing transformation and growth. A huge thank you to Naomi Janzen for being an amazing mentor through EFT Universe and now via Peta Stapleton.

I am so appreciative of Liz Germain for being my business coach as I had to pivot from doing my makeup and art, to this healing work at the beginning of the pandemic. You helped me so much; I am forever grateful. A huge shout out and thank you to The Foundation Of Spiritual Development in San Rafael for supporting me in really learning how to own my space and ground, clear, and protect it. Thank you to Lisa Kay for being my spiritual mom and always supporting me with the more spiritual aspects of continuing my healing and growth.

A huge thank you to Padre Paul and the Celebrating Life Ministries community. You have shown me that miracles are here and happening. You supported my connection to God and my highest self. Thank you to all my past business coaches and mentors. I have learned so much from so many of you: Satema Gali from Shield Maiden, Railey Molinario, Mike Sherbakov from Passion to Profit and the Greatness Foundation, April Berezay from Women's Empire, Jeff Slayter from Jeff and Kane, RC Peck, Penelope Jane Smith, Bill Walsh, Michelle Masters, and so many others.

A special thank you to Rachel Adler for believing in me in that Meisner class and taking me under her wing. Thank you to Rachel's class assistant, Javier Galito Cava, for always speaking wisdom and love over me. Thank you to Bobby Weinapple from Seydways Theatre in San Francisco for speaking words of encouragement to me in his ongoing stretch class.

Thank you to my mom for birthing me, gifting me this life, and being there in the really hard times. Thank you to my step-in dad for stepping into our lives when we were little. A huge thank you to my godfather and his family for being so loving and being such a bright light for me in my life. I love you guys.

A huge thank you to all my clients who have trusted me to work with them through their most vulnerable experiences, and for referring me to your friends. Huge thank yous to my C-Love Sparkle Babes (Paola, Priscilla, Ashley, and Jessenia) for being a part of the magic with me.

A huge thank you to my Burning Man Family and community for supporting my daughter and me for all these years. Truly appreciated.

Thank you to everyone who has been a part of this journey. Your support, love, and belief in me have made all the difference.

Tribute to Humanity

The trenches of humility
That's where I'm from
The bottom of life
Where each day is a struggle to survive
You better be well equipped with your tactics
Or get swallowed alive
There are no silver spoons
No eloquent manners
No Ivy League educations
Only self-taught life lessons
Where the survival of the fittest
The strongest
Is the instructor
Where nothing is given
All is earned
For every advancement forward
There were a lot of mistakes
And hard lessons learned

You get no plaque
No diploma
Only a humble heart
And a heart full of compassion
One for all
All for one
To all my fellow beings
In the trenches...

Cassandra Love Lambert, June 2008

C-LOVE

Books That Changed My Life

Dyer, Wayne. *Real Magic: Creating Miracles in Everyday Life,* 1992.

Van der Kolk M.D., Bessel. *The Body Keeps the Score: Brain, Mind, and Body in the Healing of Trauma,* 2014.

Roth, Ron PH.D., *The Healing Path of Prayer: A Modern Mystic's Guide to Spiritual Power,* 1997.

Aron, Elaine N., *The Highly Sensitive Person: How to Thrive When the World Overwhelms You,* 1996.

Katz, Mabel. *The Easiest Way: Solve Your Problems and Take the Road to Love, Happiness, Wealth and the Life of Your Dreams "Special Edition,"* 2009.

Cameron, Julia. *The Artist's Way: A Spiritual Path to Higher Creativity,* 1992.

Williamson, Marianne. *Enchanted Love: The Mystical Power of Intimate Relationships,* 1999.

Williamson, Marianne. *A Return to Love: Reflections on the Principles of a Course in Miracles,* 1992.

Walsch, Neale Donald. *Conversations With God: An Uncommon Dialogue*, 1995.

Hicks, Esther & Hicks, Jerry. *The Vortex: Where the Law of Attraction Assembles All Cooperative Relationships*, 2009.

Beckwith, Michael Bernard. *Spiritual Liberation: Fulfilling Your Soul's Potential*, 2008.

Ruiz, Don Miguel. *The Four Agreements: A Practical Guide to Personal Freedom*, 1999.

Ruiz, Don Miguel. *The Mastery of Love: A Practical Guide to the Art of Relationship*, 1997.

Coelho, Paulo. *The Alchemist*,1993.

Ferrini, Paul. *Dancing With the Beloved: Opening Our Hearts to the Lessons of Love*, 2001.

Allender, Dr Dan B. *The Wounded Heart: Hope for Adult Victims of Childhood Sexual Abuse*, 1990.

Whitfield, Charles L. *Healing the Child Within: Discovery and Recovery for Adult Children of Dysfunctional Families*, 1987.

Jeffery, H.B. *The Principles of Healing*, 1939.

Hover-Kramer, Dorothea. *Creating Healing Relationships: Professional Standards for Energy Therapy Practitioners*, 2011.

Lane, Janai. *Spirit Led Instead: The Little Tool Book of Limitless Transformation*, 2013.

Willhite, Thomas D. *Path to Liberty: The Life Success Manuscripts*, 1978.

To YOU from the Author ;-)

When I felt called to write this book, I had no idea what I was getting myself into. When the opportunity to write this book arose, felt like a gift from the universe—a Godsend that landed right in my lap. Every part of me screamed, "Yes, do it—it's time," even as I trembled with fear at the prospect. I never realized just how much work goes into writing a book, especially a memoir. Revisiting some of these memories was incredibly difficult, but it also allowed me to see the extensive healing I've undergone. I am truly amazed that I was able to do this.

I am deeply honored that you chose to pick up this book and support the message it carries. If anything within these pages has resonated with you, please share your thoughts with me and tag me on social media at www.instagram.com/c_love_lambert. Consider buying a copy for a friend or relative who could use the inspiration. Your support helps spread this powerful message further. Thank you for being a part of this journey.

I have always believed in the power of gifting and spreading love—it's the foundation of every business I've ever started. As a token of my appreciation for joining me on the *Into the Light* mission, I'm excited to share with you the first three keys to the Pain into Power Process. These keys are designed to help you regain your confidence and power. Thank you for being a part of this transformative journey.

Go here to claim it: https://cassandralovelambert.com/3-keys

At the end of this book, I want to share a poem that holds a special place in my heart, first introduced to me in an acting class many years ago. Initially part of our acting curriculum, I've come to see how beautifully this poem mirrors the journey of healing. It's called "There's a Hole in My Sidewalk: The Romance of Self-Discovery" by Portia Nelson. If you find yourself on a path of self-discovery, like I have, this poem speaks to the courage to embark on a new path, one that you truly deserve. I encourage you to look it up—I promise, it will resonate deeply with you.

C. Love Lambert

Printed in Dunstable, United Kingdom

82895874R00198